Hudson Waterfall Guide

FROM SARATOGA AND
THE CAPITAL REGION
TO THE HIGHLANDS
AND PALISADES

Russell Dunn

BLACK·DOME

Published by

Black Dome Press Corp.
1011 Route 296, Hensonville, New York 12439
www.blackdomepress.com
Tel: (518) 734-6357

First Edition Paperback 2006

ISBN-13: 978-1-883789-47-3

ISBN-10: 1-883789-47-8

Library of Congress Cataloging-in-Publication Data

Dunn, Russell.

  Hudson Valley waterfall guide: from Saratoga and the capital region
to the highlands and palisades/Russell Dunn.— 1st ed.

      p. cm.

  Includes bibliographical references and index.

  ISBN 1-883789-47-8

1. Hiking—Hudson River Valley (N.Y. and N.J.)—Guidebooks.
2. Hudson River Valley (N.Y. and N.J.)—Guidebooks. 3. Waterfalls. I. Title.

  GV199.42.H83D86 2005
  917.47'30444--dc22

                                        2005026854

**Outdoor recreational activities are by their very nature potentially
hazardous and contain risk. See "Caution: Safety Tips," page 6**

Cover photograph: *Bash Bish Falls*, Robert Near, RJNPhoto.com

Map illustration: D-ZINE, Inc., N.Y.C.

Design: Toelke Associates

Printed in the USA

10 9 8 7 6 5 4 3 2 1

To the unique and wonderful experience

of being in a men's group for twenty-five years.

Thank you, Joe Zoske, John Kucij, Tom Ciancetta,

Tim Farley, Jim Raymond, Lee Bowden, Ken Jacobs,

Craig Kennedy, Lars Tourin,

Charles Rhynhart, and Jim Murphy

for your love and support,

and for tolerating my occasional

lapses of attendance in order

to complete this book.

Contents

West Side of the Hudson River:
From Catskill to Newburgh 154

CATSKILL REGION (See *Catskill Region Waterfall Guide: Cool Cascades of the Catskills & Shawangunks* for an extensive directory of waterfalls in the Catskill region.)

Foreword

The Hudson River School painters of the nineteenth century captured on canvas the awe-inspiring beauty of the region that gave its name to America's first indigenous class of renowned artists. The pioneers and giants of the school, including Thomas Cole and Frederic E. Church, employed realism, vivid color and striking clarity to capture the extraordinary scenic qualities and sense of place of the Hudson Valley. Through their work, they defined the American landscape and indeed the character of the New World for people in this country and in Europe, an identity that has lasted for generations.

Some artists of the same period imbued in their art emotional, moral and spiritual content that earned them the title "Knights of the Brush." George Inness believed—and demonstrated through his work—that an artist can serve as a conduit of the "vital force" in human beings ... and even for divine inspiration. He viewed nature as possessing "living motion" that fueled and interacted with the force of nature and human vitality. He said, "The greatness of art is not in the display of knowledge, or in material accuracy, but in the distinctness with which it conveys the impressions of a personal vital force, that acts spontaneously, without fear or hesitation."[1]

Many of us who have kayaked on the Hudson, hiked in the Highlands, or spent a moment in a quiet glen have experienced that sense of the divine in the ethereal beauty around us. The region's waterfalls capture and embody the powerful movement and spiritual dimension of life—perhaps with greater force and clarity than any other natural phenomena. The falling waters of the Hudson Valley hold an intangible sense of the mystical that excites and inspires, seeming to link heaven and earth with a dynamic hurtling force.

The region's falls link us to our economic and cultural history, while often now serving as favored destinations for quiet, contemplative walks in nature. They feed and add drama to swimming holes, fishing streams, and provide subjects for today's Hudson River painters.

Foundry Brook Falls in Cold Spring fueled major industrial operations through much of the nineteenth century. Just downstream of the cascades, the West Point Foundry churned out cannons that helped decide the outcome of the Civil War, produced pipes for the New York City water system, and forged the country's first steam locomotives. Scenic Hudson has preserved the site—now largely retaken by nature—and the falls are a popular destination for hikers.

In Beacon, the falling water of Fishkill Creek powered a mill owned by the city's founding mother, Madam Brett. Today, a meandering trail leads to a viewpoint where the waters cascade over a dam.

In Annandale-on-Hudson, a chocolate factory and mill in the shadow of Montgomery Place, once a part of the Livingston family holdings, have now given way to scenic walks along the dramatic falls and cascades emptying into Tivoli Bay.

These are just a few of the places on tributaries of the Hudson that not only add to the world-class beauty and quality of life in the region, but also provide avenues for emotional relief, solace and inspiration for residents and visitors to the region. Those who pick up this extraordinary waterfall guide by Russell Dunn will find countless paths to these and other magical places in the Valley.

A generation ago, citizens of the Hudson Valley launched the modern environmental movement by standing up to a proposal that would have defaced Storm King Mountain, an icon of the Hudson River School painters. The movement is as vital as ever in the Hudson Valley today. Never before has there been greater opportunity to forge a new path of sustainable economic development that will provide a foundation for nurturing the human spirit for generations to come. Just as the waters flowing over the falls from Shaupeneak Ridge seem to provide an endless source of energy and beauty, so too can the human spirit—reconnected with nature's inspiring powers—fuel a vision that can assure many more generations of art, nature and sustenance here in the Hudson Valley.

Ned Sullivan
President
Scenic Hudson
September, 2005

Scenic Hudson is dedicated to protecting and restoring the Hudson River, its riverfront and the majestic vistas and working landscapes beyond as an irreplaceable natural treasure for America and a vital resource for residents and visitors. It is the largest environmental group focused on the Hudson River Valley. www.ScenicHudson.org

1. "American Artists. George Innes," *Harper's Weekly: A Journal of Civilization* 11:550 (13 July 1867): 433. As cited in Adrienne Baxter Bell, *George Inness and the Visionary Landscape* (New York, George Braziller, Publishers, 2003), p. 31.

Flow of the River Valley

Dear traveler, do you see?
Look deeply, for it
runs through the water—history

of days forgotten and eons past,
dissolved in snow and summer rain
bathing this land, a valley vast

born high in lakes and rivulets
cascading down, cutting deep the earth
as streams and creeks twist and step

through generations of births and deaths
countless seasons, the soul of time
flowing, eroding, both sap and sweat

blood and rain, to weave a liquid tapestry
of the earth in all its forms and
inspiring harmony.

Dear traveler, can you hear?
In youth it trickles through the cracks
growing stronger year to year

from quiet flow to mighty roar
sliding, rolling down—down to field
and farm on valley floor

this fluid song of life not seen
often, but for its mist arising, till a journey
through the forest green

canopied in oak and pine,
and framed by arms of snow white birch
shows the source of endless time.

Sit, take it in—the whole of it,
so much to learn
so worth the trip.

Caution

Keep in mind that nature is inherently wild and unpredictable, so play it safe and don't act recklessly. Outdoor recreational activities are by their very nature potentially hazardous and contain risk. All participants in such activities must assume the responsibility for their own actions and safety. No book can replace good judgment. The outdoors is forever changing. The author and the publisher cannot be held responsible for inaccuracies, errors, or omissions, or for any changes in the details of this publication, or for the consequences of any reliance on the information contained herein, or for the safety of people in the outdoors.

SAFETY TIPS

1. Always hike with two or more companions. There is always safety in numbers. Should an accident occur, one or more can stay with the victim while another goes for help.
2. Bring a day pack loaded with survival items such as extra layers of clothes, matches, a compass, water, high-energy food (e.g., Gorp or Power Bars), mosquito repellent, an emergency medical kit, duct tape (for quick repairs), rain gear, and sun block.
3. Treat waterfalls with the respect they deserve. Don't get too close to the top, where an inadvertent slip can send you tumbling over the edge. Many waterfalls send up a spray, so keep an eye out for slippery rocks and maintain your footing. Whenever possible, approach waterfalls from the base.
4. Apply ample portions of insect repellent to prevent mosquitoes and black flies from targeting you, and don't be stingy with sunscreen if you are going to be exposed to the sun for any length of time. Remember that you can get sunburned even on a cloudy day if conditions are right. Wear a long-sleeved shirt and long pants.
5. Wear good hiking boots for proper traction and ankle support.
6. Be aware of the risks of hypothermia, and dress accordingly.

Keep in mind that the temperature doesn't have to be freezing to cause the onset of hypothermia. If you become accidentally wet or immersed while hiking during the spring, fall, or winter, return to your car immediately unless the temperature is higher than 70 degrees. Also be cognizant of the dangers of hyperthermia (overheating) and always drink plenty of water when the weather is hot and muggy. Stay in the shade whenever possible, and use the stream near the waterfall in which to cool off if you begin to feel overheated.

7. Stay vigilant for others who may not be attentive to those around them. During hunting season, wear bright colors and make frequent sounds so that you will not be mistaken for a wild animal (which you will be if a hunter accidentally takes a shot at you, and you get riled up!) If you are standing near the base of a large waterfall, keep an eye out for people at the top, especially kids, who might impulsively toss a rock over the edge without first checking to see if there is anyone below.

The Hudson is an extremely powerful river.

8. Stay on trails whenever possible. If you leave a path to explore on your own, keep in mind that you may encounter obstacles not described in this book, and you could get lost. Staying on trails is also good for the environment, causing less erosion. Do not consider bushwhacking through the woods unless you are an experienced hiker, you have a compass with you and know how to use it, you are prepared to spend several days in the woods if necessary, you are with a group of similarly prepared hikers, and you have notified someone as to your destination and your estimated time of return from the hike.

9. If you follow a creek upstream to a waterfall, you cannot get lost as long as you follow the creek back downstream to your starting point.

10. Don't presume to be a master rock climber by trying to free-climb rock walls in deep gorges. Many of the gorges containing waterfalls have walls made of shale or slate—not particularly stable rocks to grab hold of if your life is depending on a firm support. Stay on trails. When the going is steep, maintain three points of contact whenever possible.

11. Heed all signs and trail markers. Be on the lookout for possible changes in topography or trails following the date of this book's publication. Trails may be rerouted due to blowdown, heavy erosion, the sudden appearance of a lake or bog because of beaver activity, or any number of other unanticipated events. Trails, or portions thereof, occasionally become closed off. If you see a posted sign, go no further.

12. Always let someone back home know where you are hiking and your expected time of return. Clearly discuss with him or her what actions should be taken if you are not back at the appointed time.

13. Always know where you are. Guidebooks, topographic maps, and compasses are essential if you venture out into the wilderness. A GPS unit is also worth bringing along. Nothing, however, is a substitute for good judgment and basic common sense.

14. Never jump or dive off rocks or ledges into inviting pools of waters around waterfalls. Too many people have slipped and tumbled onto the rocks below, or have collided with unseen and unknown hazards below the water's surface.
15. Stay away from overhanging precipices of ice. People have died when blocks of ice have suddenly broken off from the rock face.
16. Watch out for hunters during deer season, even if you are on well-traveled trails.
17. Avoid cornering any wild animal at the bottom of a deep gorge as you approach a waterfall. If the animal has nowhere to retreat and feels threatened, it may seek a way out that goes right over you.
18. Do not drink untreated water. Giardia is not a pleasant memento to bring back from your hike.

And remember: If you carry it in, carry it out!

WILL WATERFALLS ALWAYS CALL?

Like the wind howling through tall stands of hemlocks, or ocean waves pounding against the shoreline, waterfalls are the voice of nature, powerful and majestic, beckoning and mesmerizing. It is a voice that roars in the springtime, summoning hikers from miles away with its thunderous cry. In summer it is a voice that becomes more gentle, more soothing, whispering like a quiet mountain breeze, luring hikers to repose on flat rocks below the cascading waters while they rest their weary spirits. Waterfalls are important to our spiritual side, for they represent nature at its grandest and most sublime—unfettered, wild, awesome.

Waterfalls are more than just manifestations of water, however. They are creatures of rock as well, spinning and swirling like living dynamos under towering escarpments and in deep ravines. When the dry days of summer arrive, greater portions of gorges and ravines emerge as swelling streams turn into trickles and waterfalls transform into stony cliffs of moss-covered ledges. Potholes, rock formations, cracks and crannies, obscured during the spring rush of released snowmelt, become visible to the eye.

And perhaps best of all, waterfalls are tireless performers, always ready to put on a show that is guaranteed to dazzle the eyes. All you need to do is show up, and there they are. But the question lingers as we begin to move through the second millennium—will the beauty of waterfalls always be there in the years to come?

The answer is a guarded "maybe."

From a geological standpoint, it is in the nature of waterfalls to be short-lived, much like shooting stars. Most of the cascades that we now look upon were set into motion following the end of the last ice age, no more than 10,000 years ago. Many were born even more recently. Like spring-wound clocks, all of these waterfalls are slowly running down—and the bigger the cataract, the faster the process of disintegration.

Mt. Ida Falls. Waterfalls were the driving force behind the Industrial Revolution

Take Niagara Falls, for example, America's premier waterfall. At one time the great falls of the Niagara River were breaking apart and advancing upstream at the prodigious rate of six feet per year. Fortunately for the section of Niagara Falls known as Horseshoe Falls, the rate has slowed to two feet per year, primarily because huge volumes of water have been siphoned off for power generation and released below the falls. Still, during the last 10,000 years, the incessant process of erosion and disintegration of the bedrock has caused Niagara Falls to travel up the Niagara River about seven miles from where it originated, birthed by the flood waters of retreating glaciers. Engineers estimate that in another 25,000 years, the process will come to an end when Niagara Falls, or whatever remains of it, finally reaches Lake Erie and can recede no further. At that point the falls—and if left unattended, parts of Lake Erie as well—will disappear forever.

Large cataracts like Niagara Falls are shorter lived than smaller falls because they create more self-destructive energy. The greater the quantity of water crashing down onto the bedrock below, the more powerful is the jackhammer force created and the quicker the undermining of the integrity of the waterfall's base. Waterfalls that possess only a modest flow of water and are formed in bedrock that is highly resistant to weathering will be comparatively longer lived.

Through erosion, waterfalls recede upstream and move uphill. When a waterfall has gained its maximum elevation or reached a point where the underlying bedrock changes sufficiently in composition so that waterfall formation can no longer be sustained, the cascade flattens out, leaving behind an inclined streambed descending into the valley. There is nothing we can do to halt this process. We can slow it down by damming up the falls or siphoning off vast quantities of its waters, as was done at Cohoes Falls in Cohoes, but a waterfall's eventual self-destruction is as inevitable as any other of nature's eternal cycles of birth and death.

Niagara Falls again serves as a ready example. In 1969 engineers dammed up the less spectacular American section of the falls for five months so that they could study how to slow down the erosive process and stabilize the falls. In the end it was realized that nothing significant could be done to save the falls; in fact, removing

High Falls (Philmont). Waterfalls come in all shapes and sizes.

the huge blocks of talus at the base of the American Falls would only have made matters worse. The falls were humbly "turned back on," and the clock of self-eradication continues to slowly tick.

Many of the most spectacular waterfalls of New York State have been pressed into industrial service and used for power generation, thereby usurping them and removing them from public viewing. This began in the mid-seventeenth century with undershot and overshot waterwheels, and continued right into the nineteenth and twentieth centuries with turbines and generators replacing the now obsolete waterwheels. Like beasts of burden, waterfalls were put under yoke, domesticated, and all too often desecrated in the process. Once waterfalls began to be valued primarily for the work they could generate, their natural beauty became a secondary consideration. As a variety of mills and factories took root by the falls, homes, businesses, and finally entire towns and cities sprang up as well. As a result, many large cascades were engulfed and swallowed up by communities that became increasingly bound to and economically dependent upon them.

By the mid-twentieth century, however, humanity's dependency on waterfalls began to change as other forms of energy became more readily available and increasingly cost-effective. Slowly but surely, the demands of power generation turned away from hydroelectric to fossil fuels, and in the process, the waterfall-dependent factories and mills that had once been so bountiful no longer prospered, were gradually abandoned, fell into ruin, or were demolished. Thus many of New York State's waterfalls that were previously harnessed and subjugated to industry have returned to a seminatural state. All that remains of these previous enterprises are old foundations, cinder blocks, pipes, and bits of brick and glass. The hulking buildings and factories that once blighted the scenery have been swept away as if by the hand of God.

With fossil fuel reserves diminishing, the day may come, as it did in bygone centuries, when energy providers may again view waterfalls as an untapped source of renewable, nonpolluting, and continuously available energy, and appropriate the falls for utilitarian purposes. If such a time does come, it will heighten tensions between the techno-expansionists and environmentalists as they grapple with how to meet the esthetical and technological needs of a changing society that is energy-dependent. As one who loves waterfalls, it is a day that I hope will never come.

It would seem then that since waterfalls have survived the ravages of thousands of years of natural erosion and, more recently, the ravages of the industrial revolution—coming through with only a nick or two and an occasional blemish—that we should not necessarily be worried about their ability to endure for millenniums to come. What's more, the creation of state parks in New York has ensured that some impressive waterfalls will be preserved into the foreseeable future. Shouldn't this be enough to satisfy waterfall lovers?

The problem is that there are countless waterfalls notable for their geological or historical pasts that have not been similarly protected. It is these waterfalls that we need to be concerned about, and these waterfalls constitute the majority of cascades in New York State. A number of these waterfalls have already been altered, with more and more landowners building private homes near the tops or bottoms of the cascade. In the majority of cases, the land has been posted and the waterfalls have "disappeared"—at least as far as the public is concerned.

It is a sobering thought to realize that a waterfall's fate may ultimately be determined by one individual. In theory, at least, landowners have the right to dynamite "their" waterfalls if they want to, blasting into eternity a natural phenomenon. Maybe the waterfall proved troublesome because it attracted a raucous crowd or became a legal liability. But imagine! In one second of impetuous action, a landowner could destroy forever what nature had taken millenniums to fashion.

To be fair, however, the problem of waterfall desecration today is far more the cause of visitors than property owners. Waterfall areas are favorite party sites. Litter, graffiti, and smashed bottles mar many a site. Waterfalls provide swimming holes, areas to climb, dangers to brave, and hard rock surfaces, all of which can cause injury—and lawsuits. Even though a visitor may be trespassing, if that unwelcome visitor gets hurt, it is all too often the landowner who is blamed or held liable and forced to mount a legal defense against charges that are unfair and groundless. Is it any mystery,

Waterfalls were an integral part of the lives of Native Americans, colonists and early industrialists—often at the same time.

then, why many landowners close off access to waterfalls on their property?

Then there are the inevitable despoilers who are not satisfied to wait until they die before seeing their names carved in rock. They write with garish Day-Glo paint or carve their initials onto the rocky surfaces with chisels, thus defacing the rocks for decades to come. Who really cares whether Jim loves Kim, or Karen, or even Tim? These desecrations detract from the waterfall's natural beauty and make it less enjoyable for all those who follow.

For those who love waterfalls and aspire to a higher level of social conscience and responsibility, please pick up a few bottles or pieces of litter and cart them away each time you visit a waterfall. Always leave it better than you found it. This may not be fair, but waterfalls are for everyone, so it is everyone's responsibility to help in their preservation.

TYPES OF WATERFALLS

A fairly consistent nomenclature has developed for describing and cataloguing waterfalls. The use of such a system, however, is like trying to paint a great work of art by dabbing at a canvas with a broad brush; there is little opportunity for refinement and subtle textures. Most waterfalls exhibit a complexity and variability that transcends size, shape, flow, and composition. Still, for those who like broad categories, here are a few to consider:[1-5]

Plunge Fall—This type of waterfall typically forms when a stream drops vertically to the foot of the fall. Taughannock Falls at Taughannock Falls State Park in the Finger Lakes is a perfect example of a plunge fall. Sometimes plunge falls are called cataracts, but that term is generally reserved for waterfalls that are created on powerful, high-falling streams. When the stream races over a pronounced, overhanging ledge and then plunges straight down, another variety of plunge fall is produced, called a *Hanging Fall.*

Cascade—This type of waterfall forms when its falling waters remain in contact with the bedrock. Generally, a cascade is characterized by a horizontal length that is greater than its vertical height. Cascades are frequently called *slides* or *chutes* when they are gently

Many native American legends are formed around waterfalls.

inclined. Cascades with multiple drops and ledges are occasionally called *Staircase Falls.*

Fan Fall—This is a waterfall whose base is wider than its top.

Curtain Fall—This is a waterfall whose sheet of water seemingly hangs like a curtain. Curtain falls are sometimes called *bridal veils*, particularly when they have a delicate look and texture.

Horsetail Fall—This is a very steep cascade. Its waters drop nearly vertically, but still manage to remain in touch with the bedrock.

Punchbowl Fall—This is a waterfall that is produced as water is forcefully expelled through an opening at the top of the fall and then dropped (seemingly poured) into a pool below.

Some waterfalls are *multi-tiered,* meaning that they consist of a number of separate and distinct drops, but are close enough together so that the drops can be viewed as a whole. Others are considered to be *serial* (or in a *series*), meaning that although they are formed one after the other on the same stream, they cannot be viewed as a whole.

As to when a waterfall is a waterfall, and when it is not, I will leave that to your discretion. T. Morris Longstreth, in *The Catskills,* devotes an entire chapter to the subject.[6] Truly, there can be no right or wrong answer. The matter is strictly subjective and ultimately determined by one's personal judgment. A one-foot-high fall that normally might be passed unnoticed could suddenly look wonderfully appealing when encountered on a secluded stream in deep woods after a laborious, five-mile hike on a ninety-degree summer day!

WATERFALL RECORDS

The subject invariably comes up—which waterfall is the highest in the world, or in New York State, or in the Hudson River Valley region? Human beings are driven by insatiable curiosity when it comes to collecting records on how fast, far, high, heavy, big, small, slow, loud, etc., anything animate or inanimate is. So, here are a few records that waterfalls have achieved:

Highest Waterfall

In the world—Angel Falls (Salto Angel) on the Upper Tributary of the Rio Caroni in Venezuela, at 3,212 feet high.[1] Angel Falls contains a single drop of 2,648 feet. The waterfall is named after American pilot Jimmy Angel.[2]

In the United States—Yosemite Falls on Yosemite Creek in California, at 2,425 feet high. Yosemite Falls actually consists of three distinct drops of 1430 feet (upper), 574 feet (middle), and 320 feet (lower).[1,2] Ribbon Falls, also in Yosemite National Park, is the tallest single-plunge waterfall at 1,612 feet.

In New York State—Taughannock Falls on Taughannock Creek near Ithaca is the highest single plunge, at 215 feet (but see below).

In the Hudson River Valley region—Greenbrook Falls on Green Brook is the highest cascade, at 250 feet, while Kaaterskill Falls on Lake Creek is the highest two-tiered falls, at 231 feet high.

Widest Waterfall

In the world—Khone Falls in Laos, at 6.7 miles wide. Its flood flow has approached 1.5 million cusec (cubic feet per second).[2]

In New York State—Niagara Falls, at 3,600 feet wide (a total of 2,500 feet for Horseshoe Falls and 1,100 feet for the American Falls).[3]

In the Hudson River Valley region—Cohoes Falls on the Mohawk River, at 600 feet in width.

Greatest Flow of Water

In the world—Boyomoa Falls in Zaire, with a flow of 600,000 cu. ft. sec.[2,4]

In New York State—Niagara Falls.

In the Hudson River Valley region—Baker Falls (the last dammed waterfall on the Hudson River) and Cohoes Falls (at the terminus of the Mohawk River).

Deadliest Waterfall

In the world—Niagara Falls. By 1900 more than 1,000 people had committed suicide by jumping in the river above the falls and going over the top. The list has been steadily growing since then.

In the Hudson River Valley region—Both Bash Bish Falls and Kaaterskill Falls are contenders for this dubious title of distinction.

Largest Drowned Waterfall

In the world—130-foot-high Guaira Falls on the Alto Parana River between Paraguay and Brazil was obliterated when construction on the Itaipun Dam was completed in 1982.[2,4] The falls previously flowed with a volume twice that of Niagara Falls!

In the near-Hudson River Valley region—Devasego Falls on Schoharie Creek was once referred to as a "miniature Niagara" because of its horseshoe shape. It vanished under impounded waters when the Schoharie/Gilboa Reservoir was completed in 1924.

First Daredevil to Go over Niagara Falls in a Barrel

The feat was accomplished in 1901 at the Horseshoe Falls on the Canadian side of Niagara Falls. The most amazing facts of all

Devasego Falls now lies buried under the Gilboa Reservoir— a sad fate for a once renowned waterfall.

are that the daredevil was a woman—Annie Edson Taylor—and Ms. Taylor accomplished the stunt at age sixty-three, *and* in an era that was most discouraging about women engaging in any activities that were adventurous or daring.

ACCESSING WATERFALLS: DEGREES OF DIFFICULTY

The waterfalls described in this book are generally more readily accessible and involve a less demanding hike to reach than the ones contained in *Adirondack Waterfall Guide: New York's Cool Cascades* or *Catskill Region Waterfall Guide: Cool Cascades of the Catskills & Shawangunks,* which explore the mountainous regions of New York. Therefore, most treks in this book will fall into an "easy" to "moderate" category. The longest hike contained herein is a moderate, three-mile trek to Greenbrook Falls along the shoreline-based Palisades trail.

Easy—Less than 1.5 miles one-way, with mostly even terrain and minimal elevation change.
Moderate—Up to 2.5 miles one-way, with mixed terrain and some elevation change.
Difficult—Significant elevation change and mixed terrain, possibly including some rock scrambling.

The waterfalls have been intentionally selected to provide something for everyone, including falls that are accessible by the elderly, infirm, and disabled, as well as by the able-bodied hiker. A number of waterfalls are located at roadside and thus can be viewed through a car window. Some of the hikes involve a trek over rough ground or up a steep slope, but very few require negotiating a distance greater than 0.4 mile.

The geographic territory covered consists not only of the Hudson River Valley, but includes lands to both the east and west of the valley. In a few cases, it is necessary to drive distances of up to twenty miles from the valley to get to a particular waterfall, but these are the exceptions and not the rule. Many of the waterfalls are located in parks and nature preserves. Parks in a rural area will generally provide more of a wilderness experience, creating the feeling of being in deep woods. Parks that are found in or near more urban environments have a different ambiance to them, generally with more noise, more traffic, more people, and more signs of human visitation such as litter and graffiti. In heavily populated areas, just getting to your destination may prove to be a significant part of the adventure. If you are planning to drive through areas where traffic is bumper-to-bumper, write out the directions in advance or memorize them so that you don't have to fumble around and get distracted while driving. Better yet, designate a companion to be your "navigator" and let him or her do the stressful work of getting you to the trailhead.

Several waterfalls in this book are listed as "historic" and are not accompanied by directions. This means that the waterfall is historically significant, but is inaccessible at this time because it is on private land.

GETTING THERE

No serious outdoor travel adventurer should be without a Delorme's *New York State Atlas & Gazetteer,* which can be purchased at virtually any book or sporting goods store. The *Atlas & Gazetteer* is a collection of large-scale topographical maps that enable you to see the main routes and highways in conjunction with major surface features, such as streams, lakes, and mountains. The *Atlas & Gazetteer* is indispensable for helping you make your way through eastern New York State as efficiently as possible and for assisting you in locating the general area where each waterfall can be found. Match the coordinates listed in this book with those contained in Delorme's *New York State Atlas & Gazetteer,* fifth edition.

Here's how it works: the coordinates "p. 32, A/B4" in this guidebook, for instance, instruct you to open the *Atlas* up to page 32, scan down the vertical side of the page until you are midway between letters A & B, and then move horizontally across the page until you reach an imaginary vertical line coming down from number 4. The waterfall will be located close to where the horizontal and vertical lines meet.

There are other kinds of maps that are indispensable as well, especially if it is detail that you want. Topographical (topo) maps, for instance, are particularly helpful because they show in minute detail the topography of the landscape. If your exploration takes you into popular hiking areas, trail maps such as those published by the ADK (Adirondack Mountain Club), Mohonk Preserve, Palisades Interstate Park Commission, and New York–New Jersey Trail Conference, Inc., just to name a few, will show you where to go and how to get there. Trail maps also enable you to combine your waterfall hike with side trips to other interesting sights such as mountain tops, gorges, lakes, expansive sinkholes, and unusual rock formations, which you might otherwise miss.

Some nature preserves contain kiosks that often will provide pertinent information, including a map of the hiking trails.

The Hudson River Valley region is crisscrossed by a number of main routes and major highways that will help you get you from one hiking destination to the next in the most expeditious manner possible:

East Side of the Hudson River

Rt. 22 runs north/south between Hoosic Falls and Brewster.

Rt. 4 runs north/south between Fort Ann and East Greenbush.

Rt. 7 runs west/east between Troy and Hoosic Falls.

Rt. 2 runs west/east between Troy and Petersburg.

Rt. 20 runs west/east between Rensselaer and New Lebanon.

The **Taconic State Parkway** runs north/south between
East Chatham and the New Croton Reservoir.

Rt. 9 runs north/south between Glens Falls
and Croton-on-Hudson.

Rt. 9G runs north/south between Hudson and Rhinebeck.

Rt. 44 runs west/east between Poughkeepsie and Amenia.

Rt. 9D runs north/south between Wappingers Falls and the Bear
Mountain Bridge.

I-684 runs north/south between Brewster and Bedford.

West Side of the Hudson River

I-87 runs north/south between Lake George and Nyack.

Rt. 32 runs north/south between Glens Falls and Kingston.

Rt. 9W runs north/south between Albany and the Palisades.
Palisades Interstate Parkway runs north/south between
Bear Mountain State Park and Englewood Cliffs.
I-287 runs east/west between Nyack and Suffern.
Rt. 202 runs north/south between Suffern and Oakland.

Bridges Crossing the Hudson River

Dunn Memorial Bridge (Rt. 20)—Between Albany and Rennselaer
Rip Van Winkle Bridge (Rt. 23)—Between Catskill and Hudson
Kingston–Rhinecliff Bridge (Rt. 199)—Between Kingston and
Rhinebeck
Mid-Hudson Bridge (Rt. 44/55)—Between Highland and
Poughkeepsie
Newburgh–Beacon Bridge (I-84)—Between Newburgh
and Beacon
Bear Mountain Bridge (Rt. 6)—Between Bear Mountain
State Park and Peeksville
Tappan Zee Bridge (I-87 & I-287)—Between Nyack and Tarrytown

TAKING WATERFALL PHOTOS

You don't have to be an expert to take good pictures of waterfalls, but it helps to understand the basic working principles of your
camera and to realize that waterfalls can be very temperamental
subjects at best.

Contrary to expectations, bright, sunny days create the worst
possible conditions for photographing waterfalls. The human eye
can accommodate extreme differences in dark and light, but the
camera lens cannot. On a sunny day the contrast between the sear-
ing white of a cascade and the darkness of the surrounding trees and
bedrock is simply too great for any camera to handle. If you set the
exposure to adjust to the water's brightness, the surrounding
bedrock and brush will end up dark and indistinct; if you set the
exposure to the relative dimness of the bedrock and trees, then the
cascade will become a featureless smear of white. When faced with
such conditions, there is no way to win. All you can hope to achieve

is a begrudging compromise. Optimum conditions for shooting waterfalls are when the sky is bright, but not casting shadows. Photos will come out with less contrast, leaving the waterfall properly exposed and the bedrock and trees still clearly defined.

In terms of where to stand when photographing waterfalls, your choice may be dictated by the waterfall's physical layout. For instance, if the falls are encased in a deep canyon, it may prove impossible to get down to the bottom of the gorge for a picture. In such cases your best photo may end up being a shot from the side of the canyon, looking diagonally across at the falls. In another instance you may be able to get down to the base of the waterfall, but may find yourself unable to progress downstream in order to get a more panoramic shot of the falls. The only possible picture then may be a close-up shot directly from the waterfall's base. You must rely upon your own ingenuity and creativity. Every picture does not have to represent the classic waterfall pose as taken straight on, downstream from the base.

Pictures often can be taken from the top of a waterfall, but there is more danger in doing so and the results are hardly exemplary, since the effect is akin to standing at the edge of a cliff and looking out into the valley.

You may want to consider including people sitting or standing next to the falls in order to capture the waterfall's size and dimension.

Many of the professionals who photograph waterfalls prefer to use slow shutter speeds so that the motion of the waterfall is blurred, creating a buttermilk effect. In my opinion this technique is overdone, serving only to make the waterfall look unnatural. How many cascades appear creamy to the naked eye? The practice started in the mid-1800s when primitive cameras could only take blurry pictures of moving objects because of slow shutter speeds and the films available at that time. As a result the public grew accustomed to viewing pictures of unnatural-looking waterfalls as "natural," and photos of natural-looking waterfalls as "unnatural."

The only true rule of thumb, of course, is to take whatever kind of picture you like. There is an infinite number of ways to combine the elements of water, rock, life, motion, and light whenever you point a camera at a waterfall, so get out and just enjoy!

Acknowledgments

No book of this nature could be written without building on the work of the many writers and explorers who have gone before. I remain forever indebted to those brave adventurers of past centuries who risked life and limb as they ventured into the unknown, uncharted regions of the Hudson Valley and its vast network of tributaries to chronicle the region's natural wonders. Many of these writers are quoted in the endnotes of this book.

I am also deeply indebted to my contemporaries—the regional writers who have included information on waterfalls in their own books, and from whom I have liberally drawn upon whenever appropriate.

This book would never have been written were it not for the love and support of my wife, Barbara Delaney, who has gamely accompanied me on nearly every hike in this book. You will read about only a fraction of the adventures we have undertaken. All too often a particular waterfall lead or a promise of a secret glen with a wondrous cascade has led us to a dead end—to a stream that is waterfall-less or on private, inaccessible land. Be thankful that these fruitless hikes are not ones that you will have to undertake as well.

I thank Bob Drew, whose encyclopedic knowledge of geography is a continuing resource for me, and whose amazing collection of 125,000 postcards has often supplemented my own collection of antique postcards of waterfalls. All postcard illustrations in this book are from the author's collection.

Special thanks go to: Warren Broderick, Senior Archives and Records Management Specialist at New York State Archives, who brought to bear his extensive knowledge of Rensselaer County, its waterfalls, and Native American legends in his critical review of sections of this book; Neil Schaefer for his input on the Harriman Park region; Tim Neu for generously sharing his knowledge of the Ashokan Field Campus and its history, and to Bob Ingalls for reviewing the section on Rensselaer County waterfalls.

Proofreaders Matina Billias, Natalie Mortensen, and Ed Volmar performed an invaluable service.

I am extremely grateful to Ned Sullivan, president of Scenic Hudson, for penning the foreword to this book, in which he captures the beauty, artistic heritage, and history that the Hudson Valley has to offer.

As always I am amazed at how Ron Toelke and Barbara Kempler-Toelke can take the text and breathe life into it, animating the words and images through their artistry and graphic design.

I also thank Robert J. Near for allowing us to use his photograph of Bash Bish Falls for the cover of this book, giving a face to *Hudson Valley Waterfall Guide*.

I am pleased and proud to have my son, Adam R. Dunn, join me on the "About the Author" page by way of his line drawing. *Dionondahowa Falls*.

Finally, this book would never have become a reality were it not for the magical wordsmanship of my editor, Steve Hoare, whose hand has moved unerringly over the pages you are reading, shaping it into its present form; and to my dear publisher, Debbie Allen, whose imprint is also everywhere in this book, and who somehow manages to take what starts off as pages of words and, each and every time, miraculously turns them into a finished book.

The Federal Dam at Troy represents the line of demarcation where the Hudson River becomes tidal.

Introduction

WATERFALLS OF THE HUDSON RIVER VALLEY

The Hudson River is New York State's longest and most dynamic river. In 1872, Verplanck Colvin traced the roots of the mighty river up to Lake Tear of the Clouds on the shoulder of Mount Marcy and to a small tributary rising from Indian Pass, both located in the High Peaks region of the Adirondack Mountains.[1] Although the Hudson River begins its journey as a tiny, insignificant trickle of water, by the time it reaches Troy, in the Capital District region (falling over 4,000 vertical feet in the process), it has become an enormously powerful, raging torrent of water. This fact will be made abundantly clear to you should you decide to take a rafting trip down the Hudson River Gorge in early May.

Below Troy, however, the temperament of the Hudson changes markedly. The river slows down to a more leisurely pace, widens out, and becomes tidal—all the time continuing to grow in volume as additional tributaries feed into it from a watershed totaling over 13,390 square miles. By the time the Hudson River arrives at the Atlantic Ocean, 325 miles from its starting point, it has passed through five distinct physiographic sections of eastern New York: The Adirondack High Peaks; the folded Appalachians; the Hudson Highlands; the New England Uplands; and the New Jersey Lowlands. It has also passed close by the Catskill Mountains, New York State's second-highest mountain range, which lies to the west of the river.[2]

Ironically, even when the Hudson River reaches the sea and seemingly disappears from sight, it still has not fully run its course. From New York Harbor the stream pushes its way out for another ninety miles through the Atlantic Ocean following an ancient river bed. It finally dissipates when it arrives at the edge of the Continental Shelf and drops into the Hudson Canyon.[3] It is believed that this fossil riverbed dates from a time when sea level was considerably lower (when the last ice age drew vast quantities of water out of the ocean, locking it up as ice on the northern continents), and that the Hudson River once actually ran another ninety miles before reaching the ocean.

Although the Hudson River is relatively small when compared to a number of other distinguished rivers in the United States (most notably the Mississippi, which at 2,348 miles in length is over seven times as long), it makes up for what it lacks in size and stature with its majestic scenery and charm. According to a twentieth-century author, Wallace Nutting, "The Hudson is lord among the rivers of America. It is not surpassed by any river in the world, and it is often and appropriately called the Rhine of America."[4]

The Hudson is an old river, born about 65 million years ago when a series of stupendous geological events raised the entire region. During this period of uplift, the proto–Hudson River (ancestor of the present-day Hudson) cut a wide swath between the Taconics to the east and the Catskills to the west. Not surprisingly, this forerunner of the modern-day Hudson was a considerably more powerful river, draining out the Great Lakes through the Mohawk River, driven by the prodigious meltwaters of glaciers in retreat. If the Hudson River were still this size today, the topography and geography of the valley would be unrecognizable.

To be sure, the Hudson River is already less energetic in this century than it was one hundred years ago. In March of 1930, the Sacandaga Reservoir (known since 1968 as the Great Sacandaga Lake) was created so that the Sacandaga River—a main spigot to the Hudson River—could be "turned off" during springtime to prevent the rising Hudson from flooding over its banks and overpowering a number of river towns along its banks from Glens Falls to Albany.[5]

To many visitors the lower Hudson River resembles a fjord, with massive mountainous uplifts on both sides of the valley. Moreover, the Hudson's channel has been cut so deep that the river actually stays at sea level all the way up to the Federal Dam at Troy, thus making it truly an arm of the Atlantic Ocean and therefore even more subject to tidal variations.[6,7] It is the Hudson River's deep waters, augmented by occasional dredging, that allow large ships—even ocean-faring vessels—to journey upstream as far as 145 miles from the sea to the Port of Albany. The fact that the Hudson River is nearly at sea level all the way up to Albany is also the reason why the "salt line" from the Atlantic Ocean occasionally advances as far north as Newburgh, some sixty miles up from The Battery in New York City.

Native Americans called the Hudson River *Skatemuc* or *Mannahatta*, meaning "the great river of the mountains." They also called it *Muhneakantuck*, meaning "the river that flows two ways," reflecting the fact that the river is tidal and seemingly reverses direction on a regular basis. The Dutch initially christened it the *Nassau*, after the reigning family of Holland. Then they called it Prince Mauritius, after a Dutch soldier who was known as Maurice of Orange.

The river has been called the North River, distinguishing it from the East River, which is downstate, and the South River between New Jersey and Pennsylvania.[3,8] Today, none of these earlier names are remembered. The river is known worldwide as the Hudson, in honor of Henry Hudson, whose vessel the *Half Moon* sailed upstream to Albany in 1609.

Most people believe that the Hudson River was "discovered" by Henry Hudson, but in actuality it was visited by Europeans much earlier than 1609. Giovanni da Verrazzano, sailing for Francis I, King of France, wrote that he came upon the river while exploring the coast of North America in 1524. It is unlikely, however, that Giovanni ventured further upstream than New York harbor. Then, in 1525, a Portuguese explorer sailing under the flag of Spain sighted the Hudson River while traveling along the eastern coast from Rhode Island to Maryland, but he also left the river unexplored.[9] It was left to Henry Hudson to discover the true potential of the Hudson River although, ironically, he considered his expedition a failure because he had not accomplished his primary objective—to find an easy passage to the Orient.

Hudson's epic voyage opened the door to European colonization of New York. Within a decade, the area near the mouth of the Hudson River was colonized by the Dutch, and soon other European nations followed, moving up the Hudson River Valley and outward in increasing numbers. With different countries competing for territory and control of the Hudson River, warfare was inevitable. In fact, over one-third of all battles fought during the Revolutionary War took place in or near the Hudson River Valley. Not surprisingly, several of the waterfalls in this book have war-related histories. Though Hudson Valley waterfalls may have witnessed some of the carnage of war, they remained untouched and unaffected, and stand now as they did two to three centuries ago, peaceful and serene.

The upper Hudson River has produced a number of cascades along its course from Hadley, in the southern Adirondacks, to Hudson Falls, north of the Capital District. From the Capital District to the Atlantic Ocean, however, there are no waterfalls or dams on the river. If there were, the Hudson River would not be affected by the tides. Fortunately, the Hudson River is blessed with many tributaries of all sizes and lengths, and it is to these tributaries and to neighboring streams in some of the outlying areas that we will turn in order to enjoy the waterfalls of the Hudson River Valley region as we proceed downstream from the southern Adirondacks to the Palisades.

MAPS

MAP KEY:

1. Rockwell Falls
2. Curtis Falls
3. Palmer Falls
4. Glens Falls
5. Bakers Falls
6. Fall in Pilot Knob
7. Buttermilk Falls (Fort Ann)
8. Kane Falls
9. Dionondahowa Falls
10. Middle Falls
11. Center Falls
42. Cascade on Fish Creek

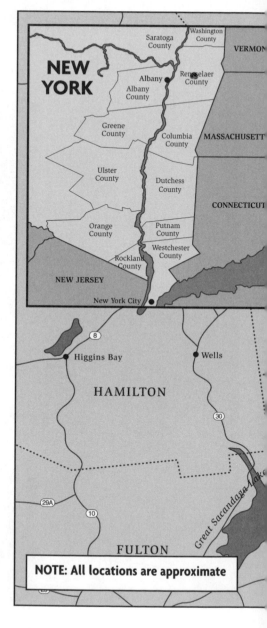

NOTE: All locations are approximate

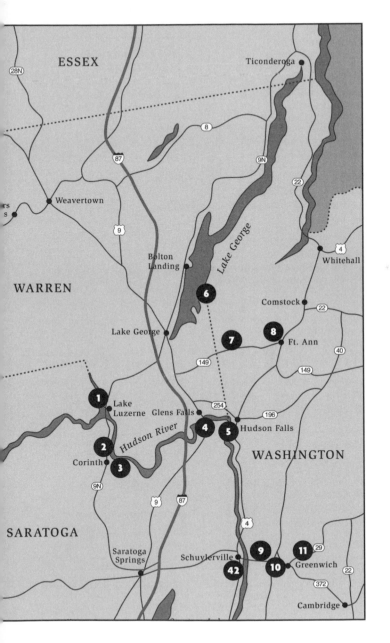

MAP KEY:

12. Buttermilk Falls (Schaghticoke)
13. Great Falls of the Hoosic
14. Hoosic Falls
15. Falls on Goulds Creek (north)
16. Falls on Goulds Creek (south)
17. Factory Hollow Falls
18. Mount Ida Falls
19. Eagle Mills Falls
20. Falls on Little Hoosic
21. Falls on Coon Brook
22. Falls on Wynants Kill
23. Barberville Falls
24. Falls at Rensselaer Technology Park
25. Red Mill Falls
26. Fall on Upper Wynants Kill
27. Fall on Burden Lake Road
28. Falls on Black River
29. Mattison Hollow Cascade
30. Falls on Tsatsawassa Creek
31. Falls in East Nassau
32. Fall on Moordener Kill
33. Falls on Muitzes Kill
34. Fall on Mill Creek
35. Falls in Valatie
36. Davenport Falls
37. Falls in Beebe Hill State Forest
38. Stuyvesant Falls
39. Rossman Falls
40. Fall on Fitting Creek
41. Fall on Claverack Creek
43. Buttermilk Falls (Cohoes)
44. Cohoes Falls
45. Buttermilk Falls (Albany)
46. Falls on Lower Normans Kill
47. Fall on Vloman Kill
48. Falls on Coeymans Creek
49. Ravena Falls
50. Falls on Coxsackie Creek
51. Falls on Tributary to Cob Creek.

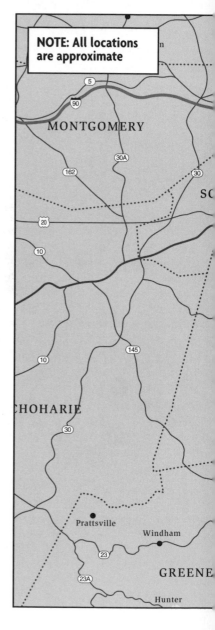

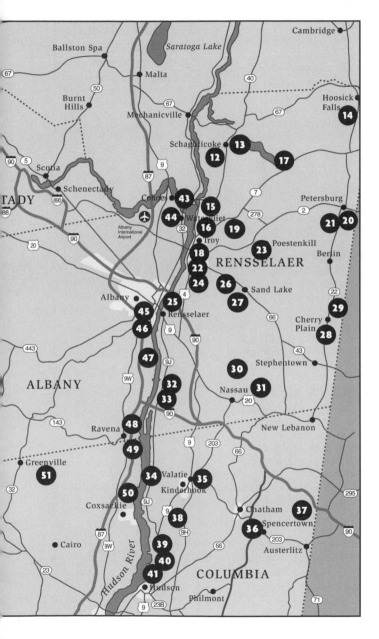

NOTE: All locations are approximate

GREENH

Hunter

Tar

Phoenicia

ULSTER

Kerhonkson

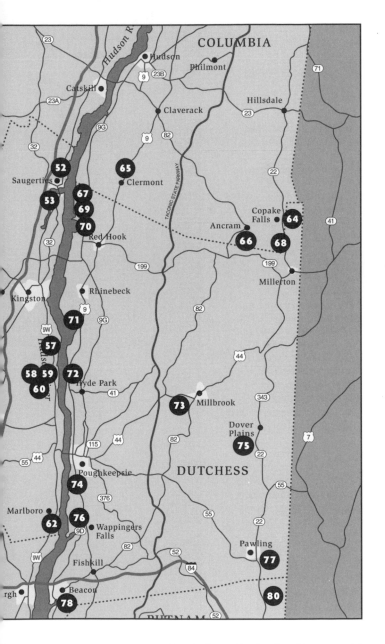

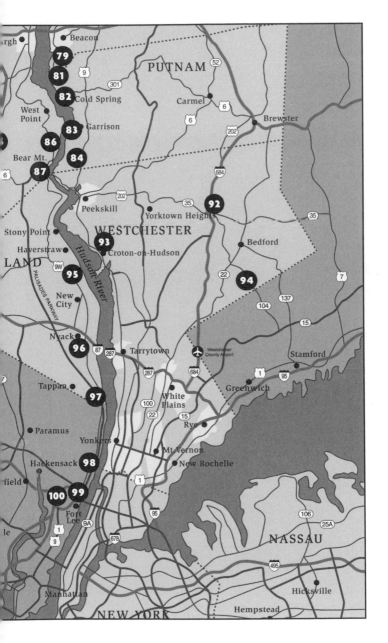

Waterfalls bridge the past and the present.

UPPER HUDSON RIVER

THE INDUSTRIAL SECTION

With the exception of Rockwell Falls (located between the hamlets of Hadley and Lake Luzerne), all of the falls to the southeast of the upper Hudson River—Curtis Falls, Palmer Falls, Spier Falls, Glens Falls, and Bakers Falls—are dammed, and have been for over a century. Each one of these industrialized waterfalls tells a similar story of how the addition of a dam increased the height of the falling waters, thereby amplifying the power that could be generated when the fall's potential energy was converted into kinetic energy. The impoundment of a sizable body of water above the falls also ensured that a reliable source of power was always available whenever summoned by the mills and factories. It was in this way that the waterfalls on the upper Hudson River were tamed.

ROCKWELL FALLS

Location: Hadley/Lake Luzerne (border of Warren & Saratoga counties)
Delorme *New York State Atlas & Gazetteer*: p. 80, B3
Accessibility: Roadside

Description: Because of Rockwell Falls' exceptional beauty as well its ideal location—only a stone's throw away from a well-traveled bridge that connects Hadley with Lake Luzerne—it is one of the most frequently photographed waterfalls on the Hudson River or in the Adirondacks.[1-3]

The waterfall is a twelve-foot drop at the mouth of a ruggedly cut glen formed on the Hudson River just upstream from the Hudson's confluence with the Sacandaga River, a major stream in its own right that flows northeast from the Great Sacandaga Lake (an artificially created reservoir). The glen is a picturesque area and remains a favorite destination for boaters and paddlers.

History: The area by the fall has seen its share of industrialization in past centuries. In the 1700s, Jeremy Rockwell erected the first sawmill on the west bank of the river. At one point the top of the fall was dynamited so as to widen the passage of water to make it more suitable for power generation.

Today the area appears pristine. Little evidence remains that the fall was ever touched by the hand of man.

Directions: From Saratoga Springs, drive north on Rt. 9N to Corinth. From the traffic light at the northern end of Corinth, continue north on Rt. 9N for 4.5 miles and then turn left onto Bay Road just as you begin to enter the outskirts of Lake Luzerne. Proceed northwest for 0.4 mile, then turn left onto Bridge Street. You will immediately cross over the "Bridge of Hope" from where, looking north, stunning views of Rockwell Falls can be obtained. Park off to the side of the road at either end of the bridge.

CURTIS FALLS

Location: Corinth (border of Warren & Saratoga counties)
Delorme *New York State Atlas & Gazetteer*: p. 80, B/C3
Accessibility: Roadside

Description: Curtis Falls is a set of ledge falls on the Hudson River formed at a crucial point where the river, after flowing northeast from the Hudson Gorge near Riparius, turns sharply east at the "Big Bend."[1]

The view of the falls is not a pretty one, marred by a long dam spanning its top and the hydroelectric plant sitting next to the base of the falls along the southwest bank. Under normal conditions—when water is being siphoned off for power generation—all that you will see will be mounds of bedrock and some rivulets.

History: Curtis Falls was named after Warren Curtis, Jr., who founded the Corinth Electric Light Company in 1896. His utility was a provider of limited service: "No electricity was supplied on moon-lit evenings or after midnight any evening."[2] Besides furnishing electricity, the plant also produced wood pulp, which was pumped downstream for a short distance to a paper mill.[3]

Beginning in 1913, Curtis Mills, home of the Corinth Electric Light Company, became a more reliable source of electrical power and maintained operations until 1950, when the business was purchased by New York Power and Light.

An historic marker at the pull-off overlooking the top of the dam points out that the site was once at the end of an old iron bridge built by the Owego Bridge Company in 1896. Previously to that bridge, crossings had been made at Jessup's Ferry. The new bridge, which spans the Hudson River just upstream from the dam and falls, was built in 1954.

Pagenstecher Park, from where views of the falls can be obtained, is named after Albrecht Pagenstecher, the first president of the Hudson River Paper Mill. Pagenstecher had purchased the land from the Palmers, who had acquired it from Edward Jessup.[3,4] The park was donated to Corinth in 1919 by the heirs of Pagenstecher's estate.

Directions: From Saratoga Springs, take Rt. 9N into the village of Cornith and proceed north for a short distance until you reach the stoplight at the northern end of town. Turn right onto East River Drive and go east for less than 0.1 mile. Just before you cross over the bridge spanning the Hudson River, turn right onto River Street. Follow River Street for 0.1 mile and then turn left as River Street continues, paralleling the Hudson River. Immediately, you will see a pull-off to the left from where the top of the dam can be viewed, as well as a portion of the fall below. Continue on River Road for another 0.1 mile and you will reach Palmer Avenue. Turn left onto Palmer Avenue and drive east for 0.05 mile, then turn left again into Pagenstecher Park. (As soon as you cross over the railroad tracks you will be in the park.) From the high, fenced-in overlook along the north side of the park, you can obtain distant but clear views of the fall. Keep your expectations low; the waterfall is not especially attractive because of its continued industrial use.

Curtis Dam. Many falls were dammed to increase the power of their water flow.

3

PALMER FALLS

Location: Corinth (border of Warren & Saratoga counties)
Delorme *New York State Atlas & Gazetteer*: p. 80, B/C3
Accessibility: 0.3-mile hike, one-way, to an overlook
Degree of Difficulty: Easy

Description: Palmer Falls is a seventy-foot-high dammed waterfall formed on the Hudson River.[1,2] It has also been known as Jessup's Great Falls. Sadly, the fall is frequently reduced to ledges of bedrock because of a dam across its top that diverts vast amounts of water for power generation.

With the demise of the paper plant next to the fall, there is no way to predict at this time what changes may occur to Palmer Falls in the future. One might hope that the fall will return to its former state of glory, but there is no assurance that this will ever happen.

History: A sawmill owned by Ira Haskins was erected near Palmer Falls around 1804. Later, in 1820, a gristmill and woolen factory were established. In 1859, Thomas Brown built an edge tool factory, and then in 1866 he began operating a woolen mill. The site became further industrialized in 1869 when the Hudson River Pulp and Paper Company began productions at the fall. The factory quickly became renowned as one of the first plants to produce pulp from wood. In 1898 the mill became part of a constellation of twenty mills that formed the International Paper Company.[3] The Curtis/Palmer Hydroelectric Company has provided a small park and overlook of the fall and dam from atop the north bank of the river.

Directions: Leaving Saratoga Springs, proceed north on Rt. 9N until you reach Corinth. When you come to the stoplight at the northern end of town, turn right onto East River Drive and immediately cross over the Hudson River. Drive north for 0.7 mile, then turn right onto Call Street and proceed uphill, going east, for another 0.7 mile.

When you see a sign that states "Scenic Overlook," pull into a parking area on your right. The park is open from sunrise to sunset, Memorial Day through Labor Day.

Follow the well-maintained path downhill for 0.3 mile to the overlook. Be prepared for a letdown, however, if you are visiting at a time when the Hudson River is running at anything but full throttle.

International Paper Company Mill, Corinth. The paper company is gone, but Palmer Falls and the dam remain.

4

GLENS FALLS

Location: City of Glens Falls (border of Warren & Saratoga counties)
Delorme *New York State Atlas & Gazetteer*: p. 81, B4-5
Accessibility: Roadside

Description: Glens Falls is the most famous (and at one time the most visited) waterfall on the Hudson River.[1-5] The fall is formed where the river begins a wild descent of nearly fifty feet over a series of broad drops and plunges. A long, U-shaped dam crowns the fall.

Until 1961 a spiral staircase descended from the Rt. 9 bridge to a rocky island in the center of the river directly in front of the fall. From there tourists could visit Cooper's Cave (immortalized in James Fenimore Cooper's *The Last of the Mohicans*) and view Glens Falls head-on from the level of the river. In 1961 the bridge was replaced and the staircase was demolished. The cave had been deemed unstable at that time and unsafe as a tourist attraction. Recently, however, a new, $15 million, four-lane bridge—the Cooper's Cave Bridge—has been built with a small observation balcony on the east side of the bridge. In addition a lower, pedestrian bridge has been constructed with an observation deck overlooking Cooper's Cave and providing views into the gorge, complete with interpretive signs to highlight the fall's history.[6]

History: Glens Falls is named after John Glen, Jr., who operated an early mill at the fall. Originally the fall was known as Wing Falls, after Abraham Wing, who founded a settlement of the Society of Friends (Quakers) in 1763 and operated a sawmill at the waterfall by 1765.

Native Americans called the falls *Chepontuc,* meaning "a difficult place to get around."[7] This name has never been as apt as now; with all of the sluiceways and factory buildings lining both sides of the gorge by the fall, approaching the waterfall from its banks is nearly impossible.

The site has provided waterpower for lumber, plaster, paper, and lime-kiln mills. During the twentieth century, limestone was mined to make Portland cement and provide building stone. Over the last century, the area has been a major paper manufacturing center.

The hydroelectric plant next to the observation deck was built in 1993–94 and is the newest industrial addition to the site. You can see two enormous pipes coming down from the sluiceway along the south bank. These enter the power plant after going underground.

Directions: Take Rt. 9 either south from Glens Falls or north from South Glens Falls to the Cooper's Cave Bridge. The observation deck overlooking Cooper's Cave and providing views of the gorge and the fall is accessible off River Street at the southwest end of the bridge.

Glens Falls was once a pristine waterfall—but that was over 300 years ago.

5

BAKERS FALLS

Location: Hudson Falls (border of Saratoga & Washington counties)
Delorme *New York State Atlas & Gazetteer:* p. 81, B5
Accessibility: Roadside or via canoe
Degree of Difficulty: Easy, either by land or water

Description: Like Glens Falls, Bakers Falls is formed on the Hudson River and is a natural wonder that has been exploited and substantially modified in order to extract work from its falling waters.[1-5] As a result the natural beauty of the limestone falls and the gorge has been greatly compromised.

Not counting the dam at the top, Bakers Falls has a total drop of sixty-eight feet. The present dam is 1,015 feet in length and curved like a bow to ensure that the maximum possible volume of water can flow over the top of the dam without causing a bottleneck. In earlier times, timber crib dams served as a barrage.

History: Hudson Falls was originally known as Sandy Hill. The first mill in the area was erected in 1765 by Albert Baker, for whom the falls are named.[6] In the early 1800s the industries at the falls turned to paper manufacturing.[7] Old ruins are clearly visible below the falls along the east bank. An old stone bridge lies between the new bridge and the top of the dam.

The falls are presently used for power generation by Hudson Falls Hydroelectric, which has a powerhouse in nearby Fenimore (named after author James Fenimore Cooper, who made the fall at Glens Falls famous).

Directions: From the Adirondack Northway (I-87), get off at Exit 17N and head northeast on Rt. 9 for 1.3 miles. Turn right onto Rt. 197 and drive east for 4.8 miles, crossing over the Hudson River and Rogers Island, until you come to Rt. 4. Turn left onto Rt. 4 and drive north for over 2.0 miles to Hudson Falls. When you come to a stoplight, turn left onto John Street and drive west for 0.2 mile. Turn right onto Sumpter Street and drive north for 0.2 mile. Turn west onto Bridge Street (which immediately crosses the Hudson River). As soon as you cross over the bridge (at 0.2 mile from Sumpter Street), you will see a parking area to your left where limited views of Bakers Falls can be obtained.

If you continue southwest for less than another 0.2 mile, you will come to a left-hand turn down a gravel road that will take you to a lower parking area. Partial views of the fall can be obtained from the rocky shore here. For optimal, unobstructed views of the falls, launch a canoe or kayak from here and head up to near the base of the falls, keeping a respectable, safe distance away from the hydraulics.

Bakers Falls is the last dammed waterfall on the Hudson River.

NORTHEAST OF THE HUDSON RIVER

Although not directly on the Hudson River or its tributaries, the following three falls are relatively close at hand and deserve mention. The latter two—Buttermilk Falls and Kane Falls—are historically significant enough to have been specifically mentioned in Delorme's *New York State Atlas & Gazetteer*.

6

FALL IN PILOT KNOB RIDGE PRESERVE

Location: Lake George (Washington County)
Delorme *New York State Atlas & Gazetteer*: p. 81, A4-5
Accessibility: 1.5-mile walk with moderate changes in elevation
Degree of Difficulty: Difficult

Description: This twenty-foot-high waterfall is formed on a tiny creek that possesses a limited watershed. For optimal viewing this hike should be taken early in the season when sufficient water is flowing to animate the fall.

History: This unnamed waterfall is located in the 223-acre Pilot Knob Ridge Preserve, an area of protected land whose name is derived from nearby Pilot Knob Mountain. Pilot Knob was named for the fact that early river men would use the 2,180-foot nubble to help guide them at night through the dangerous reefs at the north end of Ripley Point, south of Pilot Knob.[1]

Several decades ago, a developer illegally cleared the land, constructed a mile-long road up to the top of a high hill, and built a house in the general vicinity of the present gazebo. Many landowners and concerned citizens became upset over what had happened to the previously unbroken continuity of the Pilot Knob range, and they demanded that something be done about the house that blighted the horizon. Through a series of fortunate circumstances, the land was confiscated by local authorities, the house was demolished, and the property was returned to the Zug family. A decade later the Zug family graciously sold the land to the Lake George Land Conservancy at well below market value.[2] The Pilot Knob Ridge Preserve is an example of what concerned citizens and local authorities can accomplish even in instances when land has been privatized and seemingly removed from the public domain.

The area has also seen some tragedy. In 1969 a Mohawk Airlines plane with fourteen passengers crashed near Pilot Knob, killing all aboard.[3]

Directions: From the Adirondack Northway (I-87), get off at Exit 20 for Fort Ann and Whitehall. Turn left onto Rt. 9 and drive north for 0.5 mile, then turn right onto Rt. 149 and drive east for 4.7 miles. At a traffic light turn left onto Rt. 9L and drive north for 4.6 miles. When you reach the waters of Lake George, where Rt. 9L veers to the left, continue straight onto Pilot Knob Road. Drive north from this point for 0.7 mile and park in a designated area on your right for the Pilot Knob Ridge Preserve.

From the parking area, follow the red-blazed trail as it wends its way steadily uphill for over 0.4 mile. At the top of the main hill, you will come to a gazebo with wonderful views of Lake George. From the gazebo, follow the road for less than a hundred feet and then take the trail (which becomes blue-blazed) heading off into the woods. From this point, the hike to the fall is roughly 1.2 miles.

You will come to a junction where the blue-blazed trail makes a large loop, going off both to the left and straight ahead. Continue straight ahead for 0.1 mile and you will see the fall upstream as you cross over the creek. It is relatively easy to scamper over to the base of the fall from this point, or you can follow the blue-blazed trail uphill for over 0.1 mile to the top of the fall.

BUTTERMILK FALLS
(Fort Ann)

Location: West Fort Ann (Washington County)
Delorme *New York State Atlas & Gazetteer*: p.81, A5
Accessibility: Roadside, but views are seasonal

Description: This medium-sized waterfall is formed on a tiny stream which rises from Sly Pond and The Three Ponds to the north, eventually flowing into Halfway Creek. Buttermilk Falls has the distinctions of having a road named after it and being identified on Delorme's *New York State Atlas & Gazetteer.*

Directions: From the Adirondack Northway (I-87), get off at Exit 20 for Fort Ann and Whitehall. Turn left on Rt. 9 and drive north for 0.5 mile, then turn right onto Rt. 149 and drive east for 6.0 miles. Turn left and drive northeast on Buttermilk Falls Road for 1.4 miles. The waterfall will be visible off to your left in the woods.

Bear in mind that the waterfall is on private property. Stay on roadside.

This trip should be combined with one taken to visit mammoth Shelving Rock Falls (see *Adirondack Waterfall Guide: New York's Cool Cascades,* p. 196).

KANE FALLS
(Historic)

Location: Fort Ann (Washington County)
Accessibility: On posted land; not open to the public

Description: Kane Falls is formed on Halfway Creek, a medium-sized stream that rises from Wilkie Reservoir, east of Lake Luzerne, and flows into the Champlain Canal at Fort Ann.[1] The fall is approximately fifty feet in height and descends over a series of steep drops.

History: Kane Falls has over 400 years of recorded history. Centuries ago the area surrounding the fall was called "the Warpath of the

A Revolutionary War blockhouse once stood at Kane Falls.

Natives" because of its strategic location at the northern terminus of the "Great Carrying Place" between Fort Edward and Skenesboro (present-day Whitehall).[2]

In 1765 the waterfall was the site of a Revolutionary War blockhouse and a sawmill. At that time it was briefly called Cheshire Falls, possibly after the man who erected the first sawmill. The mill provided a ready supply of lumber to General Benedict Arnold, whose fleet was assembled in nearby Whitehall.[3] After the Revolutionary War, the waterfall was acquired by John Wray, who later sold it to Charles Kane for whom the fall is named. Kane erected several mills and forges, and as his production of cables and anchors increased, the mills came to be known as the Kane Iron Works.

Since then, other mills have occupied the fall including a pulp mill, carding mill, the Kane Falls Woolen Mill, and the Bridgeport Wood Finishing Company.

Eugene Ashley of Glens Falls once installed a generator to supply electricity to Fort Ann, and Niagara Mohawk once had a power station at the site.

Detailed directions cannot be given at this time because the falls are on private property.

CAPITAL REGION

The Capital Region is geologically defined by its strategic location at the confluence of two mighty river valley systems—the Hudson River, flowing north to south, and the Mohawk River, coming in from the west. The two rivers converge at Waterford. There, the Mohawk River flows into the Hudson River after making its way between a series of small, interlaced islands, the most historically significant of which is Peebles Island, home to tiny Buttermilk Falls. Waterford's name came naturally; it was one of the few places along the Hudson River where it was possible to ford the water without a boat or a ferry.

A second distinguishing geological feature of the Capital Region is that it marks the northernmost point where the Hudson River is tidal (at the Federal Dam in Troy).

The region's third distinguishing geological feature is that it rests in the basin of what used to be glacial Lake Albany, which explains why part of the area is so broad and flat.

Although the Mohawk River is the Hudson's main tributary, it is by no means the only stream that carries a significant volume of water. The Batten Kill, flowing in from Vermont, produces several notable waterfalls along the way, including Dionondahowa Falls. The Hoosic River, racing down from Massachusetts, produces several noteworthy waterfalls as well, including the Great Falls of the Hoosic.

The Capital Region's long history of hydropower industrialization is not surprising when you consider that the area is at the hub of a vast network of natural waterways augmented by railroads, highways, and canals.

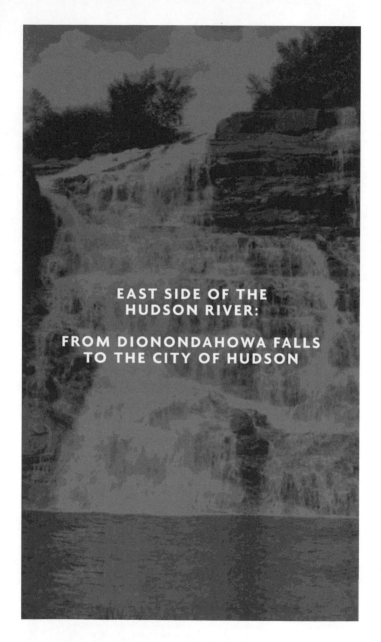

EAST SIDE OF THE HUDSON RIVER:

FROM DIONONDAHOWA FALLS TO THE CITY OF HUDSON

DIONONDAHOWA FALLS

Location: Near Greenwich (Washington County)
Delorme *New York State Atlas & Gazetteer*: p. 81, C/D5-6
Accessibility: Short walk over uneven terrain; canoe/kayak paddle
Degree of Difficulty: Easy by land or water

Description: Dionondahowa Falls is an impressive, thundering cataract formed on the Batten Kill, a sizable river that rises north of Manchester, Vermont, and flows into the Hudson River several miles downstream from the fall.[1-6] The Batten Kill runs for over twenty miles through Vermont and twenty-four miles through New York State.[5]

The fall is roughly fifty to sixty feet high and has been hewn out of a deeply formed gorge. Benson J. Lossing wrote of the fall in the mid-nineteenth century: "For about three hundred feet above the great falls, the stream rushes through a narrow rocky chasm, roaring and foaming; and then, in a still narrower space, it leaps into the dark gulf which has been named the Devil's Caldron, in a perpendicular fall of almost forty feet."[7]

Dionondahowa Falls has also been called the Great Falls of the Batten Kill, and Big Falls.[5,6,8]

History: The origin of the name Dionondahowa is somewhat obscure, but according to one source it is the Iroquois name for the river. Another source contends that Dionondahowa may have something to do with the Native American name for the conical hills that have formed on the south side of the river.[9]

The Batten Kill was named after an early settler named Bat.[10]

Around 1880 several industries were erected near the waterfall. Two paper mills—one built by the Bennington Falls Paper Company, another by the Ondawa Paper Company—were established on the east bank of the stream. Both mills originally manufactured manila wrapping paper. The Bennington Falls Paper Company was owned by two families from Hoosic Falls by the names of Stevens and Thompson. Eventually the plant came to be known as the Stevens & Thompson Paper Company, specializing in the production of tissue paper. The plant came under the ownership of John Bright in the 1930s, then of Robert Stevens in the 1940s.[6]

Also near the falls were a powerhouse operated by the Hudson Valley Electric Railway, and a primitive electric plant operated by Gardner & Rich that provided electricity to Greenwich and Schuylerville.

In the early 1900s a recreational area called Dionondahowa Park was established along the west bank of the river opposite the former Stevens & Thompson Paper Company mill. People came from as far away as Troy and Glens Falls to be entertained by band concerts, to picnic, and to engage in sports activities.[11]

The present public access to the falls and the viewing areas are provided through the generosity of Dahowa Hydro.

Directions: From the village of Schuylerville (junction of Rtes. 29 East & 4), take Rt. 29 east across the Hudson River and continue east for nearly 2.5 miles. Before reaching the intersection of Rtes. 29 & 40, turn left onto Windy Hill Road and drive north for 0.6 mile. You will come to a parking area on the right with a sign stating "Welcome. Dionondahowa Falls. Viewing Area. Dahowa Hydro."

Park and follow the trail down to the top of the gorge. There is a series of lookouts and observation decks along the rim that allow you to see the fall and the gorge safely.

It is also possible to canoe up to the falls on the Batten Kill if you put in above the upper dam at Clarks Mills.

This view of Dionondahowa Falls is as you would see it from canoe or kayak.

10

MIDDLE FALLS

Location: Near Greenwich (Washington County)
Delorme *New York State Atlas & Gazetteer*: p. 81, C/D5-6
Accessibility: Roadside
Description: Middle Falls is a medium-sized, block-shaped, twenty-foot-high waterfall formed on the Batten Kill, a large stream that rises north of Manchester, Vermont, and flows into the Hudson River several miles downstream from the fall.[1-4]

The fall is located directly below a bridge spanning the Batten Kill. From the east side of the bridge can be seen a dam that impounds a small body of water. Old ruins are visible on the north bank next to the fall.

History: Gerrit G. Lansing built the first mill at Middle Falls, along the east bank. The tiny hamlet of Arkansaw formed around this mill. Later, Lansing's mill was sold to Joseph Heath who operated a gristmill, a fulling mill, and plaster grinding mill.

The southwestern side of the river at Middle Falls was settled in 1766 by Nathan Tefft and his son Stanton. Although the Teffts were primarily farmers, it is believed that they also operated a sawmill at the site.

Arkansaw later became known as Galesville, presumably after John Gale (or his son Frederick), who operated a grist and flour mill, a sawmill, and a land plaster mill. Just before his death in 1848, Gale went into partnership with two associates and built a three-story brick mill next to his gristmill. Initially the building served as a woolen mill. Later it was used for making shoe shanks, and still later it produced cotton mesh underwear. In the 1920s the building was destroyed by fire.

In the 1880s the name of the hamlet changed to Middle Falls.[5]

In 1892 the Consolidated Electric Company leased the land around the fall and built an electric power station to service Schuylerville, Greenwich, and Cambridge. In 1927 the company merged with the Adirondack Power & Light Company and went through successive mergers until it was finally acquired by Niagara Mohawk.

The present dam next to the Rt. 29 bridge was built in 1900.

Directions: From Schuylerville (junction of Rtes. 4 & 29 East), take Rt. 29 east for over 3 miles until you reach the village of Middle Falls, right after you pass by the junction of Rtes. 29 & 40. At 0.4 mile from the junction of Rtes. 29 & 40, Rt. 29 crosses over a bridge that spans the Batten Kill. Immediately park off to the side of the road. There are limited but sufficient views of the fall and dam from the top of the bridge.

Middle Falls was named for its position between two other waterfalls on the Batten Kill.

CENTER FALLS

Location: Center Falls (Washington County)
Delorme *New York State Atlas & Gazetteer*: p. 81, C/D6
Accessibility: Near roadside
Degree of Difficulty: Easy

Description: This waterfall, which is fairly wide and dammed, is formed on the Batten Kill, a large stream that rises north of Manchester, Vermont, and flows into the Hudson River west of Clarks Mills.[1-3] The waterfall and dam are approximately twenty feet high.

History: In the early days, Center Falls was known as Hardscrabble because of the difficulty of the climb to get there by horse from Greenwich.[4] The hamlet was settled by Smith Barber and Nathan Rogers and became a lumbering district.[2]

Directions: From Schuylerville (junction of Rtes. 29 East & 4), drive east on Rt. 29 until you come to Greenwich. From the junction of Rtes. 29 & 372 in Greenwich, continue east on Rt. 29 for a little over 2 miles. As soon as you pass the Hollingsworth & Vose plant on your right, turn right onto Center Falls Road and drive south for 0.1 mile, crossing over the Batten Kill in the process. Turn right onto Cozy Hollow Road and pull over immediately when you see the signs indicating access to Center Falls.

Walk down to the stream for an excellent view of the fall and dam from the south bank.

Public access is permitted across private lands, courtesy of Hollingsworth & Vose. Obey all rules and regulations, and remember that you are there as a guest.

BUTTERMILK FALLS
(Schaghticoke)

Location: Southwest of Schaghticoke (Rensselaer County)
Delorme *New York State Atlas & Gazetteer:* p. 67, A/B4-5
Accessibility: Roadside

Description: This pretty cascade is formed on Tomhannock Creek, a medium-sized stream that flows out of the Tomhannock Reservoir and into the Hoosic River west of Schaghticoke.[1] The fall is over ten feet high and fairly broad.

A second, taller waterfall, 0.1 mile downstream, can be seen as you drive in from Rt. 29 along Buttermilk Falls Road. Take note, however, that both falls are on private land and can be observed only from roadside.

A third waterfall, known as Hidden Falls, is further upstream, but it is located in deep woods and is also on private property.

History: The waters producing Buttermilk Falls come from the Tomhannock Reservoir (which, in turn, is formed by several smaller creeks) located in Pittstown. The reservoir is approximately six miles long and two miles wide, covers 1,750 acres, has an average depth of twenty-one feet,[2] and furnishes water to Troy and several other nearby towns.

A mill dating back to the early 1700s once operated below the waterfall.[3]

Ann Eliza Bleecker wrote *The History of Maria Kittle*—which many scholars consider to be America's first novel—while living near the falls. In one passage of the novel, Ms. Bleecker wrote, "the roaring of Tomhanick dashed with rapidity its foaming waters among the broken rock."[3]

Directions: From I-87 (the Adirondack Northway), get off at Exit 9 and drive northeast on Rt. 146 for 2.2 miles. When you come to the junction of Rtes. 146 & 236, turn left onto Rt. 146 and drive northeast for another 2.7 miles. When Rt. 146 comes to an end at a stop-light, turn left onto Rtes. 32/4 and drive north into Mechanicville, proceeding for 1.5 miles. Turn right onto Rt. 67, go east for 0.1 mile, and then turn right, following Rt. 67 south for 0.3 mile to a stop-light. Turn left and follow Rt. 67 as it crosses over the Hudson River. Proceed east on Rt. 67 for just over 3 miles. As soon as you cross over Tomhannock Creek, turn right onto Buttermilk Falls Road and drive southeast for 1.4 miles. You will reach a point where the road veers sharply to the left after crossing a tiny bridge. The cascade is visible there from the side of the road.

The Great Falls of the Hoosic. Much of the Hoosic's water has been diverted for power generation.

13

GREAT FALLS OF THE HOOSIC

Location: Schaghticoke (Rensselaer County)
Delorme *New York State Atlas & Gazetteer*: p. 67, A/B5
Accessibility: Roadside

Description: There are several falls and a large dam on the Hoosic River, a medium-sized stream that rises from the Cheshire Reservoir south of Adams, Massachusetts, and flows into the Hudson River near Stillwater.[1,2] There is much to see from the top of the Schaghticoke bridge spanning the Hoosic River. Upstream is a mighty dam, nearly perpendicular to the bridge, which diverts a significant portion of the river through a channel paralleling the stream to a power plant downstream. Below the bridge are several cascades that become more pronounced when less water is flowing through the gorge. From the west side of the bridge, you can see the ruins of an old factory near the base of the bridge, as well as the ruins of the old cotton mill, 0.1 mile further downstream. Both are along the north bank. If you look downstream closely enough, you will notice the distant brink of a large waterfall that extends across the entire width of the stream. This is the Great Falls of the Hoosic, a broad, fifteen-foot-high wall of rock with deep chasms worn into the bedrock at several places along its length. There are more chasms downstream from the base of the falls along the north bank.

History: Hoosic is a Native American word for "stony country." Schaghticoke comes from the Algonquian word for "mingling of the waters" (namely, the Hoosic River and Tomhannock Creek). The Hoosic River and its main tributary, the Little Hoosic, have also been called Wappennakuis, or "Fresh River," a name that may have derived from the Abenaki tribe.[2]

The Schaghticoke Woolen Mill was a main industry in the village of Schaghticoke, beginning in 1864. At its peak it employed 175 workers and processed 145,000 pounds of Australian wool each month. The mill was demolished in 1932 after sitting idle for nearly a quarter of a century. The factory sat along the north bank directly next to the Great Falls of the Hoosic.[3]

In 1909, Russell Parsons, representing General Electric, secured land rights at Schaghticoke and erected a 12,000-kilowatt plant. Power produced by generators downstream from the falls was transmitted by a line of towers twenty-two miles long to Schenectady, where General Electric was based.

Directions: From the Adirondack Northway (I-87), get off at Exit 9 in Clifton Park and take Rt. 146 east for 2.2 miles. Turn left at the junction of Rtes. 146 & 236, and drive northeast on Rt. 146 for 2.7 miles until Rt. 146 comes to an end at a stoplight. Turn left onto Rtes. 4/32 and proceed north into Mechanicville, continuing for 1.5 miles. At a stoplight, turn right onto Rt. 67, drive east for 0.1 mile, and then turn south, following Rt. 67 for 0.3 mile to a stoplight. Turn left and continue on Rt. 67 as it crosses over the Hudson River. From the east end of the bridge, follow Rt. 67 east for 5.4 miles until you come to the junction of Rtes. 67 & 40. Turn left onto Rtes. 67/40 and proceed northeast. At 0.5 mile you will reach the high bridge that spans the Hoosic River. When you get to the end of the bridge, at 0.7 mile, turn right at a blinking light onto Main Street. Park along the side of the road on Main Street.

Return on foot to the bridge, where you will have excellent views looking down from both sides of the bridge into the gorge and at the several cascades below.

14

HOOSIC FALLS

Location: Hoosick Falls (Rensselaer County)
Delorme *New York State Atlas & Gazetteer*: p. 67, A7
Accessibility: Roadside

Description: Hoosic Falls consist of a series of small cascades formed on the Hoosic River, a sizable stream that rises from the Cheshire Reservoir in Massachusetts and flows into the Hudson River across from Stillwater.[1]

Gordon's 1836 *Gazetteer* states that the village of Hoosick Falls "has a fall here of 40 feet within 12 rods, affording fine water power, nearly all of which is unemployed; contains 1 Baptist and 1 Presbyterian churches, grist, saw, oil, carding and cloth dressing mills, 2 large factories, [and] a manufacturing of shearing machines."[2] What is most interesting about this passage is that the writer listed the large number of industries at the falls, but still considered the river to be nearly "unemployed."

When the water level subsides a bit during the summer, numerous potholes that have been carved out by the river's swirling waters become visible.

Hoosic Falls was at one time a main industrial center.

History: Hoosic is an Algonquian word meaning "stony," or "stony country." The river's name has also been spelled Hoosac and Hoosick at various times in the past.[3] Native Americans called it Wappennakuis, or Fresh River.[4]

The village was settled by Dutch and English pioneers and became incorporated as Hoosick Falls in 1827. In 1784, Joseph Dorr erected a carding and fulling mill along the north bank of the river. Soon a flax mill, a distillery, and a sawmill were established as well. In 1786, Benjamin Colvin built a gristmill along the south bank of the Hoosic River. The first bridge over the Hoosic River was constructed 1791, for the first time linking the two sections of the village of Hoosick Falls without the need of a ferry or boat crossing. In 1823, Joseph Gordon put up a cotton factory on the south bank, and in 1831 the Tremont Cotton Factory was erected on the north bank.

In 1865 an enormous tract of land next to the northern end of the bridge became the site of the Walter A. Wood Mowing & Reaping Machine Company, which endured until 1924 when it went into receivership and closed. During its heyday the plant consisted of forty-one buildings and employed 2,000 workers. Over one million farm machines were produced during the plant's lifetime.[1,5,6]

A dam once crossed the river at the top of the falls, but no evidence of it remains today.

The famous folk artist, Grandma Moses (Anna Mary Robertson, 1860–1961), lived only a few miles from Hoosick Falls.

Directions: From Troy, go northeast on Rt. 7. At the junction of Rtes. 22 west & 7, turn left onto Rt. 22 and drive north until you reach the village of Hoosick Falls, where Rt. 22 turns abruptly right opposite Church Street. Instead of turning right and continuing on Rt. 22, proceed straight ahead. Within several hundred feet you will cross over a large bridge spanning the Hoosic River.

Park either in town or at the back of the parking lot used by Allied Signal. The falls can be readily seen by standing at the north end of the bridge and looking downstream.

15

FALLS ON GOULDS CREEK AT NORTH END OF OAKWOOD CEMETERY

Location: Lansingburgh (Rensselaer County)
Delorme *New York State Atlas & Gazetteer*: p. 67, B/C4
Accessibility: Short hike, less than 0.2 mile
Degree of Difficulty: Easy to moderate

Description: There are two cascades that have formed on Goulds Creek, a small stream that rises east of Oakwood Avenue and is impounded at the Oakwood Cemetery, where it forms two small ponds.[1-3] According to old records, Long Lake (the larger of the two ponds) covers five acres and is twenty-five feet deep in places. Undoubtedly the depth of the ponds has decreased slightly over the years from sedimentation. From Long Lake, Goulds Creek descends rapidly through a series of steep ravines and is finally channeled underground just east of the intersection of 111th Street and 9th Avenue, and thence out into the Hudson River.[4] Both cascades are downstream from the outlet of Long Lake. The upper cascade, which is the smaller of the two, is located at the outlet of Long Lake and is roughly fifteen feet in height. The lower—and by far the larger—cascade is located downstream from where the ravine changes direction from north to west, forming a series of pitched descents some fifty feet in height. This area is known as the Devil's Kitchen.

History: The Oakwood Cemetery has a rustic history that dates back to 1849. Its lakes and ponds have been artificially created, and many of its shrubs and trees are not native to the area. Of the many famous people buried here, undoubtedly the most celebrated of them all is Sam Wilson, who many believe was the original "Uncle Sam" popularized by political cartoonists.

According to Warren Broderick, "A remarkable carved stone face effigy of Native American origin was found some years ago in Devil's Kitchen at the base of the lower waterfalls."[5] This suggests that Goulds Creek and its waterfalls were visited for many centuries prior to European settlement.

Directions: From I-787, get off at the Troy Exit (9E) and take Rt. 7 east. As soon as you cross over the Hudson River and begin driving up a long hill, turn left onto Rt. 40. Proceed north for 1.1 miles. Turn left and drive into the Oakwood Cemetery. Proceed north for over 0.7 mile until you pass two small bodies of water, one on each side of you. Immediately turn left and drive west for another 0.2 mile, paralleling the north side of the pond until you reach the end of Long Lake (the larger of the two ponds), where the outlet can be found. Park the car off to the side of the road and follow the trail that parallels the west bank of the ravine.

You can also access the ravine by continuing north on I-787 past Troy towards Cohoes. Just before you reach the city of Cohoes, turn right onto Rt. 470 and proceed east. Cross over the Hudson River and then turn right onto Rt. 4. Drive south for one block and turn left onto 111th Street, now going east. Park at the intersection of 111th Street and 9th Ave. Walk to the end of 111th Street, where a cement block drain channels Goulds Creek under Lansingburgh. Hike up and over the Uncle Sam Bikeway and continue east up a gully to the main cascade. The second cascade is further up the ravine near the top of the escarpment.

16

FALLS ON GOULDS CREEK AT SOUTH END OF OAKWOOD CEMETERY

Location: Lansingburgh (Rensselaer County)
Delorme *New York State Atlas & Gazetteer:* p. 67, B/C4
Accessibility: Roadside

Description: This noteworthy cascade is formed on a tiny stream that rises near Oakwood Cemetery. The stream is impounded next to the cemetery's crematorium, and ultimately flows into the Hudson River after being channeled under the streets of Lansingburgh from the base of the escarpment.[1] The cascade is roughly thirty feet high and formed at the top of a gully cut into the eastern escarpment, directly to the north of the crematorium.

There are lower falls as well, which are located just above the Uncle Sam Bikeway (an abandoned railroad bed).

If you stand at the south end of the crematorium and look across the valley, you can get a distant but still astonishingly clear view of Cohoes Falls.

History: The Gardner Earl Crematorium—Oakwood Cemetery's centerpiece—is a Romanesque structure that was built in the late 1800s.

The three-mile-long Uncle Sam Bikeway, which is located at the base of Oakwood Cemetery along the western border of the property, was opened to the public in 1981. It is located on a portion of the former rail bed of the Troy & Boston Railroad.

Directions: From I-787, get off at the Troy Exit (9E) for Rt. 7 and proceed east. As soon as you cross over the Hudson River, Rt. 7 turns into Hoosic Street. Begin following Hoosic Street uphill, and then immediately turn left onto Rt. 40. Head north for 1.1 miles and turn left into the entrance for the Oakwood Cemetery and Crematorium. You will soon come to the crematorium and chapel, which will be on your left. After passing the crematorium, at

0.2 mile, take your first left, which leads down a steep hill (and eventually out onto 101st Street in Lansingburgh). As soon as you start down the steep hill, you will notice a ravine off to your left. Park and walk over to the ravine, from where you can see the main cascade.

There are more falls in a lower section of the ravine. Continue downhill along the main road for 0.3 mile from the crematorium and turn right into section Q. From the edge of the ravine at the end of the tiny road leading in to section Q, you can look down at several cascades.

Or better yet, continue downhill on the main road for another 0.2 mile. You will cross over the Uncle Sam Bikeway and exit from Oakwood Cemetery. Turn left onto 7th Street and then immediately turn left again onto Garden Court. Drive to the end of Garden Court and park. From the end of the street, walk up onto the Uncle Sam Bikeway and proceed north. Within 0.2 mile you will come to a series of cascades on your right at the terminus of the ravine that you saw earlier from above. From here the stream is channeled underground, where it remains for the rest of its journey under Lansingburgh and into the Hudson River.

17

FACTORY HOLLOW FALLS

Location: Near the Tomhannock Reservoir, Factory Hollow
(Rensselaer County)
Delorme *New York State Atlas & Gazetteer*: p. 67, B5-6
Accessibility: Roadside

Description: Factory Hollow Falls is formed on Sunkauissia Creek,
a small stream that rises in the hills east of Lake Lorraine and flows
into the Tomhannock Reservoir a short distance downstream from
the falls. Prior to the reservoir's creation, the stream flowed directly
into Tomhannock Creek. The falls consist of a series of small ledge
drops, beginning just upstream from the bridge.

The main waterfall, downstream from the bridge, is three or
four feet high and is formed in a more constricted section of the
streambed. Near the base of the falls, along the north bank, can be
seen the stonewall ruins of an old factory building. Also on the
north bank, next to the bridge, are several stone benches facing the
stream. There is a painted piece of old machinery made to look like
a centerpiece. It would seem that some effort has been made to turn
this site into a little park, but a park that is probably intended only
for the landowner's private use.

History: The Tomhannock Reservoir and its out-flowing stream are
named after the hamlet of Tomhannock (previously known as
Reed's Hollow), which is located on Otter Creek, a tiny tributary to
the reservoir. The name was originally spelled Tomhenack, but was
gradually modified over the years. The reservoir is not large when
compared to the Great Sacandaga Lake north of Amsterdam, or the
various reservoirs contained in the Catskills, but at 0.5 mile long
and two miles wide, it is still of respectable size and large enough to
provide water for Troy and several other communities.[1,2]

In the mid-nineteenth century, several mills were built along
the creek in a section known as Sherman's Mills. One of the mills

was a textile and weaving mill run by Wilbur Sherman. There also were a sawmill and a flax mill. Later, a paper mill was erected, and a shirt factory, gristmill, and cider mill were added at the beginning of the twentieth century.[3]

Directions: From I-787, get off at exit 9E for Troy and drive east on Rt. 7 for over 11 miles. As soon as you have crossed over the Tomhannock Reservoir, 6.3 miles from the junction of Rtes. 7 & 278, turn left onto Reservoir Lake Road (Rt. 115) and proceed north for 1.2 miles. Turn right onto Factory Hollow Road (a hard-packed dirt road) and drive east for 0.6 mile. At the fork in the road, bear left onto Holbritter (or Hollerbrader) Road, which takes you immediately across a small bridge that spans Sunkauissia Creek. Park off to the side of the road. The tiny falls are mostly downstream from the bridge.

18

MOUNT IDA FALLS

Location: Troy (Rensselaer County)
Delorme *New York State Atlas & Gazetteer*: p. 67, B/C4
Accessibility: Roadside; steep walk down a hill for a closer view
Degree of Difficulty: Easy

Description: Mount Ida Falls (also known as Poestenkill High Falls and sometimes, though less often, Wire Mill Falls) is one of those natural treasures in the heart of the Capital District that is not heavily visited despite the occasional burst of publicity whenever a novice rock climber has to be hauled out of the gorge. Mount Ida Falls consists of a series of cascades totaling 175 feet in height formed on the Poesten Kill, a medium-sized stream that rises principally from Dyken Pond (a 173-acre lake northeast of East Poestenkill) and flows into the Hudson River at downtown Troy.[1-4] The falls are located near the mouth of the Poesten Kill Gorge, an immense ravine of black shale whose cascades and adjacent hills and flatlands along the southern rim were incorporated into a park in 1976 and listed in the National Register of Historic Places.

As soon as you drive into the parking area, your attention will immediately be riveted by the three main cascades, each one successively taller in height. There is also a block cascade, some fifteen feet high, which is formed several hundred feet downstream from the base of the main falls.

Several miles further upstream, just past the point where Rt. 2 crosses over the Poesten Kill, is an elongated cascade to your left that can be seen from roadside.

History: The name Poestenkill likely derives from the Dutch word *poesten,* meaning "foamy."[6]

The Poesten Kill Gorge has been significantly altered over the last few hundred years by the numerous factories, mills, and industries that have exploited the Poesten Kill's waterpower.

Ghostly ruins from some of these old mills still remain in the gorge.

The Poesten Kill's long industrial history goes back as far as 1660 when Jan B. Wemp constructed a mill on the stream, and continued for three centuries until 1962 when the Manning Paper Mill burned down. In between, there has been a variety of sawmills, gristmills, paper mills, and cotton mills along the north bank of the stream.[1-5]

In 1840, Benjamin Marshall drilled a 600-foot tunnel through the gorge's solid rock wall in order to channel water for power generation to his cotton factory and to a number of others mills along the stream.

A dam was created upstream from the top of the gorge so that power could be generated for the Excelsior Knitting Mill, which was located along the north bank. The dam impounded a body of water that is known today as Belden's Pond.

Interestingly, despite the continuous presence of industries, the Poesten Kill Gorge was a favorite spot at one time for swimming, fishing, and picnicking. A small bridge that once existed just down from the base of the falls made it possible for revelers to easily access both sides of the gorge.

Signs of past use (or misuse) abound in the gorge. Mine-like shafts can be found at both the base of the main cascades and at the fall just downstream from the main cascades. The shaft near the main cascades is a horizontal passageway some twenty feet in length. Long ago, water was diverted from an adjacent dam through this opening down a wooden flume (which later became a metal penstock) to mills below. Several iron spikes jut out of the bedrock at the end of this passageway. The shaft by the lower fall is primarily vertical, intersecting both the top and front of the waterfall's bedrock, constituting a turbine pit and cave.

Like many other large waterfalls, Mount Ida Falls has its own ready-made legend. In Abba Goddard's "A Legend of the Poestenkill," written in 1846, the story is told of Elsie Vaughn, a seventeenth-century European maiden who was rescued from a serpent in the Poesten Kill Gorge by an amorous Mohawk warrior named Dekanisora. Vaughn, however, felt nothing but repugnance for her rescuer and threw herself off the top of the falls rather than be his bride.[7]

Devastated by Vaughn's death, Dekanisora, according to one fanciful version of the story, kept vigil over the maiden's shattered body in a cave until he languished away and also died. Waterfall legends never seem to come with happy endings.

Directions: From downtown Troy, proceed east on Rt. 2, driving up a long, steep hill. At the top of the hill, turn right onto Rt. 66, immediately crossing over the Poesten Kill. Take your first right (Linden Ave) and follow it downhill, going west, for over 0.2 mile. The entrance to a parking area by the gorge will be directly to your right. Mount Ida Falls are clearly visible from the parking lot.

You can walk down the hill to a lower point in the gorge, called Hoboken Hollow, from where excellent views can be obtained of the main falls and the lower fall.

Mt. Ida Falls was industrialized as early as 1660.

19

EAGLE MILLS FALLS

Location: Eagle Mills (Rensselaer County)
Delorme *New York State Atlas & Gazetteer*: p. 67, B/C5
Accessibility: Roadside

Description: Eagle Mills Falls consist of a series of small cascades and rapids formed on the Poesten Kill, a fairly substantial stream that has produced notable waterfalls at both Barberville and Troy. The main cascade is downstream from the bridge and consists of a drop of four to five feet.

History: Eagle Mills was originally known as Milltown, and later as Millville. Presumably, these names derived from the numerous mills and shops that grew up at Eagle Mills during the early 1800s and 1900s.

In 1831, Defreest, Sheldon, & VanAlstyne built a flour mill on the stream. By 1836 a gristmill and sawmill had been erected and were also in full operation. Around 1851, Joseph Allen purchased the flour mill and converted it into a plant to manufacture bits and augers. Sometime later, Allen also acquired a nearby mill that made cable chains. In partnership with George Lane, he formed the Planter's Hoe Company. This proved to be Eagle Mills' main industry following the Civil War.[1,2]

If you stand at the northwest end of the bridge, you will notice old ruins along the west bank of the stream next to the bridge. Although not visible from roadside, a mine shaft goes horizontally into the side of the west bank, downstream from the bridge. After extending in for an appreciable distance, the shaft comes out again along the north bank where the stream rounds the bend.

A mill pond once existed upstream from the bridge, but came to an abrupt end around 1927 when the dam impounding it was dynamited.

Directions: From Troy (junction of Rtes. 2 & 66), take Rt. 2 east for 4.0 miles until you reach the tiny hamlet of Eagle Mills. When you arrive at Eagle Mills, park close to the old bridge where Rt. 2 crosses over the Poesten Kill. Cascades can be seen on both sides from the top of the bridge.

20

FALLS ON LITTLE HOOSIC

Location: Petersburgh (Rensselaer County)
Delorme *New York State Atlas & Gazetteer*: p. 67, B/C7
Accessibility: Roadside

Description: These small falls are formed on the Little Hoosic River, a medium-sized stream that rises near Cherryplain and merges with the Hoosic River near North Petersburgh. Walter F. Burmeister describes the Little Hoosic as "a torrential tributary," where the steepest section, in the vicinity of Petersburgh, drops one hundred feet per mile.[1]

The falls are located in a ravine of tilted bedrock that has been gradually eroded, forming a series of drops totaling ten to fifteen feet. Potholes abound in the river's bed by the falls.[2]

History: Of particular interest is the old concrete bridge that crosses the Little Hoosic just below the falls. Its style is art deco, which makes the bridge unusual and distinctive for this part of the state.[2] Prior to the bridge's construction in the 1920s, the Little Hoosic was spanned by a covered bridge at the same location.[3,4]

Take note that on the drive over from Troy, you will follow Rt. 2—the historic "Taconic Trail"—which was constructed in 1925 and follows an ancient path used by Native Americans. The name Taconic is Mohican for "wooded place." If you continue east on Rt. 2 past Petersburgh, the road turns into the "Mohawk Trail."

Directions: From Troy (junction of Rtes. 2 & 66), follow Rt. 2 for 20 miles until you reach Petersburgh (junction of Rtes. 2 & 22). Continue east on Rt. 2 for 0.3 mile farther until you cross over an old stone bridge that spans the Little Hoosic. Immediately turn right onto River Road (County Rt. 90) and park to the side. Walk back to the bridge for views of the falls from its south side.

This pretty waterfall is visible from the "Taconic Trail," where Rt. 2 crosses the Little Hoosic.

PETERSBURG
N.Y.

FALLS ON COON BROOK

Location: Near Petersburgh (Rensselaer County)
Delorme *New York State Atlas & Gazetteer*: B/C 6-7
Accessibility: Roadside

Description: This series of waterfalls is formed on Coon Brook, a small stream that rises from Taconic Lake. After passing by Sugarloaf Hill to the south, Coon Brook flows into the Little Hoosic River just south of Petersburgh.

The upper fall is a gradually inclined eight-foot-high cascade falling into a pretty glen where a pothole-shaped pool has been carved into the bedrock at the base of the fall.

The lower fall is not quite as dramatic, but equally as pretty. It is also gradually inclined and eight feet in height, and located just downstream from the base of the upper fall.

Directions: From Troy (junction of Rtes. 2 & 66), follow Rt. 2 east for twenty miles. When you come to the junction of Rtes. 2 & 22, turn right onto Rt. 22 and drive south for 0.8 mile. Turn right onto Coon Brook Road and drive south for 0.6 mile. Turn right onto Toad Point Road and drive uphill for 0.2 mile. The falls can be seen through the woods, but this is as far as you should go since the cascades are located on private property.

FALLS ON WYNANTS KILL, INCLUDING BURDEN FALLS

Location: South Troy (Rensselaer County)
Delorme *New York State Atlas & Gazetteer:* p. 67, C4
Accessibility: Short hike over variable terrain
Degree of Difficulty: Easy to moderate

Description: There are several pretty cascades formed on the Wynants Kill, a medium-sized stream that rises primarily from Burden Lake (an artificially created body of water) and flows into the Hudson River at South Troy.[1]

The Burden Pond Dam, with tiny falls at its base, can be seen at the beginning of the hike. The pond was much larger at one time, but deposits of sediment have made it shallower and turned large parts of it into a marsh.

Falls above Burden Pond. By following the nature path along the north bank of Burden Pond, you will eventually come to two small cascades that total eight feet in height. Just downstream from the cascades, near the inlet to Burden Pond, is an abandoned powerhouse. Huge pipes over three feet in diameter led to the powerhouse from Paper Mill Pond (no longer in existence), which was over 0.1 mile upstream.

At 0.05 mile upstream is the main waterfall, which is most easily seen from the top of the gorge. This cascade is eight feet high and formed where the stream abruptly changes direction. Another, smaller cascade is formed immediately at the second bend, perpendicular to the main cascade, where the stream alters direction again. The wreck of an automobile lies below in the streambed.

The pipe leading to the powerhouse is quite visible again along the south side of the gorge and crosses over the stream just above the top of the main waterfall. Less than 0.05 mile further upstream, the pipe ends at a breached dam, which once impounded Paper Mill Pond, named for the paper mill that stood along the north bank below the dam.

Don't be dismayed if you find little solitude by the falls. The trails are heavily used by dirt bikes and ATVs. There is a considerable amount of erosion evident everywhere.

Falls below Burden Pond. Several falls can also be found on the Wynants Kill downstream from Burden Pond. Accessibility is an issue, however, since there are no trails along the south bank leading to these falls, and the city of Troy has not yet made any attempts to open them up to the public.

The first fall, an eight-foot-high cascade, is immediately downstream from the Mill Street Bridge and can be glimpsed from roadside.

A short distance further downstream is a twenty-foot-high, three-tired waterfall named Burden Falls, whose historical significance was assured because of its close association with the Burden Iron Company. The falls descend over drops that are six feet, ten feet, and six feet high. Paralleling the south bank along the falls is the deteriorating sluiceway that once led from Burden Pond to the Burden Iron Company. A number of old foundations remain, including those at the site of the famous Burden waterwheel.

The stream directly below Burden Falls once followed a huge, sweeping, U-shaped bend until engineers decided to straighten out the stream and remove the kinks from it.

At some future date, Hudson Valley Community College in conjunction with the county, the city, and preservationists may open up this lower section of the Wynants Kill and turn it into a historic park.

History: Burden Pond was created in 1809 to ensure that a consistent water supply would be available for waterpower.[2] Except for the powerhouse and breached dam that once formed Paper Mill Pond (also known as Lower Smart's Pond), there are no ruins to be seen upstream from Burden Pond. Just west of the junction of Rt. 4 and Campbell Avenue, however, are the ruins of some of the riverside factories that once flourished downstream from Burden Pond. In 1807, John Brinckerhoff built on the north side of the stream a mill for converting bar iron into hoop iron and nail rods. In 1809 the Troy Iron & Nail Factory was established.[3,4]

The most memorable industry, however, was the Burden Iron Company. It was operated by Henry Burden, for whom the falls and area derive their names. In 1896, Burden constructed the legendary

The largest waterwheel in the world once operated at Burden Falls.

Burden waterwheel for power generation. The wheel measured sixty feet in diameter, twelve feet in width, and contained thirty-six buckets, each one being six feet deep. When fully engaged, the wheel could deliver 482 units of horsepower. In its time the Burden waterwheel was the largest of its kind in the world and probably served as a model for the first Ferris wheel! All that remain today are foundation ruins and the sluiceway along the south bank by Burden Falls. There is no trace of the waterwheel.

Today, the entire length of the Wynants Kill is free of mills and factories. The last factory, Portec, closed its doors in 1984.[5]

Directions: From I-787, take Exit 7E for South Troy & Watervliet and proceed east on Rt. 378. Once you cross over the Hudson River, the road automatically veers north at the end of the bridge and joins up with Rt. 4. Take Rt. 4 south, quickly turning right onto Mill Street, and drive up a long hill. Along the way, at 0.1 mile, you will see a dam to your right. Near the top of the hill, at 0.4 mile, cross over the Wynants Kill and turn left onto Campbell Ave. Immediately pull into the parking area on your left (which is right next to Burden Pond).

Walk back to the bridge spanning the Wynants Kill, cross over, and follow the well-worn nature trail that proceeds east along the north bank. Be prepared for a fifteen-minute walk to get to the first fall. A maze of trails has been created in the wide ravine leading to the falls, so always follow the trail leading towards the Wynants Kill.

There are no trails leading to Burden Falls and the old foundations of the Burden Iron Company. Accessing the falls would involve a short bushwhack along or down the south bank, and permission may need to be obtained from the city of Troy. It is to be hoped that at some future date the area will be turned into a historic site and made readily available to the public.

23

BARBERVILLE FALLS

Location: Barberville (Rensselaer County)
Delorme *New York State Atlas & Gazetteer:* p. 67, C5
Accessibility: Short, fairly level hike to top of fall; moderate descent to bottom
Degree of Difficulty: Easy to top; moderate to bottom

Description: Barberville Falls is an impressive, ninety-two-foot-high cascade formed on the Poesten Kill, a medium-sized stream that rises in the hills above East Poestenkill and flows into the Hudson River at downtown Troy.[1,2] By foresight and good fortune, the waterfall was acquired by the Nature Conservancy in 1967, thus ensuring its preservation in the years to come.[3] The fall is now located in a 119-acre nature preserve.

Barberville Falls is fashioned out of red shale and gray Rensselaer grit (greywacke). The fall widens out as the stream makes its way down over six narrow tiers, and it is best viewed when standing at its base, which can be reached by following a well-maintained trail that descends to the bottom of the gorge.

History: Presumably the falls were named after Dr. Luther Barber, the town's first postmaster.[3]

At the top of the fall can be seen the deteriorating foundation and sluiceway of a mill whose construction was started in the early 1900s, but never completed. According to legend, one of the mill partners ran off with the money and the project folded.[2] It is just as likely that the collapse of the project was caused by our country's sudden and dramatic switch from hydroelectric power to gas and oil. It was at this time that fossil fuels suddenly became abundantly available and mills no longer had to be dependent on falling water to generate power.

The old historic Moon's Hotel still stands at the bottom of the Snake Hill Cliff escarpment, next to the intersection of Rt. 4 and

Blue Factory Road and not far from the fall itself.[4] It is now an apartment complex.

Barberville Falls is said to be haunted by the ghostly sounds of a peddler and his horse, who were swept over the fall during a flood.[5]

Directions: From I-787, take Exit 5 and proceed southeast on I-90 for approximately one mile. Get off at Exit 8 for Rt. 43 & Defreestville. When you reach Rt. 4, continue east on Rt. 43 for 5.4 miles. Turn left onto Rt. 351 and drive northeast for 3.7 miles. At the traffic light in Poestenkill, turn right onto Rt. 40 and drive uphill, going east, for 1.3 miles. On the left-hand side of the road, you will notice small parking areas for Barberville Falls identified by a sign. Park there, because parking is not allowed further up the road near the fall.

Walk east along Rt. 40 for over 0.2 mile, and then turn left onto Blue Factory Road. You will immediately cross over the Poesten Kill. The fall is located directly downstream, accessible by a footpath that parallels the north bank of the stream.

Take note that a small trail leads down to the creek from the west side of the parking areas.

Barberville Falls. The Poesten Kill is a maker of big waterfalls.

24

FALLS AT RENSSELAER TECHNOLOGY PARK

Location: North Greenbush (Rensselaer County)
Delorme *New York State Atlas & Gazetteer:* p. 66, C4
Accessibility: 0.3-mile hike to first fall
Degree of Difficulty: Moderate. Special care must be taken because of slippery footing and deeply cut ravines.

Description: There are two sets of waterfall-bearing streams at this location.

Falls on Stream #1. There is a series of small to medium-sized falls formed on a small stream that rises in the hills east of the Hudson River and flows into the river north of a wastewater filtration plant.[1] The stream is sometimes called the Skipperkilldie, which is Dutch for "little stream near a mariner's house."[2]

The main fall is a twenty to twenty-five-foot-high cascade formed near the beginning of a deep ravine that has developed where the creek starts its downhill course. Downstream from the main fall, within less than a 0.1-mile stretch, can be found four more waterfalls: a gently sloping ten-foot cascade where a tiny tributary comes in from the south at the base of the main fall to produce a small cascade of its own; a ten-foot cascade that is fairly vertical; a four-foot cascade near the base of the ravine; and a three-foot fall at the very bottom.

A rectangular-shaped cement block and several bricks on the south bank by the lower-most fall suggest that the site may have had an industrial use in years past.

The little tributary feeding into the stream from the south has carved out an impressively deep ravine. The tributary also has produced a small cascade near the confluence of the two streams, and another one near the mouth of the ravine (close to the building presently housing Map Info).

Falls on Stream # 2. There is a series of six cascades formed on a tiny creek that rises east of North Greenbush and makes its way down to the Hudson River through a wetland area. Altogether, the falls total thirty feet.

It should be noted that there are several other small streams that have carved out deep ravines in the eastern Hudson River escarpment between South Troy and Rensselaer, as a quick glance at a South Troy topographic map will show. Some of these creeks have produced small falls and cascades, and can be fun to explore. If you choose to explore them on your own, be mindful of loose, slippery slopes, and be on the lookout for posted signs.

History: The trails at the Rensselaer Technology Park are part of the Hudson River Greenway Trail Network. The park consists of a number of technologically related businesses located on 1,300 acres of land.

Directions: From I-787 near Albany, get off at Exit 5 and go south-east on I-90. Get off at Exit 8 for Defreestville and proceed east for roughly 1.5 miles. When you come to the first set of stoplights, continue straight ahead on Rt. 43 for another 0.3 mile. At the second set of stoplights, turn left onto Rt. 4 and drive north for 1.5 miles. Take note along the way, at 0.5 mile, of the small falls to your right in a shallow ravine just south of a quaint cemetery. When you reach Jordan Road, turn left and proceed as follows to access each of the trailheads:

To Falls on Stream #1: Follow Jordan Road northwest for roughly 0.9 mile. Just before you reach the cul-de-sac at 0.2 mile from where Jordan Road crosses Willowbrook Road, turn left onto a road that leads up to one of the modern buildings at Rensselaer Technology Park. Park in the northwestern end of this parking lot.

From the parking lot, follow the tree and brush line west for one hundred feet. You will notice a turquoise-blazed trail that leads off into the woods. Follow the trail down into the ravine and then to the left. The trail very quickly comes part of the way back out of the ravine and then continues along near the top of the ravine for

0.2 mile. At that point you will come to a metal footbridge that spans the creek, just upstream from where the ravine deepens into a gorge. A sign on the bridge states "NYS Environmental Protection Fund: Local Waterfront Rehabilitation Program." A small, four-foot cascade is visible just downstream from the bridge at this point.

Cross over the bridge and follow the yellow-blazed trail for several hundred feet downstream along the top of the bank in order to reach the first and main fall. A long wooden fence near the top of the cascade allows you to look down into the ravine safely.

Continue following the yellow-blazed trail for the next 0.1 mile and you will encounter one small cascade after another as you proceed downstream. The trail eventually reaches the bottom of the ravine, where the gorge widens, and then crosses to the other side. From there, the yellow trail heads back upstream, providing excellent views of the falls from a different perspective. This trail tends to stay lower in the ravine, bringing you closer to the cascades. Before you return to the part of the ravine containing the main fall, however, the yellow-blazed trail veers sharply to the right and follows a very deep, narrow ravine that was cut by a tributary. The trail proceeds along the top of this ravine, going south, for about 0.1 mile. Close to the building presently housing Map Info, the trail crosses the mouth of the ravine and then follows along the top of the opposite bank, now going north. In less than 0.1 mile you will be back at the main stream. Follow the yellow-blazed trail east back to the footbridge, and then continue on the blue-blazed trail to return to your car.

To Falls on Stream # 2: Turning onto Jordan Road, drive 0.1 mile and take your first left. Bear to your right as you drive in. The road will lead you to the Technology Park Office, which is the former Philip Defreest house, built in the mid-1700s.[2] Park in the farthest parking area just south of the office building.

You will see an old, dilapidated barn behind the Technology Park Office. The trail begins from there and is blazed with orange-red markers. Follow the trail southwest as it parallels the stream. After 0.25 mile the trail crosses over the creek, goes up and across an open field, and then continues down towards the stream again.

At one point along the hike, you will find yourself at a considerable height above the stream. At about the 0.9-mile mark, the trail crosses over a bridge spanning the creek. After another 0.2 mile, or less, you will reach a point where the trail suddenly swerves to the left, pulling away from the stream. When you reach the top of the ravine, leave the trail and begin an easy bushwhack through the woods, following the rim of the creek downstream for no more than 0.1 mile. You will come to a series of six cascades that can be seen in the ravine below you.

Bear in mind that the trail is not always well-marked or easy to follow, particularly near the beginning. You will encounter no problem, however, if you remember to stay in sight of the creek at all times.

If you continue following the red-blazed trail for its entire length, it eventually will lead you down to the tracks of the former Troy and Greenbush Railroad,[2] which parallel the Hudson River. The total descent is roughly two hundred feet from the parking area.

Take note that the trails are still in transition at Rensselaer Technology Park and may be rerouted in the future.

25

RED MILL FALLS

Location: Rensselaer (Rensselaer County)
Delorme *New York State Atlas & Gazetteer:* p. 66, C/D4
Accessibility: Roadside; limited view of top of falls

Description: Red Mill Falls is a hulking cascade formed on Mill Creek, a small stream that rises in North Greenbush near Snyders Lake and flows into the Hudson River at Rensselaer. The creek has also been known as Huyck Stream[1] and Tierken Kill (or Cherken Kill), presumably after unidentified Dutch pioneers.[2,3]

The falls consist of several drops and a large cascade, totaling over eighty feet in height. Near the top of the fall can be seen a small dam. Old foundation ruins are visible on the north bank. Downstream below the falls, Mill Creek is ushered under the city through an aqueduct that carries it unceremoniously into the Hudson River.

History: In past times the falls were also known as Irwin Falls, named for W.P. Irwin, who ran a flour mill next to the cascade.

Mill Creek has been used to generate hydropower for four centuries. In the 1630s, Kiliaen Van Rensselaer established two mills and a brewery on Mill Creek. In the 1800s, flour mills were the principal industries on the stream.[1]

A poem was written about Red Mill Falls in the 1840s by an Albany poet named Alfred B. Street. The poem reads in part:

The Red Mill Falls
With one bold spring, the little streamlet sinks
Prostate below, and slumbers still and pure,
Holding its silver mirror to the sun
And open sky. It rushes from its height,
Like some bold warrior to the gladdening fray;
Then rests like that same warrior in repose,
Smiling at victory won.[4]

Directions: From I-787, take Exit 3. Cross over the Hudson River and follow Rt. 20 into the village of Rensselaer. From the first set of traffic lights after coming off the ramp, drive east, proceeding straight ahead, for 0.6 mile until you come to Rt. 9J. Turn right onto Rt. 9J, but instead of heading towards Castleton, turn immediately left and proceed under the Rt. 20 bridge, now going north on South Street. Drive north for 0.4 mile and turn right onto Aiken Ave. After driving east uphill for 0.5 mile, turn left onto Red Mill Road. At 0.2 mile you will be at the junction of Red Mill Road and Grove Street, from where the top of the falls can be glimpsed. Park far off to the side of the road.

There is no way to view the waterfall from the bottom without crossing private land. One of the present landowners has allowed public access (within reason), but it cannot be assumed that this will always be the case. One can only hope that at some point in the future the city of Rensselaer, working with private landowners, will obtain a conservation easement to the base of the fall.

A view of the upper section of Red Mill Falls.

26

FALL ON UPPER WYNANTS KILL

Location: Near West Sand Lake (Rensselaer County)
Delorme *New York State Atlas & Gazetteer:* p. 67, C/D5
Accessibility: Roadside

Description: This small, six-foot waterfall is formed on the Wynants Kill, a medium-sized stream that rises from Burden Lake and produces a significant number of falls and cascades further downstream in South Troy as it makes its way to the Hudson River.

The fall is contained in a tiny gorge that has collected a fair amount of debris and junk over the years, making it rather unappealing and anything but rustic. The waterfall is topped by a small dam. Most of the water goes through an old water gate. The dam has long been abandoned and now stands as a hulking reminder of past industrial days of the upper Wynants Kill.

This waterfall has been further degraded since the early 1900s.

History: In years gone by, the village of West Sand Lake was known as Ulines, after the town's first settler, Bernardt Uline. Like other villages with access to fairly dynamic streams, the area has had sawmills and gristmills, as well as a hosiery mill, a plow factory, and a yarn factory.

Directions: From I-787 at Albany, get off at Exit 5 and drive southeast on I-90 for about 1.0 mile. Get off at Exit 8 for Rt. 43, and drive east on Rt. 43 for nearly 5 miles from its junction with Rt. 4 until you come to West Sand Lake (intersection of Rtes. 43 & 150). From here, continue east on Rt. 43 for another 0.6 mile until you come to a small bridge. The waterfall is just downstream from the bridge, from where the top of the dam and waterfall can be seen easily.

27

FALL ON BURDEN LAKE ROAD

Location: Near Averill Park (Rensselaer County)
Delorme *New York State Atlas & Gazetteer:* p. 67, C/D5
Accessibility: Roadside

Description: This small, six-foot-high, block-shaped waterfall is formed on one of the branches of the Wyants Kill, a medium-sized stream that has produced a number of notable waterfalls near South Troy.[1]

History: The upper section of the Wynants Kill has powered a variety of factories and mills over the last two centuries. Around 1800, Thomas Thompson built a sawmill and a forge on the stream. Then, in 1825, a woolen mill was constructed, which later operated as a hosiery mill until it was destroyed by fire in 1871. In 1823, Ephraim Whittaker erected a tannery. After the property was destroyed by fire several times, it was sold to James Aken, who then proceeded to build a hosiery mill. Aretus Lyman ran a sawmill on the stream in 1820, and John P. Albertson operated a cloth dressing factory around the same time. The Wynants Kill has also played host to gristmills, sawmills, satinet mills, straw paper mills, plaster mills, cotton mills, and many other types of industries.

Around 1860, Staats D. Tompkins erected a paper mill at the fall. This property was later acquired by Eugene and John W. Merwin. In 1875, Andrew J. Smart became the new owner and subsequently began manufacturing straw paper. William Carmichael built a furnace in the same area in 1885.[2]

Directions: From I-787 in Albany, get off at Exit 5 and proceed southeast on I-90 for roughly 1.0 mile. Get off at the Exit 8 for Rt. 43, and proceed east. When you come to Rt. 4, continue driving east on Rt. 43 for nearly 8 miles until you arrive at Averill Park. When you see a turn on your left for Rt. 49, go 0.05 mile further on

Rt. 43 and turn right onto Burden Lake Road (Rt. 51). Drive south for 1.0 mile. In the process you will cross over the Wynants Kill several times. Pull over to your right as soon as you come to a tiny bridge spanning the Wynants Kill, just a short distance past Garner Road. The fall is easily seen by standing at the north end of the bridge.

Waterfalls and bridges often go together.

28

FALLS ON BLACK RIVER

Location: Taborton (Rensselaer County)
Delorme *New York State Atlas & Gazetteer:* p. 67, CD6
Accessibility: Short, 0.2-mile hike following an unmarked trail
Degree of Difficulty: Easy to moderate

Description: Two small falls are formed on the Black River, a medium-sized stream. Its west branch rises in a swamp east of Round Pond, and its east branch rises in a swampy area northwest of Spring Lake.[1] The stream flows into Kinderhook Creek near Garfield.

The falls are located in the Capital District Wildlife Management Area and are owned by New York State. The first cascade is ten feet in height, block-shaped, and formed at the mouth of a narrow chasm. A rocky centerpiece made of greywacke diverts the stream to the right and left as water goes tumbling over the top. Old ruins can be seen near its base.

The second cascade, just slightly further upstream, is five feet in height and is a smaller version of the lower fall. Between the two falls, along the pathway, is a small building foundation.

History: Taborton is a biblical word meaning "promised lands." Black River Pond, slightly south of the falls, is artificially created.

The ruins near the base of the lower fall are from an old Holcomb sawmill. Traces of the old mill race, trail race, and holding pond can be seen in the vicinity of the falls.

Directions: From I-787 in Albany, get off at Exit 5 and proceed east on I-90. In about 1.0 mile, get off at Exit 8 for Rt. 43. Take Rt. 43 east until you reach Sand Lake (junction of Rtes. 43 & 66) at nearly 9 miles from its intersection with Rt. 4. Continue straight on what is now Taborton Road (Rt. 42) and drive east for 8.5 miles, gaining altitude constantly. Turn right onto the beginning of Miller Road (also called Dutch Church Road) and then quickly bear to your right on Miller Road as it separates from Bly Hollow Road, which goes to the left. Stay on Miller Road for a total of 1.9 miles. At 0.7 mile you will pass by a secondary road (not marked, but known as Jiggs Road after a Berlin highway superintendent) to your right. At 1.8 miles you will notice that Jiggs Road reenters Miller Road on your right. Turn right at this point, cross over a tiny stream that parallels Miller Road, and then park in a small area immediately to your left.

Walk uphill along the road for 50 feet, and then follow a faint path off to the left that slowly angles away from the road. (This path may be hard to see initially. If you have difficulty locating the path, simply follow the creek downstream for 0.1 mile from where you parked. You will come to the confluence of two streams. Follow the creek on your right upstream for less than 0.1 mile to the first fall.) Very soon the path begins following an old stone wall on your right and heads down towards the stream. Within less than 0.2 mile from where you parked, you will reach the top of the first fall.

Follow the creek upstream along the path, which continues for several hundred feet, to the second fall.

There is a tiny, two-foot-high cascade another 0.05 miles further upstream.

29

MATTISON HOLLOW CASCADE

Location: Cherryplain (Rensselaer County)
Delorme *New York State Atlas & Gazetteer:* p. 67, C/D7
Accessibility: 1.4-mile hike
Degree of Difficulty: Moderate

Description: There are two cascades formed on Kronk Brook, a small stream that rises from the Taconic range and flows into the Little Hoosic River.[1] The main cascade, approximately six feet high, is known as Mattison Hollow Cascade, but has also been called Davis Cascade in the past. The upper cascade, three feet in height, serves to complement the lower one.

History: Mattison Hollow's history goes back to the 1870s and 1880s when the area's forest was heavily harvested to burn in the kilns that produced charcoal. An inclined railroad going up the side of the Taconic Hills allowed men and timber to be transported in an efficient manner.[1] Maple trees that were spared the ax supplied syrup for one or two sugarhouses in the valley.

Near the end of the drivable part of Mattison Hollow Road is a historic 1790 home.

Directions: Proceeding along Rt. 22, drive either 4.3 miles south from the junction of Rtes. 22 & 40 at a blinking light in Berlin, or 6.6 miles north from the junction of Rtes. 22 & 43 in Stephentown, and turn east onto Cherry Plain Square. Proceed south for 0.2 mile, and then turn abruptly left onto Mattison Hollow Road (avoiding George Allen Hollow Road as it goes straight ahead). Drive east for slightly less than 1.0 mile. As soon as you come to a tiny bridge crossing Kronk Brook, look to your right and you will see a sign stating "To Taconic Crest Trail" next to an old logging road that goes off from Mattison Hollow Road at an angle. Park on either side of the road before or after the bridge.

From the west end of the bridge, follow the old road uphill. The road immediately rises above and parallels Kronk Brook and Mattison Hollow Road, which remain on your left. Yellow-blazed markers soon turn into blue-blazed markers. In about 0.6 mile you will notice that you have pulled away from Mattison Hollow Road, which is far below. Continue east following the blue-blazed trail high above the ravine, which is now a precipitous drop off to your left. In another 0.5 mile the trail intersects an old logging road entering from the east. You have reached Mattison Hollow Falls.

If you continue upstream for less than 0.05 mile further, you will come to a tiny stricture in the stream where the bedrock on both sides forces the creek through a tiny flume.

30

FALLS ON TSATSAWASSA CREEK

Location: Hoag Corners (Rensselaer County)
Delorme *New York State Atlas & Gazetteer:* p. 67, D5-6
Accessibility: Roadside

Description: This small cascade is formed on Tsatsawassa (also spelled Tatsawassa) Creek, a medium-sized stream that rises from Little Bowman Pond at Taborton, and flows into Tsatsawassa Lake north of East Nassau. The stream has also been known as Tackawasick Creek.[1] The falls consist of several small drops, only part of which are visible from roadside.

Only part of the waterfall on Tsatsawassa Creek can be seen from roadside.

HOAG CORNERS, N. Y.
LOOKING EAST

FALLS AND
STREET LOOKING WEST

History: Tsatsawassa is a Mohican word for "stone mortar" (which was used for grinding grain).[2] The hamlet was named after William Hoag, whose hotel was in operation as early as 1825.[3]

The falls on Tsatsawassa Creek, like many others in the region, served as the nucleus for a number of nineteenth-century mills.[3] At one time there were as many as ten mills in the general area.

Directions: From the village of Nassau (junction of Rtes. 20 & 203), proceed east on Rt. 20 and turn left onto Rt. 66 at East Nassau. Drive north for approximately 4.3 miles until you reach Hoag Corners. (Coming in on Rt. 66 from the north, when you reach Denault Corner (junction of Rtes. 66 & 43-E), continue south on Rt. 43 for another 3.1 miles to Hoag Corners.) At Hoag Corners turn east onto Rt. 16 and drive uphill, paralleling the stream, for 0.6 mile. The waterfall is visible to your right, virtually opposite where Gardnier Hill Road comes in on your left.

Take note that the waterfall is on posted land. Remain at roadside.

FALLS IN EAST NASSAU

Location: East Nassau (Rensselaer County)
Delorme *New York State Atlas & Gazetteer:* p. 67, D5-6
Accessibility: Near roadside

Description: These small falls are formed on the upper part of Kinderhook Creek, a medium-sized stream that rises in the hills north of North Stephentown. The falls, in total, constitute a drop of no more than five feet. The riverbed is rough and ragged at the falls, with multiple ledges and small drops.[1]

History: East Nassau was originally known as Schermerhorn's, named after John W. Schermerhorn, who ran the first tavern in the area. A sawmill once existed nearby.[2]

Directions: From I-787 at Albany, get off at Exit 5 and drive southeast on I-90 for roughly 8 miles. Get off at the 11E exit for Nassau, and drive east on Rt. 20 for roughly 5 miles until you reach the village of Nassau (junction of Rtes. 20 & 203). From here, continue east on Rt. 20 for 6.3 miles. When you come to Rt. 66 North, turn left and follow it for 0.9 mile. As soon as you cross over Kinderhook Creek, take an immediate right and then a second quick right onto Tayer Road. Drive southeast on Tayer Road for 0.1 mile, and then turn right onto a small road that immediately leads to a parking area by the river. The falls are directly below the parking spot.

FALL ON MOORDENER KILL

Location: Near Castleton-on-Hudson (Rensselaer County)
Delorme *New York State Atlas & Gazetteer:* p. 66, D4
Accessibility: Roadside

Description: This small, ten-foot-high cascade is located on the Moordener Kill, a small stream that rises near West Sand Lake and flows into the Hudson River north of Castleton.[1] The stream was originally called the Mooerdnaarkill, but the name became shortened over the years. Moordener Kill is Dutch for "murderer's creek." The name has also been spelled Moerdenerkill.

The waterfall is located directly under a bridge that crosses the stream. Two tiny cascades can be seen just downstream. Directly upstream from the bridge is a medium-sized dam that rests on top of a small cascade.

Mill Rock Dam & Falls, Castleton. This fall is one of several further downstream on the Moordener Kill.

There are larger falls on the Moordener Kill that have formed downstream near the Fort Orange Paper Company, but these are located on private lands and are not accessible to the public.[2-4]

History: Like the stream Murderer's Creek, north of Athens (Greene County), the Moordener Kill has a tragic legend associated with it (though unsubstantiated by history). Legend has it that a young girl was dragged to her death along the river bank by Indians on horseback.[5]

Directions: From Rt. 20 in Rensselaer, take Rt. 9J south to Castleton, a drive of roughly 7 miles. Once you reach the village of Castleton, turn left on Rt. 150 and follow it east for 1.2 miles. You will come to a turn in the road where a small bridge crosses a stream. The fall is directly beneath the bridge. Before crossing the bridge, pull off to the left at a parking spot from where the fall can be viewed easily.

33

FALLS ON MUITZES KILL

Location: Castleton-on-Hudson (Rensselaer County)
Delorme *New York State Atlas & Gazetteer:* p. 66, D3-4
Accessibility: Roadside

Description: Several falls are formed on the Muitzes Kill, a medium-sized stream that rises in the hills northwest of Kinderhook Lake and flows into Schodack Creek south of Castleton-on-Hudson.[1]

The series of falls is situated in a ravine 0.05 mile long. The upper fall is fifteen feet high, consisting of a two-tiered cascade with an eight-foot dam capping its top. Old foundations can be seen along the north bank. It is an interesting area geologically; the bedrock has been tilted nearly vertically.

Several hundred feet down from the upper fall, a huge mound of rock has created an island that divides the stream into two halves. Each half has produced a small waterfall of its own—a broad, five-foot fall on the southern half (that can't be seen from the north bank), and an eight-foot, block-shaped fall on the northern half. Further downstream is a broad, six-foot-high fall that is visible from roadside.

History: The name Muitzes Kill goes back as far 1704, when the creek was identified as the Mutsjes Kill. There are two versions as to how this name may have come about. The most popular version is that the name arose from an incident in which a farmer's wife lost her cap in the stream. Mutsjes is Dutch for "cap."[3] But three hundred years ago the word mutsjes also meant a "small measure of brandy," and some contend that the name of the stream may have something to do with this definition of the word. The Muitzes Kill was known to early Native Americans as Paponicuck. Mohicans frequented the falls, where they would obtain furs from the Mohawks and then trade them with the English.

The area was settled in the 1700s by German Palatines and Dutch. In the 1800s and early 1900s a gristmill, a sawmill, a carding mill, a fulling mill, a plaster mill, a cider press, a cooperage, and a woolen mill could be found along the creek.[2]

Directions: From I-787 at Albany, take Rt. 20 east into Rensselaer and then turn right onto Rt. 9J. Drive south on Rt. 9J until you reach the village of Castleton-on-Hudson, a drive of roughly 7 miles. At the intersection of Rtes. 9J & 150, continue south on Rt. 9J for another 0.9 mile. When you come to Rt. 1, turn left and drive east for over 0.1 mile. The lower fall is next to the east end of the Agway Farm Service building, and easily visible from roadside.

The uppermost fall is located directly opposite the turnoff for Van Hoesen Road (Rt. 4), before you cross over the Muitzes Kill on a tiny bridge.

Only a portion of the middle cascade can be glimpsed from the road.

FALL ON MILL CREEK

Location: Near Stuyvesant (Columbia County)
Delorme *New York State Atlas & Gazetteer:* p. 52, A3-4
Accessibility: Roadside

Description: This pretty, ten-foot-high waterfall is formed on Mill Creek, a small stream that rises southwest of Kinderhook and flows into the Hudson River midway between Poolsburg and Stuyvesant.

Directions: From I-787, take Exit 3 into the village of Rensselaer. From Rt. 20, turn right onto Rt. 9J (towards Castleton-on-Hudson) and drive south. Continue for approximately 15.5 miles and you will pass over Mill Creek. After another 0.5 mile (for a total of roughly 16 miles), turn left onto Gibbons Road and drive uphill for 0.6 mile. Turn left onto Hollow Road and drive north for 0.2 mile. The waterfall is off to your right, but difficult to see until you turn around at 0.3 mile and drive back. As you go south, the fall is readily apparent. The fall is next to an attractive house with an unusual shape. Remain at roadside.

Approaching on Rt. 9J from the south, the turnoff to Gibbons Road is 1.5 miles from the blinking light at the tiny hamlet of Stuyvesant.

FALLS IN VALATIE

Location: Valatie (Columbia County)
Delorme *New York State Atlas & Gazetteer:* p. 53, A4
Accessibility: Roadside

Description: There are two, parallel, dammed cascades that are separated by a rocky island in the middle of Kinderhook Creek, a fairly large stream that rises northeast of Nassau and joins with Claverack Creek to form Stockport Creek just before the combined stream enters the Hudson River. Both falls are ten feet high and are capped by a dam that—along with the island buttress of rock in the middle of the stream—forms one continuous barrage across Kinderhook Creek. The dam serves to impound a small body of water.[1]

Immediately downstream from the falls is an impressive gorge where old foundation walls speak of past industrial times. Spanning the top of the gorge, a short distance south of the Rt. 203 bridge, are two sets of large pipes that also hearken back to the village's past industrial days. Next to the falls, on the south side of Kinderhook Creek, is a tall white building with a sluiceway next to it.

History: The word Kinderhook comes from *Kinders Hoeck,* Dutch for "children's point." According to legend the name arose when passing ships sighted Native American children playing along the bank of the river.

Valatie is Dutch for "little falls."[2]

In the past, Valatie was a notable manufacturing center. Sawmills and gristmills were evident by the late 1600s. Nathan Wild, an English immigrant, operated a cotton mill shortly after 1817. By 1825, Wild was using the first power loom in the state. Both Kinderhook Creek and the Valatie Kill played host to a collection of paper mills, sawmills, and plaster mills. In fact, for a short time, until 1832, the town was known as Millville.[3] The overlook by the falls is at the site of the former Beaver Cotton Mill, which according to an historical plaque was built around 1820 and destroyed by fire during the blizzard of 1888.

Additional Point of Interest: Along the south bank of the river is Pachaquack Park, a delightful tract of land with trails that provides overlooks of the river below. *Pachaquack* is Mohican for "cleared meadow," and it is believed that the area was routinely used by the Mohicans as a meeting place.

To reach Pachaquack Park from the Beaver Cotton Mill Overlook, drive over the Rt. 203 bridge and immediately turn right at a sign pointing the way to Pachaquack Park. Follow the road for less than 0.1 mile to the parking area. On the way out be sure to follow the one-way signs, which take you out through a development of new homes called Little Falls Estates.

Directions: From I-90, going southeast from Albany, get off at Exit 12 for Hudson (the last exit before the NYS Thruway) and drive

A view of the falls in Valatie from under the Rt. 203 bridge.

THE FALLS
VALATIE N.Y.

south on Rt. 9 for 4.5 miles. At the junction of Rtes. 9 & 9H-South, follow Rt. 9 southeast for another 1.1 miles to the edge of Valatie. Turn left onto Main Street where a sign points the way to Rt. 203. Immediately you will cross over the Valatie Kill where, if you look to your left, you can see an old dam-created waterfall. Continue east for 0.3 mile. You will come to the Rt. 203 bridge on your right. As soon as you drive by the bridge, park in the municipal parking area on your right.

The main fall can be viewed from the Beaver Cotton Mill Overlook, which is right next to where you parked. The fall on the south side of Kinderhook Creek can be readily viewed by walking part of the way across the Rt. 203 bridge and looking upstream. Minor cascades and rapids can be seen below the bridge and slightly downstream.

36

DAVENPORT FALLS

Location: Spencertown (Columbia County)
Delorme *New York State Atlas & Gazetteer:* p. 53, B5
Accessibility: Roadside

Description: This historic waterfall is formed in a narrow gorge on a tributary to Punsit Creek. The waterfall is roughly fifteen feet high, followed by a small, five-foot cascade just downstream from the base of the upper fall.[1] Standing at the top of the bridge and looking downstream, you can see the top of the main fall directly below, with the top of the smaller fall visible further down in the gorge. Looking upstream you will notice that a small, six-foot-high dam has impounded a tiny pond.

Private residences are on diagonally opposite sides of the intersection of the road and stream.

History: According to some historical accounts, the waterfall is located at a site where an "Indian killing" took place.[1]

In the early days, Punsit Creek was called Grist Mill Brook. This was probably after Abner Hawley built a gristmill on the stream around 1760. The creek rapidly became populated by a variety of other industries, including a sawmill, a carding and fulling mill, and even a factory that made ox yokes.[2]

Directions: Going east on I-90 (the New York State Thruway) from Albany, get off at Exit B2 for the Taconic State Parkway. Proceed south on the Taconic State Parkway for 5 miles and turn off at the Austerlitz/Chatham Exit (Rt. 203). Drive southeast on Rt. 203 into Spencertown. After you have passed by St. Peter's Presbyterian Church on your right, at approximately 3 miles from the Taconic State Parkway, turn right onto Dugway Road and drive southeast for 0.5 mile. You will reach a small bridge where the falls will be directly to your right, just below the bridge. Paralleling the west bank is a seasonal road called Cross Road.

Take note that the land is posted. Remain on the bridge.

Davenport Falls. Waterfalls can be a lesson in geology.

37

FALLS IN BEEBE HILL STATE FOREST

Location: Austerlitz (Columbia County)
Delorme *New York State Atlas & Gazetteer:* P. 53, B6
Accessibility: Short, less than 0.4-mile walk along an old logging road where motorized vehicles are not permitted, followed by a very short bushwhack along the stream up to the second fall
Degree of Difficulty: Easy to moderate

Description: There are two cascades that have formed on a tiny stream rising from a swampy area in Beebe Hill State Forest (named after nearby Beebe Hill). The upper fall is a five-foot cascade formed at the outlet to a shallow swamp. The lower cascade is fairly elongated, totals twenty feet in height, and is L-shaped.

Downstream, below the lower cascade, the creek flows through a second swampy area and then, upon consolidation, re-emerges about 0.5 mile further southeast. The stream eventually becomes one of the tributaries to the Green River, which flows south into Massachusetts.

Additional Point of Interest: A nearby fire tower in the forest preserve has an interesting history.[1] It was originally built in 1928 on top of Alander Mountain in western Massachusetts. It was taken down and then reassembled on top of 1,725-foot-high Beebe Mountain in 1964. It is reached by a dirt road that goes off Stonewall Road 0.4 mile from Rt. 203 near Spencertown.

Directions: From I-90 (the New York State Thruway), get off at Exit B2 for the Taconic State Parkway. Follow the Taconic State Parkway south for 4.8 miles, exiting at Austerlitz & Chatham. Take Rt. 203 southeast for over 0.5 mile, then turn left onto Red Rock Road (Rt. 9) and drive northeast for 2.5 miles. When you reach Rt. 24, turn right and drive east for 3.0 miles. At this point Rt. 24 merges with Rt. 5 (Osmer Road). Continue southeast on Rt. 5 for 1.1 miles. Turn left onto Fog Hill Road, go 0.05 mile, and bear left into the parking area for the Beebe Hill State Forest.

From the parking area, proceed on foot and follow an old logging road marked with red blazes. This will be off to your right from the top of the parking lot. Follow the road for over 0.3 mile until you reach a swampy area on your right. The cascade will be directly to your left, 75 feet away from the road. The small stream is conducted under the road through a medium-sized drainage pipe at this point. There is no path that leads to the fall, but it is easy enough to walk through the woods up to the base.

To see the second fall, continue following the creek upstream for 0.1 mile. This is a bushwhack, but a safe one since you have the stream as your guide. You will come to the second fall right after you encounter the blue-blazed trail that crosses the stream just below the cascade. To get back to the parking area, simply follow the blue-blazed trail south for over 0.3 mile, and you will have made a complete circuit back to your car.

38

STUYVESANT FALLS

Location: Stuyvesant Falls (Columbia County)
Delorme *New York State Atlas & Gazetteer:* p. 52, B3-4
Accessibility: Roadside

Description: Stuyvesant Falls is formed on Kinderhook Creek, a large stream that rises from multiple tributaries in the area of North Stephentown and flows into the Hudson River west of Stockport.[1-3] Stuyvesant Falls consists of two distinct falls separated by 0.05 mile. The upper waterfall is quite broad, twenty-two feet high, and is capped by an expansive six-foot barrage. The lower fall is just downstream from the historic 1899 iron truss bridge that spans Kinderhook Creek. Excellent views of the top of the fall can be obtained from either end of the bridge. The cascade drops over thirty feet and consists of a huge rocky dome that splits the fall into two sections. One section plunges straight into the gorge; the other section is diverted to the left and down into a long ravine. Both sections of the creek are reunited further downstream after negotiating an island.

History: Stuyvesant Falls is named after the famous Dutch settler, Peter Stuyvesant.

The name Kinderhook (an Anglicization of *Kinders Hoeck*) is Dutch for "children's place." The name first appeared on a New Netherlands map in 1614. There is some speculation that it was Henry Hudson himself who came up with the name in 1609.

A State Education Department marker next to the bridge, dated 1932, gives a succinct history of the falls and creeks: "Prior to 1667 known as 'Major Abram's (Staats) kill' and 'Third Falls' and after 1845 'Kinderhook Creek.'"

It is believed that there were sawmills and gristmills on the falls by the 1700s. A roadside historic marker states: "Cloth Mill built by William Van Hoesen in 1800. Located where power house stands." Over the centuries a variety of mills have come and gone at the falls. The reason for its popularity is that Kinderhook Creek "has precipitous banks, which, together with the natural falls at this point, form mill-sites that are not surpassed in the county."[3] Below the lower fall, on the east side of the stream, were a sawmill, a gristmill, and a plaster mill operated by Martin Van Alstyne. Later, a paper mill was erected south of the gristmill. At the upper fall, the first paper mill in Columbia County was built in 1802 by Pitkin & Edmunds. A year later, George Chittenden purchased the mill, operating it until 1806. Later still, a seven-foot dam was put across the river, and Mill No. 1 of the Stuyvesant Falls Cotton-Mills was set into operation in 1827.[5] Howard Stone, author of *25 Bicycle Tours in the Hudson Valley,* refers to "Stuyvesant Falls, where two hulking Victorian mills stand guard over a waterfall on Kinderhook Creek." The buildings are now owned by Allied Healthcare Products, Inc.[4]

A view of the upper falls at Stuyvesant Falls.

Directions: Going southeast on I-90 from Albany, get off at Exit 12 for Hudson. Proceed south on Rt. 9 for slightly over 10 miles. At a sharp curve in the road where Rt. 9 bears right, continue straight onto Rt. 25A and drive 0.3 mile to Stuyvesant Falls, where a metal bridge crosses over Kinderhook Creek.

To access the upper fall: Cross over the bridge, turn immediately left onto Lindenwald Avenue and then turn quickly left again onto a dirt road that leads into Stuyvesant Falls Family Park. Drive to the end of this dirt road and you will be at the upper fall.

Follow the rules and regulations posted at the entrance to the park.

There are also nice views of the upper fall from roadside just north of the metal bridge spanning Kinderhook Creek.

To see the lower fall: Park off the road near the bridge and walk to either of its ends. Good views of the top of the fall can be obtained from these vantage points.

There is no way to get down to the base of the lower fall. The north bank, paralleling New Street, contains two large factories that block direct access.

ROSSMAN FALLS

Location: Near Stockport (Columbia County)
Delorme *New York State Atlas & Gazetteer:* p. 52, B3-4
Accessibility: Roadside

Description: Rossman Falls (also known as Chittenden Falls) is formed on Kinderhook Creek, a large stream that rises near North Stephentown and flows into the Hudson River at Stockport.[1,2] The fall is quite broad and roughly twenty feet high, topped off by a five-foot barrage. Unfortunately, you can get no closer to the fall than the viewing area across the stream.

History: A roadside historical marker states that George Chittenden, for whom the waterfall was named, built the county's second cotton mill on the west side of the fall sometime around 1809. (The first cotton mill in the county was built nearby at Stockport in 1828 by Benjamin and Joseph Marshall.) Some years later, Chittenden's mill was renamed Rossman Mill after J. W. Rossman; hence the fall's change in name to Rossman Falls. Rossman's Paper Mill was a brick structure 46 feet wide by 157 feet long.

Directions: Going southeast on I-90 from Albany, get off at Exit 12 for Hudson and proceed south on Rt. 9 for slightly over 10 miles. When you pass by Rt. 25A (which leads to Stuyvesant Falls), continue south on Rt. 9 for another 2.3 miles. Turn left onto Rossman Road and drive east for 0.4 mile. Just before crossing a bridge that spans Kinderhook Creek, you will see a State Education Department historical marker on the left side of the road. Park at this point. Excellent, although somewhat distant views of the fall, can be obtained from roadside.

If you are coming directly from Stuyvesant Falls, continue south on Rt. 25A for 0.2 mile. Rt. 25A then merges into Rt. 25. Proceed straight on Rt. 25 for another 1.9 miles. Turn right onto Rossman Road, cross over Kinderhook Creek, and proceed up to a view of Rossman Falls within 0.1 mile.

FALL ON FITTING CREEK

Location: Stockport (Columbia County)
Delorme *New York State Atlas & Gazetteer:* p. 52, B3-4
Accessibility: Roadside

Description: This fifteen-foot cascade is formed on Fitting Creek, a small stream that rises in the hills east of Stottville and flows into Claverack Creek at Stockport. The falls consist of several rocky drops and plunges.[1]

Further downstream on Fitting Creek, nearly at the stream's confluence with Claverack Creek, is a small cascade whose top can be seen from roadside.

History: According to an old historical marker on Rt. 25, Stockport Creek, which is formed at the union of Kinderhook Creek and Claverack Creek just before they enter the Hudson River, was once known as Abram's Creek (or Major Abraham's Kill). Abraham Staats was a surgeon from Fort Orange (now known as Albany) who traded furs on Stockport Creek in the mid-1600s. Stockport Creek is the largest tributary to the Hudson River that originates from Columbia County.

Stockport derived its name from Stockport, England.[2]

Directions: Going southeast from Albany on I-90, get off at Exit 12 for Hudson and follow Rt. 9 south for over 10 miles. Where Rt. 9 curves sharply to the right, continue straight onto Rt. 25A. Follow Rt. 25A south for 0.6 mile until Rt. 25A merges into Rt. 25. Continue straight on Rt. 25 south for another 3.2 miles. You will come to a small bridge. Look to your left, and you will see the fall on Fitting Creek. Stay on roadside to look at the fall.

If you are coming directly from Rossman Falls, drive east on Rossman Road for 0.1 mile, crossing over Kinderhook Creek. Turn right onto Rt. 25, and drive south for 1.3 miles to the fall.

FALL ON CLAVERACK CREEK

Location: Stottville (Columbia County)
Delorme *New York State Atlas & Gazetteer:* p. 52, B3-4
Accessibility: Roadside

Description: This medium-sized cascade is formed on Claverack Creek, a stream that rises north of Philmont and merges with Kinderhook Creek at Stockport before entering the Hudson River as Stockport Creek.[1] The cascade is over fifteen feet in height, with a small barrage spanning its top. The falls consist of a series of drops and plunges.[2]

Slightly further downstream, after the stream rounds a bend and continues east, a ten-foot dam can be seen next to several abandoned and derelict brick buildings.

An impressive waterfall named High Falls can be found in the village of Philmont, near where Claverack Creek rises. High Falls certainly lives up to its name. It is a massive waterfall over eighty feet high, formed on Aqawamuck Creek just downstream from a dam that impounds a small lake. Unfortunately, the fall is inaccessible to the public because private land has to be crossed along both banks of Aqawamuck Creek to reach the fall.

History: The name Claverack comes from the Dutch words *klaver rack*. *Klaver* referred to the cliffs along this stretch of the Hudson River, and rack (or "reach") was a unit of distance along the river that was used by Dutch mariners.[3]

Stottville is named after Jonathan Stott, whose woolen mills were located on the river by the fall. Previously the town was known as Springville.[2] Sawmills and gristmills run by the Van Rensselaers, including Henry Van Rensselaer,[2] were also located in the same vicinity on Claverack Creek. Ruins of nineteenth and twentieth-century factories litter the banks downstream from the falls.

Directions: Going southeast from Albany on I-90, get off at Exit 12 and proceed south on Rt. 9. From Rt. 25A, which leads to Stuyvesant Falls, continue south on Rt. 9 for another 6 miles. Turn left onto County Rt. 20 at the traffic light and drive east for 0.8 mile into the village of Stottville. You will arrive at a bridge that crosses over Claverack Creek. Turn left just before the bridge onto Town Garage Road and follow it as it parallels the creek for 0.1 mile. The first cascade is below the bridge and will come into view as you follow the road to the right and look back towards the bridge.

If you are coming up from Hudson (junction of Rtes. 9 & 23B-East), drive north on Rt. 9 for 3.0 miles and turn right onto Rt. 20.

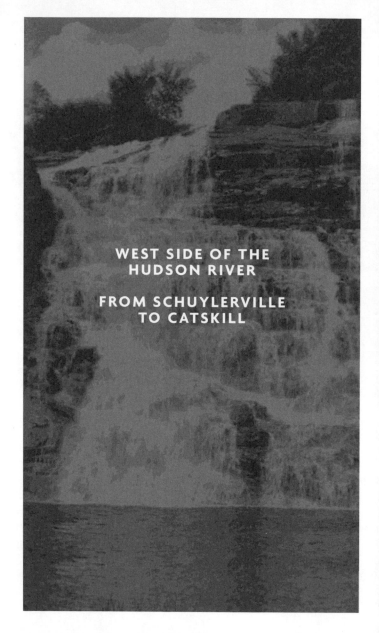

WEST SIDE OF THE HUDSON RIVER

FROM SCHUYLERVILLE TO CATSKILL

42

CASCADE ON FISH CREEK

Location: Schuylerville (Saratoga County)
Delorme *New York State Atlas & Gazetteer:* p. 81, C/D5
Accessibility: Near roadside
Degree of Difficulty: Easy

Description: This small cascade, four to five feet high, is formed directly under the Rt. 32 bridge that spans Fish Creek at Schuylerville.[1,2] This is a very small, flattened cascade, so keep your expectations low and you won't be disappointed. Fish Creek is a medium-sized stream that rises from the northern outlet at Saratoga Lake, southeast of Saratoga Springs, and flows into the Hudson River just east of Schuylerville. Fish Creek is actually the continuation of Kayaderosseras Creek, which is the inlet stream to Saratoga Lake.

Just upstream from the Rt. 32 bridge, around the bend, is a tall dam whose falling waters can be seen and heard easily from the bridge.

If you take the path northward from the Philip Schuyler House, it will lead you to a scenic footbridge that crosses a stone dam over which the waters of Fish Creek flow, forming an artificial cascade.

History: Although the cascade itself lacks notable history, its association with Philip Schuyler's house assures a tangential place in the history books. It was at Schuyler's House that military plans for the Revolutionary War were devised. Schuyler's first house was burned downed during the war by the British General John Burgoyne, who later regretted his actions when he came to know Philip Schuyler.

The original Fort Saratoga was built on the south bank of Fish Creek. When Johannes Schuyler, grandfather of Philip Schuyler, acquired the property in 1702, he erected several mills and farms.[3] Years later, when Philip Schuyler took over the land, he built the first water-driven flax (linen) mill in America.[4]

Directions: From Schuylerville (junction of Rtes. 32/4 & 29 East), drive south on Rt. 32/4 for 0.2 mile. As soon as you cross over Fish Creek, pull into the parking area for the Philip Schuyler House, on your left.

From here, you can walk over to a path leading off into the woods behind the house from where you can get a decent view of the small cascade by looking back upstream from the top of the creek bank.

Continue along this old abandoned road (part of which was once a towpath that followed next to the old Champlain Canal) and in less than 0.1 mile you will come to a footbridge that spans Fish Creek. Look down and you will see a pretty, stone, dam-created fall.

You can also see a large dam by looking upstream from the north end of the Rt. 4 bridge spanning Fish Creek.

An early view of Fish Creek at Schuylerville.

43

BUTTERMILK FALLS
(Cohoes)

Location: Peebles Island, Cohoes (Saratoga County)
Delorme *New York State Atlas & Gazetteer:* p. 67, B4
Accessibility: 0.5-mile walk over fairly level terrain
Degree of Difficulty: Easy

Description: Buttermilk Falls is a tiny cascade formed on the East Sprout of the Mohawk River just upstream from its confluence with the Hudson River.[1] During high waters the fall is barely visible, looking more like a series of prominent rapids, but in the summer it turns into a clearly defined, elongated cascade, six feet in height.

History: Peebles Island is steeped in history. Long ago it was the site of a Native American village, the Moenimines Castle of the Woodland period, located on the island's north side. Breastwork fortifications were constructed along the north and west sides of the island during the American Revolution, and the mounds remain visible even today.

The island has also been used by industries—the Cluett Peabody Company, manufacturer of shirts, was the last occupant—but it is doubtful that Buttermilk Falls was ever pressed into service for industrial purposes because of its comparatively small, innocuous size. Because it is formed on the southeast end of the island, the fall also played no role in Revolutionary War fortifications.

Directions: To get to Peebles Island, take I-787 north. Just before the highway's terminus at the city of Cohoes, turn right onto Rt. 470 (Ontario Street). Drive east for 0.6 mile, crossing over several bridges connecting the tiny islands, and then turn left onto Delaware Ave., where signs point the way to Peebles Island. Follow Delaware Ave. north for 0.9 mile, crossing over a metal bridge (which once served as a railroad crossing) and into the parking area to the northwest of the old building that is used by the NYS Parks Department.

In 2003 a second railroad bridge crossing from Waterford to Peebles Island was reconstructed and now provides an alternate access to the island, this time from the north. To reach Peebles Island from Waterford, drive 0.05 mile east on Rt. 4 from the junction of Rtes. 32 & 4 in Waterford, and turn south onto Second Street. In 0.2 mile you will come to a one-lane bridge, with a visitors center to your right, where you can cross over to Peebles Island.

From the parking area, follow a path that leads around the north end of the former Cluett Peabody building. After you walk past the building and enter an open area, you will come to a point where the trail/dirt road starts to divide. Stay on the farthest left path each time and you will eventually be directed to the east side of the island where the trail parallels the Mohawk River. Continue to follow the path south until you nearly reach the southeastern-most extension of the island. You will see Buttermilks Falls to your left, formed between Peebles Island and VanSchaick Island, which lies to the east. Take note of how the swirling rapids at Buttermilk Falls have worn an enormous semi-circular pothole into the escarpment edge of VanSchaick Island.

At certain times of the year during daylight hours, a small fee is charged to park on the island.

44

COHOES FALLS

Location: Cohoes (Albany County)
Delorme *New York State Atlas & Gazetteer:* p. 66, B4
Accessibility: Near roadside; canoe/kayak paddle
Degree of Difficulty: Easy by land; easy to moderate by water, depending upon water level and flow

Description: Cohoes Falls is a sixty-five-foot-high, 600-foot-wide behemoth that is formed near the terminus of the Mohawk River, a large stream that rises in the Tug Hill Plateau north of Rome and flows into the Hudson River between Cohoes and Waterford.[1-3] Cohoes Falls is a mighty waterfall that during the summer is typically allowed to display only a fraction of its power and glory. This is the result of vast quantities of water from the Mohawk River being diverted for power generation and for the waterways of the barge canal system that runs parallel to the north bank of the river. In the early spring or following heavy rainfall or snowmelt, however, the fall becomes dynamic and absolutely mesmerizing to behold.

During such times of heavy flow, you may also notice a tall but slender fall cascading down the north bank of the river several hundred feet downstream from Cohoes Falls. This fall is formed on an unnamed tiny tributary to the Mohawk River that normally carries little flow.

Take note of the hydroelectric plant that is adjacent to Cohoes Falls Overlook Park. Look closely and you will see a canal coming into the power plant, paralleling New Courtland Street. This canal siphons off prodigious amounts of water from the Mohawk River at a dam impoundment roughly 0.7 mile upriver.

At one time Cohoes Falls was over 1,000 feet closer to the Mohawk River's confluence with the Hudson River. The fact that it has moved upstream such a significant distance is attributable to the enormous erosive power of the Mohawk River.

History: Cohoes Falls was once as famous and heavily visited by tourists as Niagara Falls. This popularity was earned by the fall's majestic display of waterpower, its imminent location next to the Hudson River (a vital center of commerce), and its relative proximity to New York City. At that time a large hotel, called the Cataract House, sat at the top of the 175-foot precipice overlooking Cohoes Falls and afforded visitors a stupendous view of the waterfall from a series of stairs and catwalks that led down to an observation deck fifty feet below. No trace of the Cataract House remains today. It was razed when the city of Cohoes decided to use the waterfall for commerce, as opposed to tourism, and turned the fall into an industrial wonder.

There is currently talk of bringing back the glamorous days of Cohoes Falls by illuminating the waterfall at night and by restructuring the dam and power plant so that more water will consistently go over the top of the fall.

During its industrial glory days, Cohoes Falls powered numerous mills and factories along its banks, making Cohoes the leading cotton manufacturer in the United States.[4,5] The Harmony (Mills) Manufacturing Company, established in 1836, is probably the most famous and enduring of the factories to use Cohoes Falls for waterpower. In 1866, while workers were excavating the north foundation of the mills, the prehistoric bones of a mastodon (now on exhibit in the lobby of the New York State Museum) were uncovered, buried in an enormous pothole sixty feet below ground level. Look for the historic marker at the south end of Front Street indicating the site where the mastodon was exhumed.

The name Cohoes was likely a Native American term for "falling canoe" (appropriate enough if you don't paddle to shore above the fall in time),[3] "little holes" (a reference to the potholes that proliferate around the bedrock of the fall), "shad" (a commonly eaten Hudson River fish), or "island at the falls."

Directions: Take I-787 north to its terminus at Cohoes. At the junction of I-787 and Rt. 32, continue straight ahead across Rt. 32 and follow New Courtland Street northwest as it proceeds uphill, paralleling the Mohawk River (which will be off to your right). You will pass by several large buildings, also on your right. These are relics from the days of Harmony Mills. At nearly 0.8 mile from the junction of I-787 and Rt. 32, turn right onto School Street, a one-way street. Cohoes Falls Overlook Park is at the end of the road. Park wherever space is available, either on School Street or Cataract Street.

Cohoes, N.Y.,
Great Falls of the Mohawk.

At one time Cohoes Falls was second only to Niagara Falls as the premier tourist attraction in New York State.

To exit, turn right onto Cataract Street and then right again onto Front Street (both one-way streets), which take you back out to the main road.

When sufficient water is flowing, it is possible to canoe or kayak up to near the base of the waterfall. The launch point is approximately 0.5 mile downstream from the fall. From the junction of I-787 & Rt. 32, drive up New Courtland Street for less than 0.2 mile. Turn right onto a short road opposite Mohawk Street that takes you down to the river. The recreation area is open from dawn to dusk, April 15 to October 15.

BUTTERMILK FALLS
(Underground)

Location: Albany (Albany County)
Delorme *New York State Atlas & Gazetteer:* p. 66, C3
Accessibility: Inaccessible, but you can stand at the top of a metal grating and hear the stream cascading below you

Description: Over a century and a half ago the Beaverkill was a tiny tributary of the Hudson River, flowing down from the hills above Albany. The Beaverkill produced several cascades, the main one being Buttermilk Falls, named after the white, foamy suds that the breweries along the creek produced.[1] Around 1900, however, it was decided by Albany city planners to run the stream entirely underground and to incorporate it into the city's sanitation and septic system.[2,3] Today, all visible traces of the Beaverkill have vanished, but if you stand above a metal grating in the Beaverkill Ravine and listen closely, you can still clearly hear the stream as it tumbles thirty feet below you. The underground waterfall is located behind the Charles H. Shoudy Memorial Gardens, named after the former commissioner of the Albany Department of Human Resources.

History: According to historical records, the first brewery on the Beaverkill was built in the 1650s and was operated by Jacob Garritsen.[4] Much later, the Hinkel Brewery (later to be called the Dobler Brewery) was established and was allegedly responsible for producing the suds that turned the creek into white foam, thereby leading to the naming of the stream's principal waterfall, Buttermilk Falls. These sudsy waters, in turn, collected into a pond called Rocky Ledge Pool, which was located where today's Lincoln Park Pool can be found.[5]

The Beaverkill was not the only stream to be eradicated from the surface of the earth in 1917 to make room for Albany's growing city during its industrial heyday. The Rutten Kill, Foxen Kill, and Patroon Kill were also moved underground and integrated into the

Albany sewer and sanitation system. Only the Normans Kill was left untouched.[6]

In *Seventeenth Century Albany: A Dutch Profile,* Charlotte Wilcoxen writes: "On the earliest map of the Colonie of Rensselaerswyck, dating from about 1631, before any farms were actually established there, attention is called to the waterfall on that stream."[4] Rensselaerswyck was an earlier name for Albany, and "that stream" refers to the Beaverkill. Wilcoxen goes on to point out that with the availability of so much waterpower provided by the various streams coming down through Albany, there was no need for the Dutch to establish windmills as they did in downstate Manhattan. How much Albany has changed since its days as a Dutch colony is not lost on anyone who tries to locate one of these buried streams.[7]

The Beaver Kill and falls now flow underground beneath the city of Albany.

Beaver Park, Albany, N.Y.

61760

Directions: Take I-787 southwest to its terminus at Rt. 9W in Albany. From here, continue straight across Rt. 9W onto Hoffman Ave. and drive north for 0.2 mile. Turn left onto Second Avenue and drive west for 0.4 mile. When you get to Delaware Ave., turn right and drive northeast for 0.7 mile. At the intersection of Delaware Avenue with Morton and Holland Avenue, turn right onto Morton Avenue and drive east for 0.2 mile. Turn left onto Dr. Martin Luther King Jr. Blvd. and drive north for 0.2 mile. The Charles H. Shoudy Memorial Gardens will be directly on your left.

After parking the car, follow the ravine behind the Memorial Gardens for several hundred feet, going northwest. You will come to a grated manhole cover, from which you will hear the sounds of the Beaverkill as it flows downhill towards the Hudson River.

46

FALLS ON LOWER NORMANS KILL (Historic)

Location: Albany (Albany County)
Delorme *New York State Atlas & Gazetteer:* p. 66, C/D3
Accessibility: Roadside

Description: This series of small cascades is formed on the Normans Kill, a medium-sized stream that rises in East Berne and flows into the Hudson River at Glenmont, just south of Albany.[1,2] The falls are created by a huge outcropping of erosion-resistant rock located in the middle of the stream. Altogether the falls consist of a number of cascades totaling fifteen feet in height and spread out over a short distance.

History: The Normans Kill is named after an early settler, Albert Andriessen Bradt, who operated one of the first mills in the area around 1636. The Dutch called him Norman, and because he was so closely identified with the stream, the river came to be known as Norman's Kill.[3] Later, as the milling community developed, the area around the stream developed into a center called Kenwood.[4,5]

The Normans Kill is believed to be the first Indian route from the Hudson River to Schenectady. The ravine in which the falls are contained is the legendary Vale of Tawasentha featured in Henry Wadsworth Longfellow's *Song of Hiawatha.* Tawasentha is the Native American word for "place of the dead."[6] Further downstream from the falls, at the mouth of the Normans Kill, a tiny island once existed that was used by the Iroquois as an encampment for trading purposes. Later, in 1614, the Dutch built their first Hudson River fort on the island.[7]

Directions: The falls are located 0.7 mile south on Rt. 9W from the southern terminus of I-787 at Albany. They are directly below the Rt. 9W bridge that spans the Normans Kill Gorge and can only be partially glimpsed from the bridge. A much better, but fleeting, view is afforded from the NYS Thruway (I-87) bridge as you proceed north over the Normans Kill Gorge before reaching Exit 23 for Albany. Be aware that stopping on the Thruway other than for an emergency is prohibited.

Two towering bridges now span the gorge above the falls.

47

FALL ON VLOMAN KILL

Location: Near Selkirk (Albany County)
Delorme *New York State Atlas & Gazetteer:* p. 66, D3
Accessibility: Roadside; or 0.5-mile paddle upstream by canoe or kayak, water level permitting
Degree of Difficulty: Easy by canoe or kayak

Description: This small, but picturesque waterfall is formed on the Vloman Kill, a small stream that rises southeast of Voorheesville and flows into the Hudson River opposite Castleton-on-Hudson.[1] The fall is broad and twelve feet high.

Directions by Car: From the southwest terminus of I-787 at Albany, turn right onto Rt. 9W and proceed south. Cross over a high bridge spanning the Normans Kill Gorge, at 0.7 mile, and continue south for another 0.3 mile. Turn left onto Rt. 32. Drive east, going down-hill, for 0.6 mile. Turn right onto Rt. 114, which parallels the Hudson River, and drive south for 5.7 miles. Just before you cross over the Vloman Kill, turn left onto Lyons Road and drive southeast for 0.4 mile. The Vloman Kill will now be directly on your right, opposite a sign stating "Pollywick 1785." From this vantage point you can look upstream and see the waterfall off in the distance.

Directions by Water: When you turn onto Lyons Road from Rt. 114, drive southeast for 0.9 mile until you come to Henry Hudson Park (a sign states that the park is for Town of Bethlehem residents only). Next to the park (to the north) is the NYS Bethlehem Fishing Access Site, from where small boats can be launched.

Put in your canoe at the fishing access site, paddle down the Hudson River for 0.1 mile, and then follow the Vloman Kill upstream for over 0.5 mile to the base of the fall. Note that you may have to wait until high tide to make this trip. In *Appalachian Waters 2: The Hudson River and its Tributaries,* Burmeister writes that the "streamflow of the creek is normally inadequate to permit upstream canoeing. It is possible, however, to paddle upstream on the back-water of the Hudson River tidal pool for four-fifths mile to the base of a 10-foot falls."

48

FALLS ON COEYMANS CREEK

Location: Coeymans (Albany County)
Delorme *New York State Atlas & Gazetteer:* p. 52, A3
Accessibility: Roadside; canoe or kayak paddle
Degree of Difficulty: Easy

Description: This series of falls is formed on the eastern terminus of Coeymans Creek, a moderate-sized stream that rises near South Bethlehem and flows into the Hudson River by the village of Coeymans.[1-3] The uppermost fall is a fairly broad, sweeping, twenty-foot-high cascade. It is followed, slightly further downstream, by a smaller, fifteen-foot-high cascade that is more difficult to see from roadside than the upper cascade.

History: The village of Coeymans (pronounced Kwee-mans) was named after Barent Pieterse Coeymans.

In past times, Coeymans was a thriving riverside community that exported ice blocks and bricks to an insatiable New York City. With the advent of modern refrigeration and greater utilization of stone as a building material, the ice block and brick trades declined, and Coeymans contracted to its present size.

The old Coeymans House, built in 1675 by Ariantje Coeyman, is just a short distance further down Stone House Hill Road from the waterfall (0.1 mile from Rt. 144). The Coeymans House once served as an early Indian trading post.

Directions: From the outskirts of Ravena (junction of Rtes. 9W & 143), turn east onto Rt. 143 and drive east for slightly over 1.3 miles until you reach Rt. 144. At Rt. 144, turn left and drive north for less than 0.1 mile until you reach the bridge that spans Coeymans Creek. Cross over the bridge and park immediately off to the side of the road on Stone House Hill Road. You will be able to get decent views of the upper fall and into the gorge below from both sides of the road and from the top of the bridge.

The lower fall can be viewed from roadside near the junction of Rtes. 143 & 144. Extensive work was recently done on the bridge, and a nice sidewalk now follows along Rt. 144, paralleling the gorge.

The falls can be directly accessed from the Hudson River by canoe or kayak. To get there from the junction of Rtes. 143 & 144, drive south on Rt. 144 for 0.1 mile. Turn left onto Westerlo Street and drive downhill for slightly over 0.1 mile to Coeymans Landing. From here, a canoe or kayak can be launched easily. Paddle upstream on the Hudson River for a hundred yards or less, and turn into the mouth of Coeymans Creek. Paddle upstream for less than 0.1 mile and you will be at the base of the lower cascade.

49

RAVENA FALLS

Location: Coeymans (near the border of Albany and Greene counties)
Delorme *New York State Atlas & Gazetteer:* p. 52, A3
Accessibility: 0.5-mile hike along an old abandoned road, now a footpath, with an elevation change of several hundred feet
Degree of Difficulty: Moderate

Description: Ravena Falls is formed on Hannacroix Creek, a medium-sized stream that rises in the hills west of Clarksville and flows into the Hudson River just south of Coeymans.[1,2] The waterfall is located in the 113-acre Hannacroix Creek Preserve, owned by the Open Space Institute and managed by the New Baltimore Conservancy. Ravena Falls is eight to ten feet high, block-shaped, and spans the entire stream. The trail to the fall leads right out onto a promontory overlooking the cascade. The main trail also leads you to the old stone ruins of a former paper mill, as well as to several additional foundations, one being the ruins of the former town poorhouse.[3]

History: Shortly after the American Revolution, Ravena Falls was used to generate power for a gristmill. By 1826 the property had been converted into a paper mill by Nathaniel Bruce. Over the next several decades the mill passed through the hands of several owners. It burned down at least twice, but on each occasion was rebuilt. The site was subsequently purchased by a Mr. Croswell and was operated as the Croswell Paper Mill for many years. Different varieties of paper were made, including wrapping paper and wallpaper. Old-timers have been quoted as recalling seeing bales of rag coming up the river by boat or overland by train to the mill. Croswell was succeeded by his son-in-law, Stephen Parsons. The Croswell mill finally closed about 1897.[3]

Ravena Falls is by no means the only fall on Hannacroix Creek. A number of miles further upstream is an awesome gorge with falls (inaccessible, unfortunately).[4] Another falls, named Dickinson Falls, can be partially seen from roadside at the inlet to the Alcove Reservoir.

Directions: From Ravena (junction of Rtes. 9W & 143), turn east onto Rt. 143 (Main Street) and drive east through Coeymans for 1.3 miles until you reach Rt. 144. Turn right onto Rt. 144 and drive south for 0.9 mile. You will see on your right a sign indicating "Hannacroix Creek Preserve." Follow a dirt road in for less than 0.1 mile to a parking area.

Starting at the kiosk, follow the Lavern E. Irving Trail west (then south) for slightly over 0.5 mile as it first takes you uphill, and then down into the gorge. Along the way there is a blue spur trail on your right that will give you additional views of the ravine, but not of the falls. The blue spur trail reconnects with the main trail before you reach the bottom of the gorge. The main trail (the Lavern E. Irving Trail) is easy to follow since it is an old road that once led to the various mills and buildings that inhabited the bot-

DEAN'S MILL FALLS, RAVENA, N.Y.

This unique waterfall is formed upstream from Ravena Falls.

tom of the ravine. You will eventually reach a fork in the road. The road to the left leads up to some old ruins, including the poor house, and the path to the right leads to the fall. Near this junction can be seen the ruins of the old Croswell Paper Mill. Go to the right and you will be at Ravena Falls in less than 0.05 mile.

Near the beginning of the Lavern E. Irving Trail, a path going off to the left leads uphill to some pretty, but slightly obscured views of the Hudson River from upper ledges.

50

FALLS ON COXSACKIE CREEK

Location: Near Coxsackie (Greene County)
Delorme *New York State Atlas & Gazetteer:* p. 52, A/B3
Accessibility: Short, 0.1-mile hike
Degree of Difficulty: Easy

Description: There are several falls formed on Coxsackie Creek, a small stream that rises in West Coxsackie and joins with the Hudson River downstream from the falls.[1] The first cascade, visible from roadside, is a long series of small drops totaling three to four feet in height.

Downstream, there are two distinct drops that can almost appear to be one large cascade when viewed from a distance. Both falls are formed in a deep ravine where the streambed is tilted at a forty-five-degree angle and where the walls are particularly high along the south bank. The first waterfall is five feet in height and plunges over a smooth, rounded top that almost looks man-made. The second fall, just a few yards further downstream, is a cascade approximately eight feet high. From the top of the south bank, downstream from the falls, the waterfalls appear as one. The eye is fooled into seeing the falls as much higher than they actually are because of the intervening, descending water flowing between the two cascades.

Along the north bank, near the base of the lower cascade, can be seen the extensive foundations of an early mill. Just downstream from the ruins, the abutments of an old stone bridge still stand on opposite banks of the creek.

The falls are on land owned by Encon.

History: The name Coxsackie comes from the Indian word *kaak-aki.* There are several interpretations as to the meaning of this name. According to one source, *kaak-aki* refers to a "cut bank;" another source contends that kaak-aki means "hoot of an owl." The latter seems to be the preferred interpretation.[2,3]

The village of Coxsackie was settled in 1661 by Pieter Bronck of Albany. His house, which was built in 1663, is now a historical building maintained by the Greene County Historical Society.

Directions: From I-87 (the NYS Thruway), get off at Exit 21B for Coxsackie. Turn left onto Rt. 9W and drive south for 2.2 miles. At the junction of Rtes. 9W & 81, turn left onto Rt. 385 and drive east towards Coxsackie for over 0.8 mile. Just after you go under a railroad overpass, turn left onto Lawrence Ave. (opposite Firemans Park) and proceed north. At 0.3 mile the road becomes Rt. 61 (River Road). At 1.4 miles you will reach a small bridge that spans Coxsackie Creek. Cross over the bridge and park to the right, almost opposite Van Gurpin Lane.

If you are approaching from New Baltimore (junction of Rtes. 66 & 144), take Rt. 66 (River Road) south for 4.8 miles. Park to your left just before crossing over a small bridge.

The first cascade will be located just downstream from the bridge and is clearly visible from roadside. There is very little to see, and undoubtedly you will not linger for long next to the road. Take note that the stream, which initially parallels the road, abruptly turns southeast; it is shortly after this bend that the falls are formed.

To access the main falls, walk across to the south end of the bridge. You will see a little path leading off behind the guardrail. Follow this path and it will quickly become a wide trail leading you through tall pines to the top of a high ravine, from where the falls can be easily observed. The distance is not much more than 0.05 mile.

51

FALLS ON TRIBUTARY
TO COB CREEK

Location: Surprise (Greene County)
Delorme *New York State Atlas & Gazetteer:* p. 52, A/B2
Accessibility: Roadside

Description: This small waterfall is formed on a little stream that rises in a swampy area southwest of Surprise and enters Cob Creek just downstream from the falls, almost opposite Willow Brook Road. The falls consist of three small drops totaling ten feet in height, located in a small ravine almost directly facing the road. At the bottom of the falls is an attractive, circular pool of water where the stream literally does a U-turn as it rushes off in the opposite direction.[1]

Additional Point of Interest: A small stream issuing from the Coxsackie Reservoir produces a four-foot waterfall in the tiny hamlet of Climax. From the intersection of Rtes. 9W & 81, drive west on Rt. 81 towards Surprise. Look for the tiny waterfall on your right after you have gone 1.1 miles. The cascade is not always easy to glimpse, however, so don't blink as you're driving along!

Directions: From I-87 (the NYS Thruway), get off at Exit 21B for Coxsackie and proceed south on Rt. 9W for 2.2 miles. Turn right onto Rt. 81 and drive west for 8 miles. You will pass through the tiny village of Earlton about halfway along the ride. When you reach the community of Surprise, look for Willow Brook Road on your right. Drive west on Rt. 81 for slightly over 0.1 mile further. The waterfall will be on the left-hand side of the road, just after where the guardrails begin. You may not be able to see the fall from the right-hand side of the road, so turn around up ahead and come back, parking the car just east of the guardrails. From here, you can walk back thirty feet along the road and easily view the fall from roadside.

Take note that the fall is on private lands. Stay on the road.

MID-HUDSON VALLEY

As you drive along the east shore of the Hudson River between Hudson and Beacon, the mid-Hudson Valley is characterized by relatively wide-open spaces and rolling hills. Along the river's west shore between Catskill and Cornwall-on-Hudson, however, the area is markedly different and dominated by the vertiginous heights of the Catskill and Shawangunk mountains. This is an area of numerous streams and waterfalls; some are languid, and some are thunderous.

WEST SIDE OF THE HUDSON RIVER FROM CATSKILL TO NEWBURGH

Catskill Region

There are a number of significant waterfalls that have formed in the Catskill Mountains region on tributaries to the Hudson River. The most notable of these are Kleins Falls, Rip Van Winkle Falls, the Falls in Austin Glen, High Falls (at High Falls), and Buttermilk Falls—all near the village of Catskill—and Dashville Falls, Falls on the Coxing Kill, and High Falls (at Rondout Creek), which are all in close proximity to the village of Rosendale. These falls are in close proximity to the river and are described fully in the second book in this series of regional waterfalls, *Catskill Region Waterfall Guide: Cool Cascades of the Catskills & Shawangunks*. This book will skip the area already covered in *Catskill Region Waterfall Guide* and proceed south to the numerous waterfalls along the mid-Hudson River Valley, starting at Cantine Falls in Saugerties.

52

CANTINE FALLS

Location: Saugerties (Ulster County)
Delorme *New York State Atlas & Gazetteer:* p. 52, D2
Accessibility: Roadside, or easy 0.2-mile canoe paddle

Description: Cantine Falls is a dammed waterfall formed on the Esopus Creek, a sizable stream that rises on the slopes of Panther and Slide mountains from three branches and flows into the Hudson River at Saugerties.[1] The fall is formed nearly 1.0 mile upstream from the Esopus Creek's confluence with the Hudson River and is contained in a gorge whose walls are 70 feet high along the south bank and 140 feet high along the north bank.

Cantine Falls consist of a dam and waterfall that have been melded together as one and total 35 feet in height. It is not the prettiest sight for waterfall purists, however. Benson J. Lossing wrote of the falls in the mid-1800s: "A once picturesque fall or rapid, around which a portion of the village is clustered, has been partially destroyed by a dam and unsightly bridge above it."[2] Directly above the fall, on the east bank, can be seen a tiny channel where water at one time was diverted to power the Barclay Iron Works plant. Immediately downstream from the base of the fall and dam, the riverbed is so congested with large rocks that the fall cannot be approached too closely by canoeists except during unusually high water conditions.

History: The village of Saugerties began as an industrial town. Its very name is an evolution of the Dutch words *Da Zaagertijis,* for "sawmills." Later the town became a bluestone shipping center. The earliest mill was in operation as far back as 1663.

The dam at Cantine Falls was constructed in 1820 by Henry Barclay and Robert Livingston in order to power an ironworks and a paper mill. The stream was also host to factories that produced white lead, glass, gunpowder, and bluestone products. The Esopus

River at one time supposedly claimed the largest assemblage of hydropower machinery in the world. The last industry at the fall was the Martin Cantine Coated Paper Company, which was located on the north bank.[3]

The remains of several twentieth-century mills can be seen along the banks of the Esopus near the fall. Starting in 2003, however, considerable work has been done on the west bank to clear away sections of the degraded ruins and foundations.

Directions, Land Approach: From I-87 (the NYS Thruway), get off at Exit 20 for Saugerties and follow the signs east into the village of Saugerties. Once in the village, continue south on Rtes. 9W & 32 from where Rt. 212 splits off to the left. As you leave the village, Rtes. 32 & 9W take a sharp turn to the left and then cross over a bridge spanning Esopus Creek. The fall and dam are directly downstream from this point, and the top can be glimpsed from the bridge.

Cantine Falls. Many industries in Saugerties have been powered by the Esopus Creek.

To see a little more of the fall, drive back across the bridge into Saugerties. Veer to the right and follow the main road uphill towards the downtown section. Turn right onto Dock Street, 0.2 mile from the bridge. Within less than 0.05 mile you may be able to catch a partial glimpse of the fall from roadside—depending upon the season—through a sparse set of trees along the west bank of Esopus Creek, high above the stream.

Water Approach: From the center of Saugerties, follow Rtes. 32 & 9W south. As soon as you cross over the bridge spanning Esopus Creek, turn left onto East Bridge Street and drive downhill for 0.2 mile. Turn left into the Saugerties Waterfront Park, roughly a mile upstream from the confluence of Esopus Creek with the Hudson River. From here it is easy to put in a canoe or a kayak. Paddle upstream a short distance to view the fall and dam from near its base.

If you are paddling up Esopus Creek from its confluence with the Hudson, the trip is slightly longer than 1.0 mile.

Additional Point of Interest: If you are approaching Cantine Falls by canoe, the Saugerties Lighthouse, built in 1838, is certainly worth a visit. The structure degraded from lack of use in the mid-1900s, but has been brought back to life and renovated over the last decade. It now serves as a bed & breakfast. To get there: paddle downstream on the Esopus to the river's confluence with the Hudson. The lighthouse is at the mouth of the Esopus on the left.

53

GLENERIE FALLS

Location: South of Saugerties (Ulster County)
Delorme *New York State Atlas & Gazetteer*: p. 52, D2
Accessibility: Roadside, limited view

Description: Glenerie Falls is an extraordinarily broad, eight-foot-high waterfall that is formed on the Esopus Creek, a sizable stream that rises in the Catskill Mountains and joins with the Hudson River at Saugerties.[1] The fall has also been known as Mt. Marion Falls because of its proximity to the hamlet of Mt. Marion.

A short distance upstream from the main fall are two larger cascades, both of which are much higher and narrower than the visible, roadside waterfall. Glenerie Falls can be seen through the tree line along Rt. 9W. The upper falls are not as easily visible from roadside, except when the trees are leafless. Marc B. Fried refers to a distinctive "mound of bedrock protruding from the center of Esopus Creek at the brink of the upper falls at Glenerie."[3]

The falls are listed on Delorme's *New York State Atlas & Gazetteer,* which suggests that they were high-profile cascades in the past. Although the *Atlas & Gazetteer* identifies the site as Glenerie Lake Park, which would seem to imply that the falls are accessible to the public, the main waterfall and the two upper cascades are actually located on private, posted land.

History: *Esopus* is the Algonquin word for "river," but the Esopus Creek is a much less dynamic stream now than when first encountered by Native Americans, thanks principally to the Ashokan Reservoir siphoning off huge quantities of water for transport downstate.

Expansive ruins by the main fall can be seen from roadside. A leadworks once stood by the fall.[2] Between the two upper and the lower falls is an abandoned slate quarry.

An old postcard makes reference to nearby Schoentag's Hotel, whose history was intertwined with that of the fall.

Directions: From I-87 (the New York State Thruway), get off at Exit 20. Drive into the village of Saugerties and continue south on Rt. 9W. As soon as you cross over a bridge spanning Esopus Creek and leaving the village of Saugerties behind, clock off four miles as you continue south on Rt. 9W. The fall will be directly to your right at a point where the road parallels Esopus Creek, 1.2 miles after you pass by a right-hand turn to Mt. Marion.

Although it is possible to see Glenerie Falls from roadside in the summer, it is best to visit in early spring or late autumn when there are no leaves on the trees. Visiting in early spring or late fall will also ensure that you can view the upper two falls from roadside.

Glenerie Falls—almost manmade in appearance.

FALLS AT ASHOKAN FIELD CAMPUS

Location: Ashokan Field Campus, Ashokan (Ulster County)
Delorme *New York State Atlas & Gazetteer:* p. 36, A2

Description: The Ashokan Field Campus is an Outdoor Environmental Education Center and Retreat Facility that was established in 1967. It is a unit of Campus Auxiliary Services at the State University of New York, New Paltz. The campus consists of 372 acres of forest and rural countryside surrounding a nature center, a lake, and a variety of historic sites. The Ashokan Reservoir is fairly close by.

History: Long before European settlers arrived, the Esopus Indians (a contingent of the Delaware tribe) harvested fruit from trees that they planted where the campus athletic field is now located.[1] Little Native American history has survived, but much effort has gone into preserving what remains of the European culture that industrialized the area.

Directions to the Ashokan Field Campus: From I-87 (the NYS Thruway), get off at Exit 19 for Kingston. Drive northwest on Rt. 28 for nearly 12.5 miles to Shokan. Turn left onto Reservoir Road and continue south for 1.8 miles (at 1.4 miles you will cross over the Ashokan Reservoir). Turn left onto Monument Road and proceed southeast. The road forks at 0.3 mile; bear to your right. You will immediately come out onto Rt. 28A. In another 0.3 mile, turn left onto Beaverkill Road. Follow Beaverkill Road south for 1.0 mile. Turn right into the entrance for the Ashokan Field Campus. After 0.4 mile, pull into the large parking area provided by the campus.

From the kiosk, walk down a steep hill to the campus buildings below. Pay a modest day-use fee at the administrative office, where you can also pick up a handy map of the campus and its hiking trails.

54 • WINCHELL FALLS

Accessibility: 0.2-mile walk
Degree of Difficulty: Easy

Description: Winchell Falls is a broad, ten-foot-high waterfall formed on Esopus Creek, a medium-sized stream that rises from the slopes of Panther Mountain and Slide Mountain and flows into the Hudson River at Saugerties.

The waterfall is broken up horizontally into several distinct sections. Near the east bank can be seen a fifteen-foot-high cascade where water has been channeled through a sluiceway at the top of the fall. The cascade drops into a portion of the stream directly facing the ruins of a former industry. The middle section of the falls consists of a large section of bedrock that at one time was part of the falls, but which now has become an island of rock. Along the west bank, the stream drops through a small, chasm-like section of the falls. Crowning the entire length of Winchell Falls is a medium-

Unlike others, the waterfalls at Ashokan Field Campus fortunately were downstream when the Ashokan Reservoir was created.

sized dam, approximately twelve to fifteen feet in height, which impounds a small lake that is used by the campus for recreational purposes.

History: Winchell Falls is named after James & John Winchell, who established a gristmill at the falls in 1772. Around the same time, a sawmill and a fulling machine were also erected at Winchell Falls and operated until 1895. From 1895 to 1915, a mill owned by the Hudson River Wood Pulp Manufacturing Company, a subsidiary of Dupont, flourished at the falls.

Directions: From the main parking lot, proceed on foot, following the road that leads out from the south end of the parking area. Stay on this road as it continues along the top of the ridge (avoiding the road that goes off to the right and down to the athletic field and campus buildings). You will immediately pass by the tinsmith's shop and the broom shop on your left. A lake will be clearly visible to your right, far below, cradled in the valley basin. Follow the sign that directs you towards the "Covered Bridge, Barnyard & 1817 School."

Within 0.1 mile from the parking area, you will come to a gazebo on your right where old foundation ruins of a baling plant can be seen. Winchell Falls is below, but cannot be accessed from this point. Continue past the gazebo and ruins. Within 150 feet bear right, leaving the main road behind, and follow a secondary road downhill that is called the "Covered Bridge Trail." Take note that you are now on a parcel of land designated as a conservation easement and managed by the Esopus/Rondout Land Conservancy. At the bottom of the hill, turn right and follow a secondary road that leads to the base of Winchell Falls and old stone ruins. From here, be sure to follow the bank of the stream for a short distance west, paralleling the waterfall, so that you can see the dam and other sections of the falls as well.

55 • LITTLE FALLS

Accessibility: 0.1-mile hike
Degree of Difficulty: Easy

Description: This fifteen-foot-high, two-tiered cascade is formed on a tiny tributary to the Esopus Creek. The stream is a seasonal one, which means that you should only plan to visit the cascade in the spring or following significant rainfall.

Directions: From the kiosk at the west side of the parking lot, walk downhill to the main buildings comprising the Ashokan Field Campus. When you reach the bottom of the hill, follow a road to the left of Tongore Lodge, going west. The road immediately crosses over Esopus Creek and passes by a swampy area to your right. Within 0.05 mile, the road leads up to the top of a small bank. Turn left here and proceed south for less than 0.05 mile, following a well-defined trail paralleling the stream. You will see the fall to your right, dropping down from the top of a small escarpment.

56 • CATHEDRAL FALLS & UNNAMED FALLS IN GORGE

Accessibility: 0.5-mile hike from parking lot
Degree of Difficulty: Easy to moderate

Description: Cathedral Falls is formed on a small tributary to Esopus Creek. The waterfall consists of a nearly vertical, forty-foot drop over an escarpment face. It is a very impressive waterfall contained in an unusually scenic gorge.

Just before you reach Cathedral Falls, you will notice a seasonal, forty-foot cascade on the opposite side of the Esopus Creek. Unless you are visiting during the rainy season, however, you may see only a trickle of water running down the escarpment face.

History: The covered bridge over Esopus Creek was built in 1885 and originally spanned the Beaver Kill in Turnwood. By 1934 it had been deemed unsafe and was ultimately purchased by Lester

Mauring, a comptroller for the Chrysler Corporation, who moved it to his property in Olive. The bridge was subsequently sold to Frank Banks in 1955, and Banks sold it to the State University at New Paltz in 1957, including the land that has since become known as the Ashokan Field Campus. Look closely and you will notice that the bridge is held together by wooden pegs instead of nails. The sign on the bridge states: "Ten dollars fine driving over this bridge faster than a walk." How times have changed!

Directions: From the south end of the main parking lot, follow the upper road south past the tinsmith shop and broom shop. When you get to a gazebo on the right, continue straight for 150 feet and then follow a secondary road (identified as the "Covered Bridge Trail") downhill. Take note that you are now on a conservation easement. At the bottom, walk west along the road and within a moment you will reach a covered bridge that spans the Esopus Creek. Winchell Falls will be off to your right.

Cross over the covered bridge and continue uphill along the old road. You will soon come to a fork. Turn left and follow the road east for 0.2 mile, paralleling Esopus Creek. Turn left onto a secondary road and walk downhill until you reach the stream. Turn right and follow an unmarked path as it continues to parallel the stream. In less than 0.1 mile you will reach a spot where you will see a pretty, cascading waterfall to the left on the opposite side of the creek. This cascade is unnamed and seasonal. In another 0.05 mile you will come to Cathedral Falls, which is located on the same side of the creek. The trail, at this point, comes to an end when you reach the small tributary forming Cathedral Falls.

57

FALL ALONG SHAUPENEAK RIDGE

Location: Esopus (Ulster County)
Delorme *New York State Atlas & Gazetteer:* p. 36. B4
Accessibility: 0.7-mile hike along well-maintained trail, with slight changes in elevation.
Degree of Difficulty: Easy

Description: This pretty waterfall is formed on a tiny stream that merges with another, equally small creek that flows into the Hudson River at Esopus. The fall is thirty feet high and consists of a cascading upper section, followed by a ten-foot plunge over a block of bedrock into a shallow pool. Stone slabs have been placed to create steps leading down to the waterfall, and there are clusters of touch-me-nots along the way, giving the fall the feel of a rock garden.

History: The waterfall is located in the Shaupeneak Ridge Cooperative Recreation Area, a 500-acre forest preserve managed by the West Esopus Landowners Association and the New York State Department of Environmental Conservation. At one time the property belonged to a private hunting club.[1]

Shaupeneak is Unami for "people of the shore."[2] Shaupeneak Ridge is part of the Marlboro mountain range, which extends from Kingston and Marlboro and forms the western edge to this section of the valley. The ridge is formed out of Ordovician rock.[1]

Directions: From Kingston (junction of Rtes. 32 & 9W South), drive south on Rt. 9W for 8.5 miles. (Approaching from the south, continue north on Rt. 9W for 6.0 miles from the junction of Rtes. 299 & 9W, north of Highland.) Look for a sign that tells you that you are approaching the turn for Shaupeneak Ridge. From Rt. 9W turn west onto Old Post Road (Rt. 16) and drive west for 0.2 mile, crossing over railroad tracks in the process. The parking area for Shaupeneak Ridge Cooperative Recreation Area is directly to your right.

Walk north from the parking area, following a well-defined trail blazed with black-on-white markers along the base of Shaupeneak Ridge. Eventually you will pass through an old stone wall that is perpendicular to the trail. Within another 0.2 mile the trail climbs steeply up a hillside of talus rocks. When the trail splits, take the branch to the right, which leads to the base of the waterfall in less than 0.05 mile.

The upper trail follows the stream above the waterfall for a short distance, but there are no further significant cascades in the upper region. A map on the kiosk near the trailhead will give you information on how the other trails in the park are configured. Take special note of the sign warning of ticks, and heed the sign's instructions.

58

FALL #1 AT JOHN BURROUGHS SANCTUARY

Location: West Park (Ulster County)
Delorme *New York State Atlas & Gazetteer:* p. 36, B4
Accessibility: 0.1-mile walk
Degree of Difficulty: Easy

Description: This twenty-five-foot-high cascade is broken up into several small sections. It is formed on a tiny tributary to Black Creek. In dry weather the cascade is apt to go unnoticed, even though it is in fairly close proximity to the main trail.

History: This pretty cascade is located in the John Burroughs Sanctuary, a 170-acre preserve run by the John Burroughs Association. The nucleus of the preserve is Burroughs' home, Slabsides, which is a registered national historic landmark.[1,2]

Directions: Take Rt. 9W to West Park, which is 4.0 miles north of the junction of Rtes. 9W & 299 (north of Highland) and approximately 10.5 miles south of Kingston (junction of Rtes. 32 & 9W South). At West Park, turn west onto Park Lane where a roadside historic marker indicates that Slabsides is 1.5 miles westward (obviously an approximation). Drive west for 0.2 mile. Bear to the right as you cross over railroad tracks, and then proceed straight ahead on Floyd Ackert Road (ignoring the right-hand turn where a sign points the way to a transfer station and dog kennel), continuing west for 0.6 mile. Turn left onto Burroughs Drive and proceed uphill for 0.3 mile. You will see pull-offs on both sides of the road.

Park the car and walk around the green-colored barrier on the right-hand side of the road, which is the entrance path for Slabsides. Follow the dirt road downhill for less than 0.1 mile. You will come to a sign that reads: "NYS Environment Protection Fund. John Burroughs Sanctuary's Slabsides." At this point you will notice a privy on the right-hand side of the road. To the right of the privy is a trail that has been flagged with orange markers. Follow this trail downhill and it will immediately lead you across the upper third of a cascade and then to its bottom, where you can look back up and view the waterfall in its entirety.

If you are interested in seeing Slabsides, John Burroughs' rustic home, simply continue on the dirt road for a short distance further.

Slabsides. John Burroughs was a naturalist and a lover of waterfalls.

FALL #2 AT JOHN BURROUGHS SANCTUARY

Location: West Park (Ulster County)

Delorme *New York State Atlas & Gazetteer:* p. 36, B4

Accessibility: 0.2-mile walk, followed by a short, 100-foot bush-whack from road

Degree of Difficulty: Easy

Description: This ten-foot-high cascade, broken up by blocks of talus, is formed on a tiny outlet stream that issues from a pond in John Burroughs Sanctuary and flows into Black Creek just a short distance downstream from the fall.

Directions: From Rt. 9W at West Park (4.0 miles north of the junction of Rtes. 299 & 9W), turn west onto Park Lane and drive west for 0.2 mile. Bear to your right as you cross over railroad tracks, and then proceed straight on Floyd Ackert Road, going west for 0.6 mile. When you get to the left-hand turn to Burroughs Drive, continue straight ahead on Floyd Ackert Road for another 0.1 mile. Pull into the small parking area for John Burroughs Sanctuary on your left, making sure not to block the gated road.

Continuing on foot, follow the dirt road into the woods for 0.2 mile. You will come to a scenic pond whose shoreline is framed by huge upthrusts of Shawangunk conglomerate. You will notice a tiny outlet stream issuing from the north end of the lake. Follow the creek downstream for 100 feet—this requires a short bushwhack using the stream as your guide—and you will quickly arrive at the bottom of a small cascade.

FALL ON BLACK CREEK

Location: West Park (Ulster County)
Delorme *New York State Atlas & Gazetteer:* p. 36, B4
Accessibility: Roadside

Description: This cascade is made up of angled slabs of bedrock. The fall is formed on Black Creek, a medium-sized stream that rises from Lake Sunset south of Ardonia and flows into the Hudson River at Esopus.[1,2] The fall is broad, approximately four feet in height, with tilted slabs of bedrock. Below the cascade, the stream flows into a large, oval-shaped pool before changing direction abruptly and proceeding north. There are cascades further downstream, before West Park, but they are located on private land.

John Burroughs frequently visited this fall because of its close proximity to Slabsides.[3] The cascade may well have inspired Walt Whitman to write "An Ulster County Waterfall," in his book *Specimen Days,* as he and Burroughs walked along Black Creek together.[4]

Directions: From the junction of Rtes. 299 & 9W (north of the village of Highland), drive north on Rt. 9W for 4.0 miles. At West Park, turn left onto Park Lane, marked by a roadside historic marker, and proceed west for 0.2 mile. Bear right as you cross over railroad tracks, and then continue west on what becomes Floyd Ackert Road. At 0.6 mile, you will pass by Burroughs Drive. Continue straight ahead on Floyd Ackert Road for over 0.2 mile further. As soon as you cross over Black Creek, turn left onto Lalli Road and drive south for 0.5 mile. When you come to a short bridge spanning Black Creek, look downstream and you will see the top of a broad, small cascade. Take note that the fall is on private land.

FALL AT THE TUTHILLTOWN GRISTMILL & COUNTRY STORE

Location: Near Gardiner (Ulster County)
Delorme *New York State Atlas & Gazetteer:* p. 36, C2
Accessibility: Roadside; short, 0.3-mile walk if you follow the raceway up to the dam
Degree of Difficulty: Easy

Description: This small, man-made fall is at the end of a feeder canal where water is diverted from the Shawangunk Kill, a medium-sized stream that rises northeast of Port Jervis and flows into the Wallkill River at Tuthill after paralleling the Shawangunk ridge for much of its length.[1] The cascade is directly under the rear of a gristmill.

The fall, however, is not the primary attraction. The Tuthilltown Gristmill has been in continuous operation since shortly after the American Revolution. The gristmill provides a rare opportunity to go back in time over two centuries and experience being inside a real, working mill. With this image fresh in mind, one can then better appreciate the old stone and brick foundations of all the mills and factories that once stood near the various falls described in this book.

History: The gristmill was built in 1788 by Selah Tuthill when he was only eighteen years old. It was a prodigious undertaking; not only did the mill have to be constructed, but a long canal as well, so that water could be diverted from the Shawangunk Kill to power the mill's water-wheel. The present canal, which runs from the mill to a three-foot-high dam that spans the Shawangunk Kill, is approximately 3,000 feet in length and lies parallel to the river for much of that distance.

Earlier centuries used two kinds of waterwheel—undershot and overshot. Undershot waterwheels were favored in the early days because they could be made cheaply and were relatively easy to maintain. The typical undershot was constructed out of a wooden shaft eight to twelve inches in diameter, with two-by-six-foot paddles approximately ten feet long attached to the shaft lengthwise. Water flowed under the wheel, which is how the term "under-shot" arose. Unfortunately, the undershots were notoriously ineffi-cient at generating power and came to be known, rather derisively, as "flutter wheels."

Overshot waterwheels were far superior at power generation. They were larger and required considerably more craftsmanship to fashion, however, and also required more water flow to run effi-ciently. The name "overshot" arose because the flow of water went over the top of the wheel. At full flow, overshots operated at a power efficiency equivalent to a modern-day turbine.[3]

The Tuthilltown mill used an undershot waterwheel, which last-ed until the late 1930s when it was replaced by a bucket turbine. The turbine endured until the mid-1980s. Since then the mill has been episodically run by a PTO (power take off), which is diesel-powered.[2]

When people picture a waterwheel, they generally imagine a large wheel spinning briskly at the side of a mill. In reality, most waterwheels were enclosed and protected from the elements so that ice wouldn't build up during the winter and bring them to a grind-ing halt or break them into pieces.

The millstones that were used by many Hudson Valley mills were quarried at Esopus, in Ulster County.

Directions: From New Paltz (junction of Rtes. 299 & 32), take Rt. 32 south for 6.0 miles until you reach Rt. 44/55. Turn right and follow Rt. 44/55 west. At 3.6 miles you will pass through Gardiner and then cross over the Wallkill River. At 4.0 miles you will come to a blinking traffic light. Turn left onto Rt. 9 and then, after 0.1 mile, right onto Tuthill Road. Quickly turn left onto Gristmill Lane and you will arrive at the parking area for the mill within 0.05 mile.

A wooden platform next to the gristmill allows you to look at the mill, the cascade (when water is being diverted down the canal), and the Wallkill River.

To get to the dam across the Shawangunk Kill: follow the dirt road past the house next to the mill, and walk south for over 0.3 mile, paralleling the canal on your left. It is an interesting hike to take, for it depicts how much more there was to running a mill than just constructing the mill building itself.

62

WRIGHT FALLS

Location: Marlboro (Ulster County)
Delorme *New York State Atlas & Gazetteer:* p. 36, C/D4
Accessibility: Roadside

Description: Wright Falls is a twenty-foot-high dam that looms over a small, naturally formed cascade at its base.[1] The dam and fall are located on Lattintown Creek, a small stream that rises north of Lattintown and flows into the Hudson River east of Marlboro. Look closely along the north bank, and you will see a number of large, rusted cog wheels lying scattered about inside the ruins of an old mill foundation.

Further upstream, at the intersection of Western Avenue and Prospect Street, is a deeply cut ravine containing several small cascades. The brick chimney of a now-defunct factory stands alone and towers over the ravine.

Just downstream from Wright Falls is Marlboro Falls, a massive cascade located on private land and far enough from roadside to make it inaccessible. Walter F. Burmeister describes it as a one-hundred-foot drop.[2]

To the northwest, Marlboro Mountain rises to a height of over 1,000 feet above the level of the river.[3]

The village of Marlboro was named in honor of John Churchill, the Duke of Marlborough. In days gone by, a gristmill and a sawmill were mainstays of the community.[4]

Directions: From Kingston, take Rt. 9W south for roughly 22 miles until you reach the little village of Marlboro. (From Newburgh, drive north on Rt. 9W for roughly 6 miles.) Just north of a blinking traffic light in the middle of town is Lattintown Creek. Park off the side of the road by the stream and walk over to the west side of the bridge spanning the creek. Wright Falls will be clearly visible upstream from the bridge

After you have finished looking at Wright Falls, cross over the street to the east side of the bridge and peer over its side. You will be at the top of a prodigious gulf, looking down at the upper section of an enormous cascade that drops precipitously into the valley far below. This is Marlboro Falls. If you drive southeast down Dock Road (which is directly off of Rt. 9W) north of the bridge, you may be able to catch a fleeting glimpse of Marlboro Falls, providing it is early spring or late fall and the trees are bare. Just be sure to bring along a pair of binoculars since the waterfall is at some distance from the road. You will also notice a number of old foundations along Dock Road—vestiges from past industries.

Wright Falls is more dam than falls.

Wrights Falls, Marlborough, N.Y.

63

HORSESHOE FALLS

Location: Walden (Orange County)
Delorme *New York State Atlas & Gazetteer:* p. 36, D2
Accessibility: Roadside

Description: Horseshoe Falls is formed on the Wallkill River, a medium-sized stream that rises in New Jersey near Pochuck Mountain and flows into Rondout Creek northeast of Tillson.[1] The Wallkill and its various tributaries virtually single-handedly drain the entire area east of the Shawangunks.

Horseshoe Falls is crowned by a large, curved dam, which undoubtedly is the feature that gave the fall its name. (The waterfall has also been called the Great Falls of the Wallkill River.) The natural waterfall, located directly below the ten-foot-high dam, consists of an enormous, tilted rock slab roughly twenty-five feet high. The Walden Hydroelectric Project is situated directly next to the fall. If you look closely, you will see a number of foundations along the east bank downstream from the fall, as well as a faintly discernible, long-abandoned, descending road along the west bank leading away from the fall. These are remnants of past days of rampant industrialization.

History: In the 1820s, Jacob T. Walden (the town's namesake) purchased land near the falls and convinced two partners to go into business with him to produce and process woolen goods. Together they formed the Franklin Company. By the 1830s several other textile companies were also turning out woolen and cotton products at Walden. By the early 1840s, Walden and its woolen mills had become so successful that the town was producing over one-third of all the wool manufactured in the United States. By the 1850s, however, the woolen industry in Walden had declined precipitously, a victim of hard economic times that had beset the entire country.

Just as it seemed as if Walden was doomed to fade into obscurity after its decades of glory, the town suddenly burst into life again, this time thanks to the Wallkill River Knife Works, which built its factory in 1856 along the east bank below the falls. Almost overnight, Walden became known as the "cutlery capital of the country," and the town again prospered. By 1931 the Wallkill River Knife Works had gone out of business, and by World War II the buildings themselves had been reduced to crumbling bricks and mortar. The ruins that you see today along the east bank downstream from Horseshoe Falls are from this once prosperous factory.[2]

Directions: From New Paltz (junction of Rtes. 299 & 208) take Rt. 208 southwest to Walden. From the center of Walden (junction of Rtes. 208 & 52), drive west on West Main Street for 0.3 mile and cross over the Wallkill River. In doing so, you may partially see the falls upstream, off to your left. When you reach the end of the bridge, turn left onto Cross Street, which immediately leads up to South Montgomery Street. Park along the side of South Montgomery Street, from where you can obtain views of Horseshoe Falls from along the roadside.

Thanks to its waterfalls, Walden flourished as an industrial center twice.

MID-HUDSON VALLEY

EAST SIDE OF THE HUDSON RIVER:

FROM HUDSON TO BEACON

BASH BISH FALLS

Location: Copake Falls (Columbia County)
Delorme *New York State Atlas & Gazetteer:* p. 53, C/D5-6
Accessibility: 0.5-mile walk along an old abandoned road;
little change in elevation; open dawn to dusk
Degree of Difficulty: Easy

Description: Bash Bish Falls is a stupendous, eighty-foot-high water-fall formed on Bash Bish Brook, a medium-sized stream that rises from two tributaries in the highlands of Mount Washington State Forest in Massachusetts and joins with the Noster Kill south of Copake.[1-16] Bash Bish Falls is located in a 3,290-acre park that contains a variety of hiking trails. Nearby are the historic ruins of the Copake Iron Works, which operated from 1845 to 1903. Many years ago, a rustic footbridge used to span the creek slightly downstream from the base of the falls.

The waterfall is distinguished by a massive boulder of schist and granite near its top, which splits the fall into two rivulets much like a cleaver. Posted warnings should be heeded; a number of people have died at the fall over the years. There are several smaller cascades just upstream from the main waterfall, but they are inaccessible. Anyone caught trespassing in that section will be fined several hundred dollars. The upper parking area provides a way to look down into the gorge and to gaze out west across Bash Bish Valley, but there is no legal way to access the falls in the upper section of the gorge. You will have to be content with the sound of the rushing waters below.

There are two stories about how Bash Bish Falls came to be named. According to one, the name is onomatopoetic, suggestive of the bashing and bishing sounds produced by the falling waters. The more popular (and much more romantic) version is that an Indian maiden named Bash Bish was accused of being unfaithful. She was strapped to a canoe and sent over the top of the fall to her death. Her body was never found, but if you look into the veil of water at just the right angle (according to the legend), an image of the beautiful maiden can be seen as the sound of the falling waters call out "Bash Bish."[17]

Bash Bish Falls is actually located in Massachusetts, just over the state boundary line with New York. To access the fall from the main parking area, however, you need to approach from the New York State side, so in this sense, at least, it is a New York State waterfall.

History: Bash Bish Falls is one of the most often photographed falls in the Hudson River Valley region. In the early nineteenth century, it was painted by John Frederick Kensett, one of the leading landscape artists of the Hudson River School of painting.

It is believed that a rustic tavern was built near the foot of the fall in the 1850s. In 1858 the famous tightrope walker Jean Francois Gravet (whose stage name was Blondin) walked across Bash Bish Gorge, imitating his famous feats at Niagara Falls.[18]

By 1867, Jean Roemer had acquired eight parcels of land, one of which included Bash Bish Falls. Later, the fall and surrounding lands were purchased by Alfred Douglas, a prominent New York City lawyer who died at the age of forty-seven before finishing his goal of developing and beautifying the area. Under his wife Josephine's guidance, however, Douglas' lands were turned into a beautiful wooded area with luscious gardens, velvety manicured lawns, Swiss-style cottages, greenhouses, carriage houses, and barns. For years the property served as Mrs. Douglas's summer residence.

In 1879, Josephine Douglas built an inn overlooking the falls, but the business failed to make a profit and the inn was torn down in 1897. Nothing of this structure remains today.[19] By 1899, all of the Douglas property had been acquired by John Haldane Flager, an iron pipe manufacturer. Flager subsequently sold 300 acres of land in 1903 to Eugene and Margaret Vacheron. The parcel included the Douglas buildings, but not the land around the falls. Vacheron converted the estate into a country inn, enlarging the Douglas' residence considerably. The business ultimately failed and the land was being foreclosed on in 1914 when a French chef from New York City named Louis Moquin took over the property and established the Bash Bish Inn. He had even less success. The inn burned to the ground in 1918. This area was subsequently turned into a parking lot for Bash Bish Falls.

In 1923, Francis and Ella Masters purchased the falls and 400 acres of surrounding land from Flager. The Masters subsequently sold the property to the State of Massachusetts, which created the park as we know it today.[20]

Directions: From the Taconic State Parkway, get off at the Claverack & Hillsdale Exit and drive east on Rt. 23 for 7.4 miles to Hillsdale (junction of Rtes. 23 & 22). Turn right onto Rt. 22 and drive south for 4.1 miles. Turn left onto Rt. 344 at Copake Falls. Proceed east on Rt. 344 for 1.3 miles and turn into the parking area on the right for Taconic State Park.

Continuing on foot, follow a gravel road that leads from the east of the parking lot, paralleling Bash Bish Brook, up to the falls, a distance of 0.5 mile.

It is also possible to hike down to Bash Bish Falls from the upper parking lot. Proceeding east from the lower parking area, drive uphill on Rt. 344 for 1.0 mile and then pull into the upper parking area on your right. From here, you can follow a trail downhill for 0.3 mile to the base of the falls. Bear in mind that although the hike is short, it is steep and involves a descent of over 300 feet. The upper parking area also provides access to an overlook of Bash Bish Valley and the top of the gorge above Bash Bish Falls.

Few waterfalls rival the splendor of Bash Bish Falls.

BASH-BISH FALLS,
NEAR GREAT BARRINGTON, MASS.

65

FALL ON ROELIFF JANSEN KILL (Bingham Mills)

Location: Bingham Mills (Columbia County)
Delorme *New York State Atlas & Gazetteer:* p. 52: C/D3
Accessibility: Roadside

Description: This twenty-foot-high cascade is formed on the Roeliff Jansen Kill, a large stream that rises north of North Hillsdale and flows into the Hudson River south of Catskill.[1]

Directly downstream from a short bridge spanning the Roeliff Jansen Kill is a large, breached dam that has been abandoned for many years. The cascade is slightly further downstream from the top of the dam. At the east end of the dam, next to a pull-off before the bridge, is a metal gate and the machinery used to regulate the volume of water released by the Bingham Mills Dam.

History: According to the roadside historic marker located at the junction of Bingham Mills Road and Mill Road, the site was previously known as Baker's Mill. At that time, the hamlet consisted of twenty buildings including two mills, a blacksmith shop, a woolen factory, and a Methodist chapel. It was renamed Bingham Mills in honor of a local resident named Charles Bingham.

Directions: From the junction of Rtes. 9, 82 & 23, south of Hudson, take Rt. 9 and drive southwest to Blue Store. As soon as you pass through the tiny hamlet of Blue Store, 6.0 miles from the junction of Rt. 9 with Rtes. 82 & 23, turn right onto Bingham Mills Road and proceed west for 0.7 mile, stopping just before you reach a short bridge spanning the Roeliff Jansen Kill. Park to the right side of the road at a small pull-off. Relics from the dam that once impounded the waters of the Roeliff Jansen can be seen next to the east bank of the stream. It is also possible to see part of the cascade from here.

Walk out to the bridge and look downstream. The massive walls of the breached dam will be directly in front of you, slightly downstream. Still further downstream can be seen the top of a twenty-foot-high cascade. Unfortunately, the waterfall is not directly accessible. The faint path leading down to the fall from near the historic marker is on private, posted lands.

66

FALL ON ROELIFF JANSEN KILL (Ancram)

Location: Ancram (Columbia County)
Delorme *New York State Atlas & Gazetteer:* p. 53, D4-5
Accessibility: Roadside

Description: This waterfall—part dam and part cascade—totals twenty feet in height and is formed on the Roeliff Jansen Kill, a medium-sized stream that rises north of North Hillsdale and flows into the Hudson River south of Catskill.[1-4]

The dam itself is nearly fifteen feet in height and is primarily responsible for the thunderous sound of falling water that you hear as you approach the fall. Along the west bank, next to the dam, are rusted, long-abandoned pipes which once carried water for power generation.

A smaller cascade can be seen downstream from the dam, but is inaccessible.

History: Centuries ago the stream was called Saupenak by Native Americans. It came to be known as the Roeliff Jansen Kill in the 1630s, after Roeliff Jansen, the overseer of Kilian Van Rensselaer's estate.[5] At various other times, the creek has been known as Livingston Creek[1] and Ancram Creek. The town of Ancram was named after the village of Ancram, Scotland, the ancestral home of the Livingston family, whose name and history is nearly synonymous with the upper mid-Hudson Valley.[6]

A historic marker next to the bridge points out that New York State's first iron mill was located at this spot, built in 1740.[7] By the year 1743, Robert R. Livingston had established four forges in the area. Livingston's forges produced a variety of cast-iron products including stoves, firebricks, grates, pots, kettles, shot and cannon balls, and pig iron. Some of these items were supplied directly to the Continental Army during the Revolutionary War. The forge in Ancram was swept away by floodwaters, but was quickly rebuilt.

In 1854 it was converted into a paper mill.[3,7] Today, a factory that supplies fine paper to the tobacco industry stands next to the fall along the west bank.

Directions: From the junction of Rtes. 9, 23, & 82, south of Hudson, drive southeast on Rt. 82 for 11.8 miles to Ancram. (If you are approaching from the Taconic Parkway, get off at the West Taghkanic Exit and drive southeast on Rt. 82 for 6.8 miles until you reach Ancram.) At the center of the small village of Ancram (junction of Rtes. 82 & 7), continue southeast on Rt. 82 for another 0.1 mile. As soon as you cross over the bridge spanning the Roeliff Jansen Kill, turn right onto Pooles Hill Road and park immediately to your right. The dam and fall can be comfortably viewed from a square concrete platform next to the dam.

67

WHITE CLAY KILL FALLS

Location: Tivoli (Dutchess County)

Delorme *New York State Atlas & Gazetteer:* p. 52, D2-3

Accessibility: 0.05-mile walk

Degree of Difficulty: Easy; moderate scramble over rocks if you decide to go down to the streambed to get up close to the fall

Description: White Clay Kill Falls is formed on Stony Creek, a medium-sized stream that rises principally from the Tivoli Bay State Unique Area and flows into the Hudson River at North Bay.[1] Stony Creek has also been known as White Clay Kill, which is how the waterfall came to be named.[2]

The fall consists of a fifteen-foot-high cascade encased in a gorge whose bedding is tilted to nearly sixty degrees. At the base of the cascade is a large, shallow pool.[3] The waterfall is located in a 1,640-acre preserve that features an estuary whose bay waters fluctuate as much as four feet in height twice a day from the Hudson River's tides.[4-5]

History: Native Americans may have visited this waterfall as far back as 6,000 years ago. Some of the artifacts that archaeologists have excavated from the Tivoli Bay area date back to that time.[3,4]

Directions: From the junction of Rtes. 23 & 9G near the east end of the Rip Van Winkle Bridge connecting Catskill with Hudson, drive south on Rt. 9G for approximately 13 miles. If you are coming up from the south along Rt. 9G, set the odometer to zero at the blinking traffic light at the junction of Annandale Road (which leads to Bard College) and Rt. 9G, and drive north on Rt. 9G for nearly 2.5 miles.

Approaching from either direction, turn west onto Kidd Road. At 0.5 mile you will pass the upper parking area for Tivoli Bay on your left. Keep going west on Kidd Road. At 0.8 mile you will come to a tiny bridge spanning Stony Creek. Cross over the bridge and immediately park to your right in a small parking area.

Walk back across the bridge, keeping an eye out for passing cars. From the south side of the bridge you will be able to look down into the gorge and see the top of White Clay Kill Falls just a short distance downstream.

Continue walking east up Kidd Road. Within 50 feet from the bridge you will come to a trail on your right. Take the trail into the woods and you will immediately come to a trail registry. From this point follow the blue-blazed trail, which parallels the creek, for 0.05 mile. You will see a sizable pine needle-covered open area to your right, from where you can look upstream at the waterfall from a distance. If that view is unsatisfactory, follow an unmarked trail from the open area down a steep slope to the streambed below. Once you are level with the stream, it is possible with moderate effort to scramble up the streambed for a short distance to get a close-up view of the cascade. Watch out for slippery rocks.

Second approach: If you enjoy a more invigorating hike, a second approach is to drive 0.5 mile down Kidd Road from Rt. 9G (or go 0.3 mile back east from the bridge), and turn south into the area designated for Tivoli Bay. Drive down the unimproved road for 0.8 mile and you will arrive at the lower parking area just above the marshlands of Tivoli Bay. From here it is less than a 0.6-mile hike north along the blue-blazed trail to the cascade, which you will reach just before coming out onto Kidd Road.

68

FALL NEAR SOUTH BRACE MOUNTAIN

Location: Whitehouse Crossing (Dutchess County)
Delorme *New York State Atlas & Gazetteer:* p. 53 D5-6
Accessibility: Short but fairly steep ascent for 0.4 mile
Degree of Difficulty: Moderate

Description: This medium-sized waterfall is formed on a small, unnamed stream that rises from the south shoulder of South Brace Mountain in the southern Taconic Highlands.[1,2]

When you reach the ravine and begin your ascent, proceeding up a steep incline, you will pass between two large, guardian-like boulders where a lower cascade some twenty-five feet high is visible. Further uphill, near the mouth of the ravine, is the main cascade, which is roughly fifty feet in height. Be aware that this small stream is often nearly dry during the summer, so visit in the early spring when the water flow is optimal.

History: The waterfall is formed in the southern Taconics, the southernmost part of a mountainous range that extends from northern Connecticut up along the border between western Massachusetts and eastern New York State and on up to southwestern Vermont, where the highest peaks in the range can be found. Taconic is a modern spelling of the native American word Taghkannock, (or Taghanick, or Taghkanic) meaning "wooded place."[3] The southern Taconic range has produced a number of notable waterfalls. With the exception of Bash Bish Falls, however, all of these waterfalls have formed on the western Massachusetts side of the Taconic range, where the general approach is from Rt. 41. These Massachusetts waterfalls include Race Brook Falls, Bear Rock Falls, and Twin Falls in Sages Ravine.

Directions: From the intersection of Rtes. 344 & 22 at Copake Falls, drive south on Rt. 22 for 6.8 miles. Turn left onto White House Road and drive east for 0.6 mile. Turn left onto Rudd Pond Road and drive north for 0.2 mile. Proceed right onto Deer Hill Road, go east for 0.5 mile, and then take a left onto Quarry Hill Road. After 0.5 mile, pull into a small parking area on your left that is marked Taconic State Park.

Hike up the white-blazed trail for approximately 0.4 mile to the base of the falls, which is at the top of a very steep ravine.

FALLS ON THE SAW KILL

69 • FALLS ON THE SAW KILL:
BARD COLLEGE APPROACH

Location: Annandale-on-Hudson (Dutchess County)
Delorme *New York State Atlas & Gazetteer:* p. 52, D2-3
Accessibility: 0.2-mile hike
Degree of Difficulty: Easy

Description: There are several pretty cascades formed on the Saw Kill, a medium-sized stream that rises east of Red Hook and flows into the Hudson River south of Bard College.[1] The upper cascade, known as Zabriskie Falls,[2] is fifteen feet high and would be an absolute stunner were it not for the hulking ruins of a swimming pool

This lovely swimming pool is now an old cement ruin next to the upper Saw Kill falls.

and bath houses on the north bank. These facilities were once used by the college, but have long since been abandoned and desecrated by years of graffiti. Near the side of the swimming pool is a blue-colored "waterfall register." Visitors are invited to record in it any thoughts they might have about the waterfall and the area in general.

The lower falls, slightly over 0.1 mile further downstream, consist of two cascades in close proximity to one another. The upper fall is fifteen feet high, and the lower one is approximately twenty feet in height. When seen from a distance below, they appear as one long continuous waterfall. A stone arch is set into the north bank near the top of the lower cascades. It may look like a passage-way, but in actual fact it leads nowhere. The red-blazed path along the Saw Kill crosses over the top of the arch.

History: Bard College was founded in 1860 by Dr. John Bard. At that time it was called the St. Stephen's College for Sons of Episcopal Clergymen. The name was changed to Bard College in 1933 to honor its founder.

The falls are named after Captain Andrew C. Zabriskie, who constructed a nearby home named Blithewood.

The Saw Kill has served as a mill site since the mid-1700s, producing such goods as flour and woolens. W.H. Baker operated a chocolate factory on the Saw Kill until the business was relocated to Red Hook in order to expand its base of operation.[3]

Directions: From the center of Rhinebeck, proceed north on Rt. 9 for approximately 2.5 miles. Turn left onto Rt. 9G and drive north. After 1.4 miles you will observe that Rt. 199 comes in on your left from the Kingston–Rhinecliff Bridge, joining with Rt. 9G. Continue north on what is now Rtes. 9G & 199. At 4.3 miles from the junction of Rtes. 9 & 9G, turn left at a blinking light onto Annandale Road. In 0.05 mile bear to your right, which brings you out onto Rt. 103 (a continuation of Annandale Road). Proceeding on Annandale Road (Rt. 103), drive north for slightly over 0.3 mile and turn left onto Blithewood Avenue, which leads onto the grounds of Bard College. After driving west for 0.2 mile, turn left onto Bay Road (a secondary road) and follow it downhill for 0.2 mile. Park in the small parking area next to the waste treatment plant.

Walk back to Bay Road. There are now two ways to proceed, both of which involve following the "Mills and Minnows" trail that parallels the stream. To reach the lower two cascades, walk downhill along the dirt road for less than 0.05 mile and then follow a red-blazed trail to your left as it parallels the Saw Kill, passing above the falls. It is a very scenic area.

If you continue downhill from the falls, you will reach a marshy bay on the Hudson River, long favored by kayakers and canoeists from the college.

To get to the upper fall, take one of several paths leading directly to the stream from Bay Road, and follow the path upstream. Within less than 0.1 mile you will reach the upper fall, where the ruins of an abandoned swimming pool and bathhouses are visible along the north bank.

Midway between the upper and lower falls is a six-foot dam, virtually opposite across from the area where you parked.

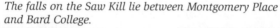

The falls on the Saw Kill lie between Montgomery Place and Bard College.

Location: See previous hike
Delorme *New York State Atlas & Gazetteer*: See previous hike
Accessibility: 0.2-mile hike
Degree of Difficulty: Easy

Description: The two cascades that appear as one when seen from a distance in the previous waterfall destination (Falls on the Saw Kill: Bard College Approach) may also be approached from Montgomery Place.[1-8] The cascades totals thirty-five feet in height, with an initial fifteen-foot drop followed by a twenty-foot descent. Near the viewing area you will see the ruins of a powerhouse built in the late 1920s that once generated electricity for the Montgomery estate. The powerhouse ceased operations in 1964, and its cement walls have been garishly painted over with graffiti.[9] Behind the ruins can be seen a large pipe. If you follow the pipe uphill, it leads to a small dam on the Saw Kill where water was impounded for power generation. Take note of the tiny gully that leads downhill from the powerhouse to the Saw Kill. At one time this gully was much deeper and carried back to the stream all the water that was taken from the Saw Kill for hydropower.

History: Montgomery Place is one of the most significant nineteenth-century country estates in the United States. It is located on 434 acres of land, some of which overlook the Hudson River. The house is a two-story Federal mansion remodeled twice (in 1840 and then again in the 1860s) by America's great mid-nineteenth-century architect, Alexander Jackson Davis. Since the mid-1860s the home has undergone substantial restorations several times. Subsequent owners were unable to properly maintain the house because of the ever-increasing cost and financial liability of owning such a large estate. In 1986 the property was acquired by Historic Hudson Valley, which immediately intervened to restore the property and return it to its present level of authenticity. Since 1992 the home has been on the list of National Historic Landmarks.[10]

The name Annandale is attributed to Mrs. John Allen, who it is presumed had ancestors from the Annandale region in Scotland.[11]

Directions: From the center of Rhinebeck, proceed north on Rt. 9 for approximately 2.5 miles. Turn left onto Rt. 9G and drive north. After 1.4 miles, Rt. 199 comes in on your left from the Kingston–Rhinecliff Bridge and joins with Rt. 9G. Continue north on what is now Rtes. 9G & 199. At 4.3 miles from the junction of Rtes. 9 & 9G, turn left at a blinking light onto Annandale Road. Within 0.05 mile bear to the left as Annandale Road turns into Rt. 103. After less than 0.1 mile, Rt. 103 crosses over the Saw Kill, where a tiny, two-foot-high cascade can be seen to your left below a small dam. In another 0.2 mile you will come to the entrance to Montgomery Place to your right. Turn in and drive down the road for 0.4 mile to the visitor center.

At the visitor center you will have two choices: you can either purchase an all-inclusive ticket that allows you to visit the mansion and tour the grounds, or you can purchase a ticket for the grounds only.

From the visitor center the falls can be accessed by one of two routes, both of which are clearly marked on the map that will have been provided to you at the visitor center. The first route involves taking an old carriage road between the site of the former conservatory and the arboretum. This leads downhill 0.3 mile to the falls. The second route follows a pathway from the north side of the mansion to the falls, a hike of slightly over 0.2 mile. Both routes are clearly marked with signs stating "Trail to Sawkill." The paths will lead you to an excellent viewing area complete with wooden rails that will allow you to easily and safely view the cascades upstream.

Montgomery Place is open daily (except Tuesdays) from April through October. Starting in November and continuing through the first two weekends in December, it is open only on weekends.

71

FALLS ON LANDSMAN KILL

Location: Rhinebeck (Dutchess County)
Delorme *New York State Atlas & Gazetteer:* p.37 A/B4
Accessibility: Roadside

Description: This broad, twenty-foot-high cascade is formed on the Landsman Kill, a medium-sized stream that rises in the hills east of Rhinebeck and flows into the Hudson River at a bay south of Rhinecliff.[1,2] Although the cascade is quite elongated, it appears tall and fairly vertical when viewed head-on from a distance.

The water level at the base of the fall varies significantly because the cove containing the fall is part of the Hudson River and is affected by the tides.

Even though it may look possible to get to the base of the fall for excellent views from its east bank, it is an exercise in futility. No views are possible because of the way the Landsman Kill turns abruptly west as it makes its way down the descending ravine.

History: In past times the Landsman Kill has also been known as Vanderburgh Creek.[3] The Landsman Kill was named after Casper Landsman, who was the first miller on the stream[4] under patentee Henry Beekman.[5] Henry Beekman Sr. was the first to erect a mill at Landsman Falls, having purchased the land sometime around 1710.[5]

Like many tributaries to the Hudson River, the Landsman Kill was heavily industrialized. Within the span of six miles, it contained four sawmills, four gristmills, two paper mills, a tannery, a plaster mill, and a carding mill.[4]

The area directly below the falls is known as Vanderburgh Cove, which extends all the way to the mouth of Fallsburg Creek.

Directions: From the stoplight at the center of Rhinebeck, go south on Rt. 9 for 0.2 mile and you will cross over the Landsman Kill. At 0.4 mile turn right onto Mill Road and drive southwest for 3.7 miles. At 0.9 mile you will cross over the Landsman Kill again where a dam-created fall on the south side of the road can be seen if you get out of your car to take a quick look. At 2.4 miles, Rt. 85 comes in on your right. Continue straight ahead on Mill Road, which now is also Rt. 85. At 3.6 miles you will again cross over the Landsman Kill. The cascade is directly below the bridge at this point, and its top can be easily viewed from the west side of the bridge.

The best view of the waterfall, however, is obtained by driving 0.1 mile further along Rt. 85 to where the curvature of the road puts you in a better position to look back at the fall head on, albeit from a distance.

At Landsman Kill Falls, the stream cascades into Vanderburgh Cove.

OGE ON RUPPERTS ESTATE, RHINEBECK, N. Y.

72

FALLS ON CRUM ELBOW CREEK

Location: Hyde Park (Dutchess County)
Delorme *New York State Atlas & Gazetteer:* p. 36 B4
Accessibility: 0.3-mile walk
Degree of Difficulty: Easy

Description: There are a number of small falls and cascades formed on Crum Elbow Creek, a medium-sized stream that rises in the hills east of Rhinebeck and flows into the Hudson River west of Hyde Park.[1,2] The first waterfall is located directly under the Rt. 9 bridge, just north of the entrance to the Vanderbilt estate and grounds. The cascade is eight feet in height and split into two sections by an island in its center. A six-foot dam sits on top of the cascade, accentuating its height and impounding a small body of water, called Sherwood Pond, that has formed on the east side of Rt. 9.

Proceeding south from the "white bridge," which is at the entrance to the Vanderbilt estate, you will see one small cascade after another as you follow the creek downstream to Dock Street where the stream, after dropping over a final dam, joins the waters of the Hudson River.

History: The name Crum Elbow Creek comes from the Dutch words *Kromme hoek,* for "rounded corner." Years later the name changed to elleboge, or "crooked elbow," a reference not to the creek itself, but rather to the Hudson River, which bends sharply just south of Crum Elbow Creek.[1,3]

The waterfalls are located on the 212-acre estate of Frederick William Vanderbilt, grandson of the shipping and railroad magnate, Cornelius Vanderbilt. The Vanderbilt Mansion—a Renaissance-style palace—was completed in 1899, having taken four years and over $2 million to finish. Frederick Vanderbilt lived at the estate from 1895 until his death in 1938.[4-6]

The elegant "white bridge" that greets you as you drive onto the grounds of the Vanderbilt estate is a Melan arch bridge. It was constructed in 1897 and was one of the first steel and concrete bridges to be built in the United States.[7]

Directions: From Hyde Park, go northwest on Rt. 41 to Rt. 9. Turn right onto Rt. 9 and proceed north for 0.2 mile. The entrance to the Vanderbilt Estate is on your left. Drive in, cross over Crum Elbow Creek via the white bridge, and follow the road up to the main parking area near the visitor center. The tour of the Vanderbilt Mansion is fascinating and highly recommended.

To access the waterfalls, walk back down to the white bridge. The first cascade can be seen from the west end of the bridge, looking upstream past a small pond to the Rt. 9 bridge. You will also notice a dam-created waterfall directly by the white bridge.

Continue downstream for several hundred feet and you will come to another dam. On the opposite bank is the powerhouse where electricity was generated for the estate. From here, all you need to do is continue following the road downhill as it parallels Crum Elbow Creek. Along the way you will see one cascade after another. Although none of these falls are large, the waters of the stream tumble continuously all the way down to Dock Street before falling over one last dam into the river.

The grounds of the Vanderbilt Estate are open seven days a week, from 9:00 AM to 5:00 PM.

There are multiple cascades on Crum Elbow Creek at the Vanderbilt estate.

73

FALLS AT INNISFREE GARDENS

Location: Millbrook (Dutchess County)
Delorme *New York State Atlas & Gazetteer:* p. 37, B/C5-6
Accessibility: 0.3-mile walk
Degree of Difficulty: Easy

Description: There are a number of pretty, artificially created waterfalls on the grounds of Innisfree Gardens to the northwest of Lake Tyrell. Pick up a map at the preserve and you will have no difficulty finding your way around the grounds.

The first artificially created fall is called the Mist Waterfall. Here, water is released as a vapor at the top of a cliff face. As the vapor condenses, it forms tiny rivulets that shimmy down the side of the cliff.

The next significant fall is called the Stone Bridge Waterfall. This fall is pretty and is framed by a stone bridge at its base, but the fall resembles a steeply descending streambed more than an actual cascade.

Truly delightful are the numerous small falls that are scattered about in an area called Waterfall Sculpture. Here, tiny streams drop over ledges and overhanging slabs of rock, producing a gentle, soothing sound that perfectly complements the peaceful ambiance of the gardens.

History: Innisfree Gardens is a 180-acre basin preserve with woodlands and gardens surrounding a picturesque, glacially created, forty-acre lake. The gardens were created by Walter Beck between 1930 and 1952. Beck's intent was to incorporate Chinese, Japanese and other Eastern influences into a work where the elements would be kept "in tension" and "in motion." Beck devised the term "cup garden," meaning that each rock, clump of flowers, collection of shrubs, trees, and so on, was arranged so as to stand alone and to be complete in itself. The gardens were given to the Innisfree

Foundation in 1959, and opened to the public in 1960 under the stewardship of architect Lester Collins.[1]

Directions: From the Taconic Parkway, get off at the exit for Millbrook. Go east on Rt. 44 for 1.7 miles. Turn right onto Tyrell Road and proceed south for 1.0 mile. Turn left into Innisfree Gardens and follow a dirt road into the interior of the preserve until you reach a small parking area at 0.6 mile.

The preserve is open from May to October 20, Wednesday to Friday from 10:00 AM to 4:00 PM, and weekends from 11:00 AM to 5:00 PM. There is an admission fee to access the grounds.

74

FALLS AT LOCUST GROVE

Location: Poughkeepsie (Dutchess County)
Delorme *New York State Atlas & Gazetteer:* p. 36, C4
Accessibility: 0.3-mile walk
Degree of Difficulty: Easy

Description: The fall at Locust Grove is formed on a little stream that rises from the east hills in the sanctuary and flows west into the Hudson River only a short distance further downstream.[1] The cascade is five feet high, but very scenic because of a footbridge and dammed pond directly downstream from the base of the fall.

According to a brochure distributed by Locust Grove: "The cascade trail leads to a stream that tumbles over rock ledges into what is probably the site of Samuel Morse's fish pond."[2]

History: Locust Grove is a 145-acre preserve with over three miles of trails that are open seasonally. The land was originally owned by Henry Livingston Jr., who operated a sawmill and a farm, with a store and landing for passing sloops. In 1830 a large part of the tract was sold to John Montgomery, who continued to farm the land.[1]

In 1847, Samuel F. B. Morse, best known as the inventor of the telegraph, bought one hundred acres of the land and the house that was on it for his summer home. Morse also continued the farming of the land. The house was remodeled in 1852. In 1895, Morse's estate was sold to William Hopkins Young and Martha Innis Young, whose family owned the estate until 1975. Today, the nature sanctuary to the west of Morse's house is known as the Annette Innis Young Memorial Wildlife Sanctuary.

Directions: From the Mid-Hudson Bridge (Rt. 44), go south on Rt. 9 for roughly 2.0 miles. The entrance is on the west side of the road at a stoplight just south of the Poughkeepsie Rural Cemetery. If you are approaching from the south, drive north on Rt. 9 for 4.0 miles from the intersection of Rtes. 9 & 9D, and turn left at the stoplight into Locust Grove.

From the main parking lot at Locust Grove, walk north past the main buildings and then west, following signs that point to the "walking trail." You will soon come to a kiosk, where maps of the preserve can be obtained. At this point you will be northeast of the Morse mansion, which is nearly straight ahead to your left. Follow the road next to the kiosk downhill. You will pass a cemetery and then, a moment later, a pet cemetery to your right. At this point you will notice a gated road to your left. Enter the preserve through this gate and follow the road downhill for less than 0.1 mile, going west. You will pass by a barn on your left. When you come to a trail junction, turn left onto the Lakeside Trail, which is clearly marked. Walk south for several hundred feet and then turn left onto the Cascade Trail, which immediately crosses over a creek via a footbridge. In less than 0.05 mile you will reach a second footbridge, which crosses a tiny creek with a small cascade directly to your left.

The grounds are open year-round from 8:00 AM to dusk. Tours of the Morse home are seasonal.

75

DOVER STONE CHURCH CAVE FALLS

Location: Dover Plains (Dutchess County)
Delorme *New York State Atlas & Gazetteer:* p. 37, B/C7
Accessibility: Fairly level 0.5-mile walk
Degree of Difficulty: Easy

Description: The waterfall contained in Dover Stone Church Cave is formed on Stone Church Brook, a small stream that rises in the hills northwest of Dover Plains and flows into Tenmile River.[1-3] At Dover Stone Church Cave the stream has carved out an unusual chasm sixty feet long, twenty-seven feet wide, and thirty feet high[2,4] where a cascade in the rear of the cave drops the stream from one level to the next.

Dover Stone Church Cave is part of a fifty-eight-acre preserve that includes not only the cave, but 4,000 + linear feet of Stone Church Brook. The preserve (and access to it) was established through the collaborative efforts of the Town of Dover, Friends of Dover Stone Church, Dutchess Land Conservancy, Dutchess county government, and the New York State Office of Parks, Recreation and Historical Preservation.

The cave and waterfall are unlike any other natural formation explored in this book. The entrance to the cave gives the appearance of a cathedral arch, hence the name "stone church." This image is further enhanced by a large rock formation inside the cave called the Pulpit Rock, from whose top one could imagine a minister preaching to a congregation standing below. Although one gets a feeling of being completely enclosed when inside the cave, it is only an illusion. Look up at the ceiling and you will see that you are actually at the bottom of a deep chasm whose walls narrow near the top, but never completely meet except at the very front of the cave.

History: The cave and waterfall have been known since the 1600s when Sassacus (chief of the Pequots) and his followers accidentally discovered the entrance while fleeing upstate from Long Island following a murderous attack by New England soldiers.[5]

The cave has been visited by European-descended Americans since the 1830s. Thousands of tourists from downstate would come to see this curious natural formation and stay at the nearby Stone Church Cave Hotel. Marriages were even performed at the cave (as they have been, also, at Lester Howe's Howe Caverns in Schoharie County, New York).

The cave also attracted artists and writers: Asher B Durand, the famous Hudson River School painter, depicted the cave in a masterful drawing in 1847; and Benson Lossing, a prolific nineteenth-century artist and writer, wrote a book titled *Dover Stone Church Cave*.[6]

The name of the town, Dover Plains, goes back to early England.[7]

Only nature would think to put a waterfall inside a "church of stone."

Directions: From the Taconic Parkway, get off at the Millbrook exit. Drive east on Rt. 44 for 3.7 miles. Turn right onto Rt. 343 and continue driving east for 8 miles. When you get to Rt. 22, turn right and within 0.5 mile you will be in the center of Dover Plains. At the traffic light near the center of the village, you will notice Mill Street (going east) and—on the opposite side of Rt. 22—a stone gazebo and stone stairs. Park in this general area.

Proceeding on foot from the stone gazebo and stairs, walk south along Rt. 22 for about 75 feet. When you reach the first driveway on your right, where a yellow sign indicates a firehouse up ahead, turn right and follow the driveway up between two private residences. This is a public easement established by the Dutchess Land Conservancy. Please respect the landowners' privacy and walk quickly and quietly.

Within 75 feet you will come to a tree line and a large white sign that welcomes you to the Dover Stone Church Cave Preserve. Follow a wide path that leads down an embankment and out onto a large field. Continue straight, heading west towards a grove of trees that extends out slightly from the edge of the woods, roughly 0.1 mile away.

When you reach the grove, continue straight ahead on a wide path. Very soon you will come to a high, wire fence with a narrow opening (presumably to prevent ATVs from entering). By now you may have noticed a stream to your left. This is Stone Church Brook.

In less than 0.1 mile you will come to a point where a footbridge made of planks crosses the stream and leads into a section of the preserve that is more park-like, with a small open field encircled by woods. The wide trail now turns into a narrow path and quickly leads into a deep gorge. Within 0.1 mile you will reach the entrance to Dover Stone Church Cave. It is possible to walk along the streambed right into the cave without getting wet, except during high water conditions. As soon as you enter the cave, you will catch a partial glimpse (and hear) the waterfall, which is in the rear of the cave.

On the right side of the cave is a large ladder to the top of Pulpit Rock, where a small platform allows you to get a better look at the waterfall and the chasm.

76

WAPPINGER FALLS

Location: Wappingers Falls (Dutchess County)
Delorme *New York State Atlas & Gazetteer:* p. 37 C/D4-5
Accessibility: Roadside

Description: Wappinger Falls is formed on Wappinger Creek, a medium-sized stream that rises from several lakes and swamplands southwest of Pine Plains and flows into the Hudson River at New Hamburg.[1-5] Between the dammed falls at Wappinger Lake and the final set of rapids, the stream drops seventy-five feet as it passes through the town.

The main falls are formed just below the Rt. 9D bridge, where an island of bedrock splits the stream into two sections. Most noticeable is an enormous water pipe. After paralleling the east bank of the stream all the way down from Wappinger Lake, the water pipe crosses over the creek just below the falls and then continues downstream along the west bank.

History: The village and creek are named after a Native American tribe called the Wappingers. Waping is a Munsee Lenape word for opossum and means "white face."[6] Wappinger Creek was originally known as the Great Wappings Kill.[6,7]

The two principal mills in the village that used Wappinger Creek for waterpower were the Dutchess Company, which made sheets and pillow cases, and the Sweet Orr Company, which manufactured overalls.[8]

Directions: From the Mid-Hudson Bridge at Poughkeepsie, drive south on Rt. 9 for roughly 6 miles. Turn right onto Rt. 9D and continue for 1.3 miles. When you reach the East Main Street bridge spanning Wappinger Creek, park off to the side of the road. If you are approaching Wappinger Falls from the south, drive north on Rt. 9D for 6.7 miles from the junction of I-84 & 9D, and park when you come to the bridge spanning Wappinger Creek.

Standing on the south side of the bridge, you can get a good view of the falls by looking straight down. For a better view, stroll over to the east end of the bridge and walk down Market Street for fifty feet. You can see the falls head-on by looking across a vacant lot.

Wappinger Falls was named after a tribe of Native Americans who occupied the region.

FALLS AND BRIDGE.   WAPPINGERS FALLS, N. Y.

77

FALLS ON DUELL BROOK

Location: Pawling (Dutchess County)
Delorme *New York State Atlas & Gazetteer:* p. 37, D7
Accessibility: 0.1-mile hike
Degree of Difficulty: Easy

Description: The falls in the Pawling Nature Preserve are formed on Duell Brook, a small stream that rises from Quaker Lake and French Lake, and flows into Tenmile River just west of the border of New York and Connecticut.[1,2] The falls are encased in a gorge that is fifty feet deep. The main cascade—the first fall—is a narrow, fissure-like waterfall approximately twenty feet high, formed where the stream cuts through the bedrock like a gleaming white knife. Further below, deeper in the gorge, is a smaller cascade approximately six feet in height.[3]

The falls cannot be readily approached from the bottom, so they must be viewed from a dangerously high precipice. Caution must be exercised when visiting these falls.

History: The preserve was established in 1959 as a refuge for plants and wildlife—in essence a living museum. It presently contains 1,060 acres of land and is owned and managed by the Nature Conservancy. The Appalachian Trail runs through the preserve from southwest to northeast.

Duell Brook was named for a Quaker family that became one of the first homesteaders in the area during the 1730s.[4] Pawling was named after Mrs. Albert Pawling of Kingston.[5]

Directions: From Pawling (junction of Rtes. 22 & 55-W) take Rt. 22 north for 2.5 miles. If you are approaching from the north, take Rt. 22 south from the junction of Rtes. 22 & 55-E for 4.1 miles. Approaching from either direction, turn east onto North Quaker Hill Road (Rt. 68) and drive uphill for 1.4 miles. Turn left onto Quaker Lake Road and go north for 1.5 miles. During part of the drive you will be making your way along the east shore of Quaker Lake. At 1.5 miles turn into the parking area on your left.

Follow the yellow-blazed trail, which will lead you to the top of the gorge and waterfalls in a little over 0.1 mile. To avoid a mishap, caution should be exercised at the top of this deep gorge.

78

TIORONDA FALLS

Location: Beacon (Dutchess County)
Delorme *New York State Atlas & Gazetteer:* p. 32, A4
Accessibility: 0.05-mile walk
Degree of Difficulty: Easy

Description: Tioronda Falls is a small cascade under a broad dam. The fall is formed on Fishkill Creek, a moderate-sized stream that rises from several tributaries in the hills east of the Taconic Parkway and flows into the Hudson River at Beacon.[1,2]

The waterfall is located in Madam Brett Park. From the cement block platform, which looks across to the cascade, you can also see to your left the old sluiceway that once carried water for power generation. Fairly close by is Fairy Island, a small patch of land in the center of the creek.

History: Madam Brett Park is a twelve-acre preserve named after Catharyna Rombout Brett, the founder of Beacon, who lived from 1687–1764. In 1708, Brett established a gristmill along the bank of the creek. The land is owned by the Scenic Hudson Land Trust, Inc., and is managed by the City of Beacon.

Beacon Terminal, located next to the park, was once the site of the Tioronda Hat Works.

The fall may also have been known as Sucker Brook Falls when an 1869 train trestle spanned the top of the cascade, connecting Dutchess Junction with Pine Plains. The trestle was dismantled when the Dutchess & Columbia line was rerouted to come in directly to Beacon.[3,4]

Directions: From the junction of I-84 and 9D (exit 11 off I-84), go southeast on Rt. 9D for 2.0 miles. When you come to a stoplight, turn right onto Tioronda Avenue (just before you reach Fishkill Creek) and drive southwest for 0.7 mile. Along the way you will see

Fishkill Creek paralleling the road to your left, as well as a series of abandoned factories. At 0.7 mile, just before you start up a small hill to South Avenue, turn left and drive through a one-lane underpass beneath a train track. Be sure to blow your horn first in case a driver is approaching from the other direction. Drive to the end of the road (less than 0.05 mile) and park in the area for Madam Brett Park, which will be on your left.

Follow the path upstream, going north, for 0.05 mile until you reach the cement block platform that overlooks the falls.

The cascades on the Fish Kill have seen many mills and factories come and go over the years.

79

FISHKILL RIDGE FALLS

Location: Beacon (Dutchess County)
Delorme *New York State Atlas & Gazetteer*: p. 32 A4
Accessibility: 0.6-mile hike steadily uphill
Degree of Difficulty: Moderate

Description: Fishkill Ridge Falls is an eighty-foot-high cascade formed on Dry Brook, a small stream that rises from the Beacon Reservoir and flows into Fishkill Creek.[1-3] There are a number of tiny cascades and falls created by boulders along Dry Brook, but nothing to prepare you for the sight of this monster waterfall as it comes into view, seemingly appearing out of nowhere.

Dry Brook got its name for a reason; be sure to time your visit to when there is adequate water flow through the ravine.

History: The trail leading up to the high fall on Dry Brook is part of the Fishkill Ridge Conservation Area that was purchased between 1992 and 1993 by the Scenic Hudson Land Trust. So far, 1,900 acres of land have been protected by the trust, whose goal is to prevent mining interests from gaining rights to the land and excavating 50 million tons of rock over the next century and a half. The land is managed by the New York State Office of Parks, Recreation, and Historic Preservation.

The area was first settled by Catherine (Catharyna) Rombout Brett and her husband Roger, who built a house and mill near the mouth of Fishkill Creek in 1708.

The city officially acquired the name Beacon in 1913 to commemorate the rectangular, thirty-foot-high pyramid of brush and wood that was set on top of Beacon Mountain to be lit as a warning should British military vessels sail up the Hudson River during the Revolutionary War. Melzingah and Matteawan were two other contenders for the community's name.[4]

Directions: From the intersection of Rt. 9D & I-84 (Exit 11 off I-84), drive southeast on Rt. 9D (Wolcott Avenue) for slightly over 2.0 miles. As soon as you cross over Fishkill Creek, continue southeast on Rt. 9D for another 0.4 mile and then turn left onto Howland Avenue, where Rt. 9D bears to the right. Go northeast on Howland Avenue for 0.5 mile until you come to a stop sign. Turn right onto East Main Street and drive uphill for over 0.1 mile. Turn right onto Pocket Road and drive uphill for less than 0.1 mile to where the road ends. This is the beginning of the trailhead, but you may not be able to park there depending upon conditions.

If parking is not available at the trailhead, drive back down to East Main Street, to one of the side streets, or to Howland Avenue and park where you will not inconvenience any of the residents.

Return on foot to the end of Pocket Road. Take note of the sign, which states: "No trespassing. No hunting, fishing, camping, swimming, or boating." Nearby you will also see white trail markers. This means that hikers *are* allowed access, but with the restrictions stipulated on the "No trespassing" sign.

The Beacon Reservoir is above Dry Brook Falls.

Go around the gate and follow the road as it leads south into the woods. On your left will be a huge water storage cistern for the city of Beacon. Next you will go past a small dam-created reservoir. Remain on the road, following the white markers. Soon the road begins to narrow, turning eventually into a path. From here on you will be following the white-blazed trail through a fairly deep ravine, with Dry Brook directly to your left. If you are visiting after heavy rainfall, you will be surrounded by falling water, as a myriad of tiny streams make their way down the walls of the ravine into Dry Brook. The hike involves a steady ascent. After 0.6 mile you will reach a point where double white markers indicate that the path is changing direction. Bear to your left, and cross over the stream. As soon as you start up the path on the east bank, you will see the waterfall looming high above you, racing down along a series of steep pitches and drops.

Take note of the wooden cross that someone has erected on the opposite bank. This suggests that tragedy is no stranger to this location. Be cautious and stay on the path to view the waterfall safely.

80

FALLS AT TUCKERS RUN

Location: Haviland Hollow (Putnam County)

Delorme *New York State Atlas & Gazetteer:* p. 33, A7

Accessibility: 0.8-mile hike along an old, abandoned road. At the beginning the ascent is steep, but it quickly levels off. Take note that you must be a resident of Putnam County or a guest in order to hike the trail.

Degree of Difficulty: Moderate

Description: The Falls at Tuckers Run are formed on Haviland Hollow Brook, a small stream that rises in the mountains of Connecticut and flows into a swampy area surrounding the Croton River.[1,2] The gorge containing the falls is known as Tuckers Run. The preserve containing Tuckers Run is called the Putnam County Michael Ciaiola Conservation Area, named after Michael T. Ciaiola, who died in 1999. Through Ciaiola's efforts, the County Land Trust expanded its dominion from six preserves to fifteen. The preserve was previously known as the Walter G. Merritt Park.

The falls begin with a six-foot-high cascade that drops into a small pool. From there, the stream cascades down another eight feet. Then the ravine—which has been fairly wide and expansive to that point—suddenly narrows significantly, turning into a short chasm where the creek cascades down twenty feet over a series of drops. From a pool at the base of the twenty-foot cascade, the stream goes over two smaller cascades as it makes its way out from the depths of the ravine.

Directions: From the south, proceed north on Rt. 22 for another 0.8 mile after you reach the junction of Rtes. 22 & 164. If you are approaching from the north from the junction of Rtes. 22 & 311, continue south on Rt. 22 for 2.3 miles. From either direction, turn east onto Haviland Hollow Road (Rt. 68) and drive northeast for 2.4 miles. Just before you cross over a small bridge, turn left into a large parking area for the Putnam County Michael Ciaiola Conservation Area.

Follow the red-blazed foot trail for approximately 0.8 mile. During the last 0.1 mile you will observe several old foundations in the woods to your right. The trail comes out on the south bank of a ravine where the falls are formed, directly behind the Walter G. Merritt campsite—an old stone and wood cabin. The falls can be viewed easily from the top of the ravine.

Keep in mind the residency requirements for visiting this nature preserve.

81

MELZINGAH FALLS

Location: Dutchess Junction (Dutchess County)
Delorme *New York State Atlas & Gazetteer:* p. 32, A4
Accessibility: 0.1-mile walk to main fall; 0.4-mile walk to upper cascades
Degree of Difficulty: Easy to first fall; moderate to upper cascades

Description: Melzingah Falls is formed on Gordons Brook, a small stream that rises in the hills southeast of Beacon and flows into the Hudson River. Along the way, the stream is intercepted by the Melzingah Reservoir. At a height of around ten feet, the cascade is not large, but it is very pretty because of the picturesque pond at the base of the fall.

There are a number of small cascades just upstream from Melzingah Falls, but they are contained in the depths of a fairly impenetrable gorge. They are relatively insignificant and, frankly, not worth the risk and difficulty in visiting them. At a distance of 0.3 mile above Melzingah Falls, however, the gorge flattens out and you'll find Melzingah Reservoir. A small cascade lies directly under the stone block dam impounding the reservoir, and there are several smaller cascades just downstream from the dam.

History: Melzingah is most likely a Native American (Delaware) name for "place of the hammer stone." Melsingah is an alternate spelling.[1]

Like many waterfalls in mid-eastern New York State, Melzingah Falls is associated with a Native American legend. The Nochpeens, a tribe that lived between what are now Beacon and Cold Spring, were periodically at war with the Wappingers. According to the legend, a young Nochpeen warrior was captured by the Wappingers. He was aided by a Wappinger maiden who had fallen in love with him, and he was able to escape before being put to death. The Nochpeen warrior and the Wappinger maiden took up residence near Melzingah Falls, concealed in a well-hidden wigwam. Whenever other Indians came by too closely, the young Nochpeen brave would appear at the top of the fall as the Great Spirit Manitou and frighten away the superstitious visitors. Later, Garrangula (an Onondaga sachem from the Iroquois confederacy) was able to broker a peace between the local warring Algonquin factions. Hearing this, the young couple came down from their hiding place to live in peace by the river. Later, when the Nochpeen brave died, legend has it that his spirit could still be seen by the fall dressed up as Manitou.[1,2]

Directions: From the traffic light in Cold Springs (junction of Chestnut Street & Main Street), go north on Rt. 9D for exactly 4.0 miles. (From the south end of the Breakneck Mountain tunnel, go north for exactly 2.0 miles). Follow these directions precisely. The trailhead and the stream are well hidden from the road, and the road is very busy. Park off to the side of the road by the trailhead, or turn around and drive back south for less than 0.1 mile to a large pull-off on the west side of the road.

Follow the blue-blazed trail east into the woods for slightly over 0.1 mile. You will come to the stream, where a three-foot-wide, twelve-foot-high dam impounds a small pond. Walk across the dam to the midway point and look upstream to see Melzingah Falls at the other end of the pond. If you continue all the way across the dam, there is an eroded, informal path that can be taken to near the base of the fall.

To see the upper cascades, return to the blue-blazed trail. At this point the path goes up a flight of wide stone steps and then becomes an old road. Follow the road as it goes steadily uphill, paralleling the top of the gorge. You will soon be high above the stream, which can be heard far below but not seen. While there are tiny cascades in the gorge along this section, they are not accessible. Melzingah Falls can be glimpsed from the top of the precipice, but only fleetingly. Within 0.2 mile or less, take an unmarked secondary road that leads off to the right. After 0.1 mile, this road will lead you up to a small dam that impounds Melzingah Reservoir. You will notice a small cascade that has been incorporated into the bottom of the dam. Just downstream from the dam can be seen several smaller cascades. They are located between a cement building that sits on the north bank and a green-shingled building on the south bank.

THE HUDSON HIGHLANDS

The Hudson Highlands constitute a unique and scenic section of the Hudson River. They begin at the "southern gate" by Dunderberg Mountain and Peekskill Bay, and extend fifteen miles upstream to the "northern gate" at the Storm King gorge. The Highlands are part of a geologic range known as the Reading Prong, which stretches from Pennsylvania to Connecticut. This range also includes the Ramapo Mountains.

The Highlands are formed predominantly of gneiss (pronounced "nice"), a metamorphic rock that was created over half a billion years ago. In the beginning the rocks constituted the base of a mountainous region that was eventually worn down to stubble by the actions of wind, rain, ice, and snow. When titanic geological forces raised the land back up again, the old base became the exposed bedrock of the present-day Highlands. The other rock that is commonly found in the Highlands is granite, an igneous rock. Storm King Mountain and Bear Mountain are two areas where granite predominates.

Many visitors have likened the Highlands to a fjord, and this is an apt comparison. The Hudson River has cut a deep channel in the Highlands through the erosion-resistant bedrock of gneiss and granite, giving the area a dynamic and chiseled look. The bedrock north of the Highlands—which is essentially composed of shale, sandstone, siltstone, and limestone (sedimentary rocks)—eroded more easily, causing the valley there to widen and become less mountainous.[1,2]

During the last ice age the glaciers had a two-fold impact on the Highlands. First, they deepened the Hudson River's channel. At Storm King Mountain, for instance, glaciers ground down the riverbed to a depth of 1,000 feet below present-day sea level. This process was accelerated by the fact that the ocean at that time was considerably lower in elevation because a huge volume of its waters was locked up in the northern hemisphere as ice. This meant that the Hudson River was still rapidly descending as it left the Highlands. When the glaciers retreated north, however, millions of tons of gravel and glacial debris were deposited in the Hudson River, returning the streambed somewhat to its former height (though not completely, since the Hudson River remains below or near sea level all the way to Albany).[3]

In addition, the glaciers plucked away some of the talus that had formed at the base of the Highlands (and Palisades) and removed it from the valley. The scattered boulders and rocks that you see today are residue from these earlier times, combined with other rocks and boulders that have fractured off over the last few thousand years from the continuing processes of expansion and contraction of the bedrock, caused by fluctuations in temperature.

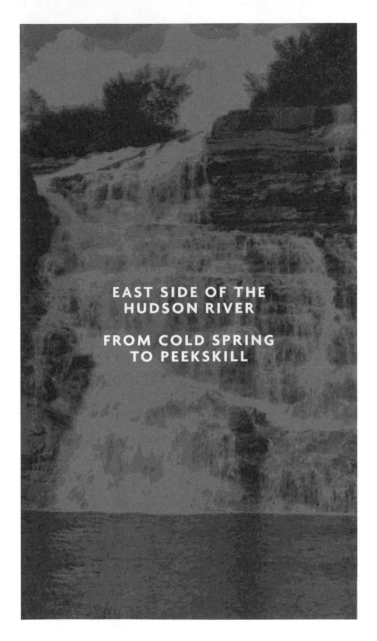

EAST SIDE OF THE HUDSON RIVER

FROM COLD SPRING TO PEEKSKILL

82

FOUNDRY BROOK FALLS

Location: Cold Spring (Putnam County)
Delorme *New York State Atlas & Gazetteer: p. 32, A4*
Accessibility: 0.2-mile walk
Degree of Difficulty: Easy, with some uneven footing

Description: There are several small cascades formed on Foundry Brook, a small stream that rises east of Schofield and the Breakneck ridges at Cold Spring Reservoir and Jacob Pond, and flows into Foundry Cove just south of Cold Spring.[1,2] The stream originally was known as Margaret's Brook, then Furnace Brook, and finally Foundry Brook. The falls are located in an eighty-seven-acre preserve.

The main cascade, a six-foot-high flume, is formed at the base of a twelve-foot-high stone dam directly under the lofty Rt. 9D bridge, all within the village of Cold Spring. Downstream for a distance of several hundred feet can be seen a number of smaller cascades, but none rise to a height of more than three to four feet. What make this hike interesting are the numerous foundations and piles of old brick that litter the relatively flat bottom of the gorge.

History: Cold Spring was founded in the eighteenth century. According to folklore it got its name from General George Washington, who dipped his cup into a local spring, took a sip, and remarked how exceedingly cold the water was.

Between Gees Point (on the west bank, near West Point) and nearby Constitution Island is "World's End"—the deepest part of the Hudson River at 202 feet. It was in this general area that colonists laid a great chain across the river, fashioned out of 2.5-inch-square iron bars, to prevent British vessels from advancing upriver.

The West Point Foundry operated on Foundry Brook between 1817 and 1884. The foundry built the first iron American ship (the cutter *Spencer*), the nation's first locomotive engine, and also produced the renowned "parrot gun," named after its inventor, Robert P. Parrott, who was appointed superintendent by the firm's industrialist, Gouvernour Kemble. In its early years the foundry produced cannons, grapeshot, and round shot. But not all of its products were for military purposes. The foundry also manufactured iron stoves, bells, plows, and even miles of cast-iron pipes for the New York City water system.[3-5] What made the foundry so successful was its close proximity to huge deposits of iron ore, and to vast forests of hardwoods along the east bank for charcoal production to enable the intense heat to be generated for iron smelting.

In 1862, Abraham Lincoln visited the foundry. Robert Parrott fired off a shell across the Hudson River to show off the power of his gun, and Lincoln is reputed to have said rather matter-of-factly, "I'm confident you can hit that mountain over there, so suppose we get something to eat."[6] The foundry was credited in Jules Verne's fictional classic *Trip to the Moon* as being the site that produced the materials for the rocket ship.

In 1897 the West Point Foundry was purchased by the Cornell brothers, who produced machines for sugar production. That lasted until 1911, when the foundry finally ceased operations altogether.

Directions: From the traffic light at the junction of Chestnut Street and Main Street in Cold Spring, go south on Chestnut Street for 0.1 mile. Turn right onto Wall Street (a one-way street), and drive downhill for 0.2 mile. Turn left onto Kimble Street and drive south for 0.3 mile until you reach a gate for the preserve. Continue past the gate for another 0.2 mile and park in the area for the Foundry Cove Preserve, directly next to the foundry's former office building, built in 1865.

Follow the blue-blazed trail upstream for 0.2 mile to the cascades.

The falls can also be accessed directly from the Rt. 9D bridge. An informal path leads down to the base of the bridge and falls from the northwest end of the bridge.

83

INDIAN BROOK FALLS

Location: Garrison (Putnam County)
Delorme *New York State Atlas & Gazetteer*: p. 32, A/B4
Accessibility: Less than 0.2-mile walk, but the trail leading to the fall is eroded
Degree of Difficulty: Moderate

Description: Indian Brook Falls is formed on Indian Brook, a small stream that rises from Catfish Pond south of Moneyhole Mountain and flows into the Hudson River at the southeast end of Constitution Island.[1-5] The waterfall is a twenty-five-foot-high cascade that drops over dark bedrock into a shallow pool of water.[1-3]

The waterfall was known in earlier times as Fanny Kemble's Bath, after the famous nineteenth-century actress, Fanny Kemble, who visited the falls in 1833 and wrote a rather dramatic (and perhaps fanciful) account of her climb up the waterfall.[4] The waterfall has also been known simply as Indian Falls.

History: The Constitution Marsh Sanctuary contains two parcels of land: the 207-acre freshwater/brackish Constitution Marsh; and further upland, Indian Brook Falls.

Virtually every article written on Indian Brook Falls includes the legend of how the falls came to be named. The story goes that Henry Hudson's crew on the *Half Moon* had become exceedingly unpopular with many Native Americans along the Hudson River because they had shot and killed a number of braves on their 1609 voyage of exploration up the river. As a result, when one of Hudson's men (Jacobus Van Horen) was captured near Garrison, the Indians were ready to extract vengeance. Fortunately for Van Horen, the daughter of the chief, Princess Manteo, fell in love with him and intervened (much as in the story of Pocahontas and John Smith). With his life spared, Van Horen was allowed to roam freely in the area. He was betrothed to Princess Manteo with the understanding that they would marry the following spring.

The story ends on an unhappy note, however. One day while swimming near the falls, Van Horen spied a European ship coming up the river and made a mad dash for it, leaving his bride-to-be behind. Following Van Horen's escape, Princess Manteo's body was found in the pool at the base of the fall. Either the princess had hurled herself off the top of the fall in despair, or she was done in by Van Horen to ensure her silence. So goes the legend of Indian Falls.[5-7]

Indian Brook Falls was well known to Native Americans.

Directions: From the east end of Bear Mountain Bridge (junction of Rtes. 6 & 9D), go north on Rt. 9D for nearly 7.5 miles (or roughly 2.7 miles north on Rt. 9D from the junction of Rtes. 9D & 403 by Garrison). Turn left onto Indian Brook Road and drive southwest for 0.5 mile. You will reach a parking area for Constitution Marsh Sanctuary. Turn left and drive uphill for 0.1 mile. You can park in front of a gate on your right, directly beneath the Rt. 9D bridge. If no parking is available there, drive back down to the main parking area for the Constitution Marsh Sanctuary, and return on foot.

Walk around the stone gate and follow the green-blazed, abandoned road that quickly leads to the stream and then crosses over it via a massive stone bridge. Turn left at the end of the bridge and fairly short (0.05 mile), but eroded in places, making it somewhat difficult to follow. The view of Indian Brook Falls, however, is well worth the effort.

FALLS AT MANITOGA PRESERVE

Location: Garrison (Putnam County)
Delorme *New York State Atlas & Gazetteer:* p. 32, B4
Accessibility: Less than 0.05-mile walk
Degree of Difficulty: Easy

Description: The waterfall at Manitoga Preserve is a pretty, artificially created, thirty-foot-high cascade that is formed on a tiny tributary to the Hudson River.[1,2]

History: Manitoga is Mahican for "spirit ground"[3] and is derived from the word *manitou,* meaning "spirit or deity." The eastern Catskill escarpment overlooking a section of Rt. 32 was called "the Wall of Manitou" by early Native Americans, and is perhaps where the word is best known (and still used).

The property that constitutes Manitoga Preserve was acquired in 1942 by twentieth-century industrial designer Russel Wright and his wife Mary. The Wrights built a home called Dragon Rock, which still stands by the pond. At the time of Wright's purchase, the land had been terribly scarred by loggers and quarrymen. It became Wright's mission to restore the land to its natural beauty and to even improve upon it wherever possible. In 1975 the property was donated to the Nature Conservancy and the Wright home was restored to its pre-1960s look. The preserve consists of seventy-five acres. It is listed on the National Register of Historic Places, and the National Trust for Historic Preservation Artists' Homes and Studios Association Sites.[4]

Directions: From the east end of the Bear Mountain Bridge (junction of Rtes. 9D & 6), drive north on Rt. 9D for 2.6 miles. If you are approaching from the north, go south on Rt. 9D for about 2 miles from Garrison. Turn east into Manitoga Preserve and follow a dirt road uphill for 0.1 mile to the parking area.

Walk past the small building on your left and follow a wide path that branches off from the main road to your left. You will immediately see an eight-foot dam intercepting a tiny stream to your left. Continue uphill for another one hundred feet and you will reach a small, dammed body of water called Quarry Pond. Look across the pond to the opposite side and you will see a thirty-foot cascade that rises above the pond. Unless you are on a guided tour, however, you are not allowed to go any further than this point.

Tours are conducted daily at 11:00 AM. Taking the tour allows you to see the rest of the grounds, including the Wright house, and to cross the stream at the base of the cascade via a small footbridge.

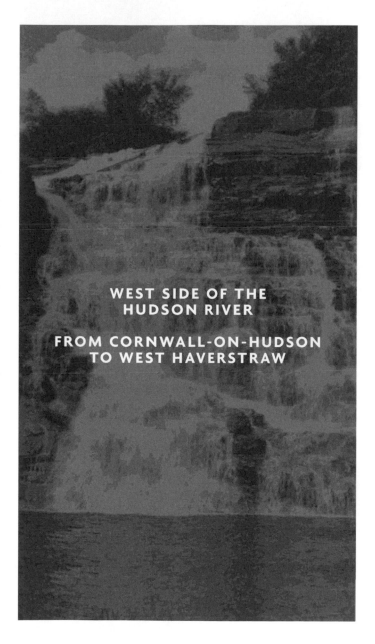

WEST SIDE OF THE
HUDSON RIVER

FROM CORNWALL-ON-HUDSON
TO WEST HAVERSTRAW

85

MINERAL SPRING FALLS

Location: Cornwall-on-Hudson (Orange County)
Delorme *New York State Atlas & Gazetteer*: p. 32, A/B3
Accessibility: 0.3-mile hike along easy, well-graded trail
Degree of Difficulty: Easy

Description: Mineral Spring Falls is formed on Mineral Spring Brook, a small stream that rises from Sutherland Pond, a spring-fed body of water with no inlets. The stream flows into Woodbury Creek at Woodbury.[1-3] The waterfall has also been known in the past as Green Falls.[2] The fall is roughly fifty feet high and cascades over a huge block of rock with significant amounts of talus at the base. Above the top of the main falls, the stream falls another thirty feet over a series of small cascades, the most significant part being a sharply slanted ledge over which a ten-foot-high waterfall drops. There are numerous large boulders strewn about in this upper section.

Mineral Spring Falls is located in a 140-acre preserve owned by the Black Forest Preserve and managed by the Black Rock Forest Consortium. It was originally purchased by the Open Air Institute. The white-blazed trail is part of the NY–NJ Trail Conference Scenic Trail.

As waterfalls go, this is a relatively safe one to visit because you arrive at the base of the fall and need go no higher to appreciate the scene.

History: Mineral Spring Falls was a popular destination for nineteenth-century visitors seeking remedy for a variety of afflictions. Tourists and wellness-seekers would arrive by train slightly north of the fall at nearby Mountainville (today the home of the Storm King Art Center) and ride in a wagon to Mineral Spring Falls, hoping that the alleged curative powers of the waters from the mineral spring would alleviate such conditions as consumption, liver and kidney disease, and rheumatism.

Old ruins can be seen to the right of the trail at the point where the path splits, with the main trail heading up the left side of the waterfall and the secondary trail leading to the rocky base of the fall.

Directions, approaching from the north: From the junction of Rtes. 17K and 9W in Newburgh, drive south on Rt. 9W for approximately 5.8 miles, passing by Cornwall-on-Hudson in the process. Turn right after you pass a green sign for Angola Road. You will immediately come upon Mineral Spring Road (Rt. 9). Turn left and drive southwest on Mineral Springs Road for 3.3 miles to Old Mineral Springs Road.

Approaching from the south: Leaving the traffic circle at Bear Mountain Bridge (junction of Rtes. 6 & 9W), proceed north on Rt. 9W for nearly 11 miles. As soon as you pass by a green sign for Angola Road, take your first right, which leads up to Mineral Spring Road. Turn left and head southwest on Mineral Spring Road for 3.5 miles to Old Mineral Springs Road.

From either of the above approaches, turn left onto Old Mineral Spring Road. In 0.2 mile you will see a pull-off to your left directly in front of a barricaded dirt road. This is the trailhead. You will also see no-parking signs, which should not be ignored. Continue on Old Mineral Spring Road for another 0.3 mile. The road at this point comes back out to Mineral Spring Road. Here, a pull-off serves as the legal parking spot for the trail.

From the parking area, walk back along Old Mineral Spring Road for 0.3 mile to the trailhead. At the unmarked trailhead for Mineral Spring Falls, follow the old carriage road up into the woods and then downhill. Within 0.05 mile you will pass a kiosk to your right, which contains a variety of information about the preserve. Continue on the trail until you reach the base of Mineral Spring Falls, no more than 0.3 mile from the trailhead. At the point where old ruins can be seen on the right, the main trail veers left up the side of Mineral Spring Falls. Take the secondary path straight ahead, which leads immediately to the waterfall's base.

86

BUTTERMILK FALLS
(In Highland Falls)

Location: Highland Falls (Orange County)
Delorme *New York State Atlas & Gazetteer:* p. 32, A/B4
Accessibility: Buttermilk Falls is on private property and cannot be accessed directly. Views can be obtained either from the Hudson River or along its east bank.

Description: This 100-foot waterfall is formed on Highland Brook, a medium-sized stream that rises west of West Point near the Hill of Pines and flows into the Hudson River at Highland Falls.[1-7] The falls are formed on a granite bedrock.

History: According to Wallace Bruce, the waterfall was christened Buttermilk Falls by Washington Irving.[1] Early Dutch settlers called the falls Boter Melck Vail, which is Dutch for Buttermilk Falls.[1,6]

Highland Brook powered a flour mill next to the falls in early years.[5,8] Around 1838 a gristmill was erected by David Parry along the south bank at the base of the falls. Power was generated by an overshot waterwheel. In addition to the gristmill, Parry also ran a resort hotel above the mill, south of the waterfall.[9]

Around 1860 a man named Cozzen built a hotel on the 180-foot-high, rocky bluff overlooking the Hudson River near Buttermilk Falls. It was called Cozzen's Hotel and could serve up to five hundred guests.[10] Later on, under new ownership, the hotel changed its name to Cranston's. A landing was constructed at the water's edge, where boat passengers could disembark to make their way up to the hotel.[3] In 1990 the hotel was acquired by the Catholic order and it is now part of the complex comprising Ladycliff College.

The village of Highland Falls, to the west of Buttermilk Falls, has been a service center for West Point Military Academy for many years.

Directions: The falls are on private property and cannot be accessed directly. They can be readily seen, however, from the Hudson River, from along the Hudson's east bank, or while riding Amtrak as it speeds through Garrison.

Buttermilk Falls—alluring, but inaccessible.

87

HELL HOLE FALLS

Location: Bear Mountain State Park (Orange County)
Delorme *New York State Atlas & Gazetteer:* p. 32, B3-4
Accessibility: 0.2-mile walk downhill to top of fall
Degree of Difficulty: Easy

Description: Hell Hole Falls is formed on Popolopen Creek, a medium-sized stream that rises from Stillwell Lake in the Forest of Dean and flows into the Hudson River just north of Bear Mountain Bridge.[1-4] The falls consist of a ten-foot-high cascade dropping into a large, oval-shaped pool, below which are a series of tiny cascades and rapids, some of which can be seen from the Rt. 9W bridge. The stream and the falls are contained in a breathtakingly deep ravine.[5,6]

Directly above the main fall are the abutments of an old bridge that once spanned Popolopen Creek. Just upstream from the falls is a massive, twenty-foot-high stone dam, which produces a spectacular waterfall of its own.

History: Popolopen Creek was named after an influential Indian.[7] At various times in the past, the stream has been known as Popolopen's Kill, Pooploop's Kill, Fort Montgomery Creek, and Montgomery Creek.[8] Hell Hole was named by cadets at West Point who were impressed by the gorge's rugged and wild terrain when venturing into the gorge to execute tactical maneuvers.

The falls have been known and visited for centuries. During the 1700s they were frequented by Revolutionary War soldiers because of the close proximity to Fort Montgomery and Fort Clinton—two colonial fortifications that were located on the north and south banks of Popolopen Creek near the stream's confluence with the Hudson River. The Hudson River narrows significantly here, forming what is called a "choke point." From a military standpoint this was highly significant because a "choke point" could force invading ships closer to shore and in range of devastating cannon fire. The other choke point was at West Point.

At the time that Fort Clinton was being erected, a pontoon bridge was constructed across Popolopen Creek at almost the identical location of today's Rt. 9W bridge.[9] Both Fort Montgomery and Fort Clinton were captured and destroyed by the British in 1777, leaving only stone ruins in their wake. Nearby, an iron chain was stretched across the river to stop the advance of British warships. It was removed by the British when Fort Montgomery and Fort Clinton were destroyed.

Hell Hole Falls. The falls are prettier than the name suggests.

In later years the area was a main exporter of iron and had many furnaces and forges. Between 1746 and 1934 over two million tons of high-grade ore and iron were extracted and shipped from the area.[10,11]

Bear Mountain State Park, which includes the gorge and falls, was created in 1910 when the Harriman family donated 10,000 acres of land to ensure that both the wilderness and historical aspects of the land would be preserved for future generations to enjoy.

Bear Mountain Bridge, which provides a vital connection between the east and west sides of the Hudson River, was built in 1924. It was the first of eight bridges to cross the Hudson River south of Albany, and it was at one time the world's longest suspension bridge.[9]

Directions: From the traffic circle at the west end of Bear Mountain Bridge (Rt. 6), drive north on Rt. 9W for 0.7 mile and park to the right in a small area provided for tourists visiting Fort Montgomery.

Walk back along Rt. 9W, going south, staying on the east side of the road. At 0.2 mile you will pass by the ruins of Fort Montgomery, which are well worth a visit. When you get to Popolopen Creek, at 0.4 mile, cross over to the opposite side of the road, keeping a sharp eye out for fast-moving traffic, and continue your walk south along the Rt. 9W bridge. While doing so, you can look upstream and glimpse the lowermost section of the cascades. At the southwest end of the bridge, 0.5 mile from the parking area, you will see an unmarked trail leading off into the woods. Follow that trail, and within several hundred feet you will join up with the main, red-colored trail (which begins just a short distance further south from the end of the bridge, where the guardrails end). Follow the red-marked trail/old road downhill for less than 0.2 mile and you will come out onto the top of a bridge abutment that overlooks the falls.

The dam upstream from the falls can be observed either from the abutment overlook or by following the red-colored trail uphill for another 100 feet.

88

CASCADE OF SLID

Location: Harriman State Park (Rockland County)
Delorme New York State Atlas & Gazetteer: p. 32, C2-3
Accessibility: 1.0-mile hike that is easy until the last 0.3 mile, when the path becomes rock-strewn
Degree of Difficulty: Moderate

Description: The Cascade of Slid is formed on Pine Meadows Brook, a small stream that rises in the swamps northwest of Pine Meadow Mountain and flows into Stony Brook 0.3 mile west of the cascade.[1-6] The fall is located in Harriman Park. Harriman Park— along with Bear Mountain Park to the northeast—was created in 1910 largely through the generosity of railroad magnate Edward H. Harriman and his wife, who donated a huge tract of land.

The Cascade of Slid is not, as its name might suggest, a natural waterslide. The fall is more like an inclined slope brimming with huge boulders. The stream drops a total of thirty vertical feet, weaving its way down, through, and over countless rocks and boulders, many of which are the size of automobiles. The entire area is virtually all rock, in fact, with little water to be seen in the dry months of summer. The fall was named by Frank Place, author of the 1923 edition of the *New York Walk Book*, after a mythical character in Lord Dunsany's book *The Gods of Pegana*.[4]

A small footbridge spans the creek at the top of the cascade.

Directions from the north: From the Bear Mountain traffic circle (intersection of Rtes. 6 & 9W) drive southwest on Rt. 6 for 2.8 miles. Get off at Seven Lakes Drive and proceed southwest for nearly 11.0 miles. The Reeves Meadow Visitors Center will be on your left.

Directions from the south: From Sloatsburg (Rt. 17) take Seven Lakes Drive northeast for 1.5 miles. Park at the Reeves Meadow Visitors Center, which will be on your right.

From the parking area, follow the red-blazed hiking trail north. Within moments Stony Brook will appear on your left. From here all you need to do is keep the stream close by to your left. At 0.3 mile the red-blazed trail veers to the right, going uphill. Continue straight ahead on what is now the yellow-blazed trail, with Stony Brook remaining to your left. Within another 0.3 mile you will reach an intersection where a white-blazed trail comes in via a footbridge that crosses over Stony Brook. Stay on the yellow-blazed trail for another 0.1 mile. You will come to Pine Meadows Brook—a tributary of Stony Brook—which comes in on your right. This is the stream that contains the Cascade of Slid. Walk across a footbridge that crosses over Pine Meadows Brook and follow the creek upstream along its north bank, which is marked by white markers. The walk at this point becomes increasingly difficult because of a multitude of rocks and boulders that are scattered about the trail and the hillside. You will reach the Cascade of Slid within 0.3 mile.

It is possible to cross over Pine Meadow Brook at the top of the fall via a footbridge and then follow the red-blazed trail back to the Reeves Meadow Visitors Center.

89

FITZGERALD FALLS

Location: Northeast of Greenwood Lake (Orange County)
Delorme *New York State Atlas & Gazetteer:* p. 32, B1-2
Accessibility: Short, 0.3-mile walk along fairly level trail
Degree of Difficulty: Easy

Description: Fitzgerald Falls is a medium-sized cascade formed on Trout Brook, a small stream that rises northeast of Greenwood Lake.[1-5] The waterfall is located in the 17,500-acre Sterling Forest.

Fitzgerald Falls is nearly thirty feet high and generally appears as a narrow cascade. The face of the fall is bearded in green moss, giving it color and a distinctive look. At the bottom of the cascade is a tiny pool that seems to have been artificially created by a semi-circle of rocks being carefully laid in place. During dry conditions the water disappears at this point, traveling virtually underground until it reemerges further downstream near the footbridge crossing Trout Brook.

Above the fall the stream deepens into a gully with a natural rock garden of enormous boulders scattered about all along the east side of the stream.

Directions: From Sloatsburg, go north on Rt. 17 for roughly 5.0 miles. Turn left onto Rt. 17A and drive west for 7.5 miles until you reach Greenwood Lake, at the intersection with Rt. 210. When you reach Rt. 210 veer to the right and continue on Rt. 17A for another 0.1 mile. As Rt. 17A bears left, proceed straight onto Rt. 5 (towards Monroe) and drive northeast for 3.7 miles. At 3.7 miles pull over and park to the right side of the road at an obvious trailhead where the Appalachian Trail crosses the road.

Follow the white-blazed hiking trail east through a meadow of thick bushes that lie under two power lines. Within 0.1 mile you will cross over Trout Brook via a tiny footbridge. In less than 0.05 mile further, you will come to a rocky streambed (which is frequently dry). Follow the trail as it continues along the side of this riverbed of stones. Within 0.3 mile from your starting point, the trail will lead you up to the base of Fitzgerald Falls.

You may follow the trail up along the side of the fall if you wish to see the top, but the views from below are more than adequate.

Fitzgerald Falls is just northeast of Greenwood Lake.

Greenwood Lake, N. Y., from Mt. Peter

90

RAMAPO FALLS

Location: Mahwah (Bergen County, New Jersey)
Delorme *New York State Atlas & Gazetteer:* p. 32, D2
Accessibility: 0.7-mile hike
Degree of Difficulty: Easy

Description: Ramapo Falls is a twenty-foot-high, nearly vertical cascade formed on MacMillan Creek, a small stream that rises from the MacMillan Reservoir and flows into Ramapo River 0.6 mile from the fall.[1,2] At the base of the cascade, the stream drops into a rocky pool and then exits, flowing over a tiny cascade. The area by the waterfall is very rugged looking, with the hillside littered extensively with small to medium-sized boulders. Several smaller cascades, two to four feet in height, can be seen just upstream from the top of the main fall.

The waterfall is located in the Ramapo Reservation County Park, a 2,000-acre preserve with over eight miles of hiking trails.[2]

Ramapo Falls is also known as Buttermilk Falls.[1] Ramapo may be a Native American word for "rugged country of the waterfalls."[3] Variant spellings are Ramapaugh, Remopuck, Ramopog, Remepog, and Ramapaw.

Directions: From the junction of Rtes. 17 & 202, proceed southwest on Rt. 202 for about 2.0 miles. Turn right into the large parking area for Ramapo Reservation County Park.

Park and follow the paved road bisecting the two parking lots into the woods. To your left you will quickly pass by the old stone foundation of a mansion that once belonged to A. B. Darling, who ran a dairy farm on the property. The road promptly leads to a kiosk and then crosses over the Ramapo River via two, wood-decked bridges that are intended now for pedestrian use only. Continue walking west along a wide expansive road for over 0.3 mile, all the while enjoying views of a scenic lake to your right known as Scarlet

Oak Pond.[2] When you get to the southwestern end of the lake, go left onto a path blazed by dark-green markers, just before the main road starts to go steeply uphill. Walk south for 0.2 mile along the green-blazed trail. A footbridge takes you over a small stream, and the trail leads up to the stone walls of an old abandoned cabin, complete with hearth and chimney. From here, follow the orange-blazed trail north as it starts uphill. The stream will now be to your right. Within 100 feet from the ruins of the stone cabin, you will see a faint, informal path leading off the orange-blazed trail towards the ravine. Follow the path and you will arrive at the base of Ramapo Falls, which is no more than 0.1 mile upstream from the spot where the footbridge crosses the stream.

If you wish, you can stay on the orange-blazed trail as it goes uphill, and then cut over to the top of Ramapo Falls. Take note, however, that the orange-blazed trail bypasses the top of the fall, which means that you must leave the trail in order to actually see the top of the falls.

91

FALLS ON BEAR SWAMP BROOK

Location: Mahwah (Bergen County, New Jersey)
Delorme *New York State Atlas & Gazetteer:* p. 32, D2
Accessibility: 1.2-mile walk along paved road
Degree of Difficulty: Easy

Description: These pretty falls are formed on Bear Swamp Brook, a small stream that rises from the east side of the Ramapo Mountain range and flows into the Ramapo River.[1] The lower fall is fifteen feet in height and very broad. After flowing over the cascade into a shallow pool, the stream continues its downward course into a lower pool and then is compressed as it exits through a narrow, shallow, twelve-foot-long flume.

The upper fall is much narrower and ten feet in height, flowing over an inclined block of bedrock. It is neither as accessible nor as pretty as the lower fall.

Directions: From the junction of Rtes. 17 & 202 (near West Mahwah), proceed southwest on Rt. 202 for roughly 3.5 miles (or just 1.5 miles south of the entrance to Ramapo Reservation County Park). When you come to Bear Swamp Road, which will be on your right, turn around and park in the small pull-off on Rt. 202 opposite Bear Swamp Road. If there is no space available in the pull-off, drive further north on Rt. 202 for 0.1 mile and park in a large area to your right. Bear in mind that no parking is permitted on Bear Swamp Road.

Begin the hike by walking over the Cleveland Bridge (the county's only functioning wood-decked traffic bridge, named after president Grover Cleveland) and down Bear Swamp Road for 0.1 mile. You will come to a point where a dirt road goes off to the right and a paved road veers to the left (crossing over Bear Swamp Brook in turn). The road you are on continues straight ahead. Proceed straight ahead to a yellow barricade where signs state: "Notice: No public land east of pipeline. Open to hunting"; and "Road to Camp Yaw Paw, 2 miles distant." The barrier may or may not be open, depending upon the time of year (but no parking is allowed from here on in any case). Walk around the barrier and follow the paved road as it crosses Bear Swamp Brook and then makes it way gradually uphill, all the time paralleling the stream, which will now be on your right. Within 1.0 mile you will reach a point where the road crosses over Bear Swamp Brook again. As soon as you walk over the bridge, look closely to your right and you will notice the hulking stone ruins of two large buildings nearby in the woods. The ruins are fun to explore, and you will notice that the stones comprising one building appear to be considerably older than those that form the other. Returning to the hike, follow the paved road uphill from the bridge for another 0.1 mile, with the stream now to your left, and you will reach a spot where a small open space is visible on both sides of the road. You will also notice signs posted on two trees to your left stating, "Wild Trout Stream." Walk up the road for another 20 feet past this point, and then take a main path to your left that leads directly to the lower fall.

To get to the upper fall, you can either bushwhack along the creek upstream for 0.05 mile, or go back to the road and walk uphill for another 0.05 mile, and then bushwhack over to the stream, which is 100 feet away. Either way, the upper fall is more difficult to access than its lower companion.

EAST SIDE OF THE HUDSON RIVER

FROM CROTON-ON-HUDSON TO OSSINING

FALLS AT MARION YARROW PRESERVE

Location: Lake Katonah (Westchester County)
Delorme New York State Atlas & Gazetteer: p. 33, B/C6-7
Accessibility: 0.7-mile hike
Degree of Difficulty: Easy to moderate

Description: This tiny waterfall, consisting of a thirty-foot descending streambed with a four-foot cascade at its top, is formed on the outlet stream to Hidden Lake.[1,2] The stream, in turn, is a tiny tributary of Indian Brook. Although the red-blazed trail is called the Fall Trail, and although the waterfall is written up in a preserve guidebook and described as a "30-foot cascade," the appearance is more of an inclined streambed than a waterfall, so expectations should be kept low. On the other hand, the pond forming the stream is exceedingly beautiful and well worth a visit in its own right.

The cascade is located in the seventy-eight-acre Marion Yarrow Preserve, which is part of a larger grouping called the Indian Brook Assemblage.

Directions: Take Exit 6 off I-684 for Katonah and Cross River, and go east on Rt. 35 for 1.9 miles. Turn left onto North Salem Road and drive north for slightly over 0.2 mile. Turn right onto Mount Holly Road and proceed east for 1.1 miles. Turn left at 1.1 miles onto a continuation of Mount Holly Road. At 0.4 mile from this turn, you will pass by a right-hand turn for Holly Hill Road. At 0.8 from the initial left-hand turn, you will reach the Marion Yarrow Preserve, which is on your right. Park in the limited space provided.

Follow the green-blazed lake trail for roughly 0.4 mile until you reach the east side of the lake. From there, follow the red-blazed Fall Trail downhill for under 0.3 mile to the cascade.

FALLS AT CROTON GORGE PARK

Location: Near Croton-on-Hudson (Westchester County)
Delorme *New York State Atlas & Gazetteer:* p. 33, B/C4-5
Accessibility: Roadside

Description: The Falls at Croton Gorge are formed on the Croton River and have been incorporated into the Cornell Dam at the New Croton Reservoir.[1,2] The Croton River is nearly one hundred miles in length. It rises northeast in the Pawling Mountains and flows into the Hudson River at Croton-on-Hudson. Along the way it is intercepted by a series of reservoirs belonging to New York City.

The falls at Croton Gorge Park are massive and consist of three tiers totaling seventy to eighty feet in height. The dam itself is stupendous. In fact, except for the Great Pyramid of Giza, the Croton Dam is reputed to be the largest hewn stone structure in the world.

Even the falls are dwarfed by the enormity of the Croton Dam.

Croton-on-the-Hudson, N. Y. Spillway, Croton Dam.

History: Originally the river was known as Kitchawn (Kitch-a-wong), a Native American word meaning "large and swift current." The name later changed to Croton, which was either the name of an Indian sachem or a corruption of the word Kenotin, meaning "wind or tempest."[3]

The 180-foot-high Cornell Dam was started in 1892 and completed in 1906. The dam is 2,400 feet in length and holds back 30 billion gallons of water. It is 216 feet thick at its base and 21 feet thick at its top.[2] It superseded a smaller, fifty-foot dam, part of which was swept away by floods in 1841 while under construction. What survived from this early dam now lies buried under the waters of the reservoir. The reservoir continues to provide water to the Delaware and Catskill aqueduct system.

Directions: From Croton (junction of Rtes. 9 & 129) take Rt. 129 northeast for 2.3 miles. Turn right into the entrance for Croton Gorge Park and drive over 0.2 mile to the parking area. Be prepared to pay an admission charge depending on the season. The falls are on the north side of the dam and are easily viewed as you drive in and cross over a bridge spanning the Croton River in front of the dam.

From the parking area, walk back to the south end of the bridge to look at the falls more leisurely, or stroll down to the side of the dam for a lateral view.

94

HAVEMEYER FALLS

Location: Bedford (Westchester County)
Delorme *New York State Atlas & Gazetteer:* p. 33, C6-7
Accessibility: 2.3-mile hike over rolling terrain
Degree of Difficulty: Moderate to difficult

Description: Havemeyer Falls is a medium-sized cascade formed on a small tributary to the Mianus River, a moderate-sized stream that rises near Greenwich, Connecticut, is quickly intercepted nearby to form the S. J. Bargh Reservoir, and eventually flows into the Long Island Sound. The waterfall consists of a ten-foot cascade falling into a pool of water.[1-3] From there the stream drops over a lower, eight-foot cascade of boulders, and after another twenty-five feet of streambed, reaches the comparatively still waters of the reservoir.

The Old Mill, Bedford, New York. Even artificial waterfalls are pretty.

THE OLD MILL, BEDFORD, NEW YORK

Above the top of the falls, where a stone slab footbridge crosses the stream, can be seen a pretty, three-foot cascade.

Havemeyer Falls is located in the 719-acre Mianus River Gorge Preserve, which is managed by the Mianus Gorge Preserve, Inc. The preserve got its start in 1955 when the Nature Conservancy purchased sixty acres of land, forming a nucleus around which additional land has since been acquired.

Another fall, Safford Cascade, can also be seen along the red-blazed trail nearly midway through the hike to Havemeyer Falls. Safford Cascade is formed on a tiny tributary to the Mianus River and consists of a five-foot-high cascade above a wide, steeply descending streambed filled with moss-covered boulders.

History: The gorge and preserve are named after Mayanos (or Mayanne), a Wappinger Confederacy Indian chief who was killed near the gorge in 1664.

The Mianus Gorge Preserve is notable for being the nation's first registered National Historic Landmark. In addition to the wildness of the gorge itself, the preserve boasts 350-year-old hemlocks, many of which stand over one hundred feet high.[4]

Originally the S. J. Bargh Reservoir dam was to be 275 feet in height, but after much debate a compromise was reached to restrict the dam's height to 257 feet, thus sparing the gorge and sections of the forest from being inundated.[5]

Directions: From the junction of Rt. 172 & I-684 (east of Mount Kisco), drive east on Rt. 172 for a total of 3.6 miles, passing through the village of Bedford in the process. When you come to the stoplight east of Bedford, turn right onto Long Ridge Road and drive south for over 0.5 mile. Turn right onto Miller's Mill Road, which immediately crosses over a stream. Look to your right as you cross the stream and you will see a dam-created fall. In less than 0.1 mile, turn left onto Mianus River Road and drive south for 0.6 mile. The parking area for Mianus Gorge is on your left.

Follow the red-blazed trail south for roughly 2.3 miles to Havemeyer Falls. Return on the blue-blazed trail to give your hike some variety.

In transit you will pass by Safford Falls between marker #4 for the Fording Place and marker #6 for Rockwell Breach—the narrowest point in the gorge.

Keep in mind that the park is only open from 8:30 AM to 5:00 PM daily and is closed from December through March. Trail maps are provided at the kiosk and are wonderfully descriptive. Be sure to place a donation in the box provided.

THE PALISADES

WEST SIDE OF THE HUDSON RIVER

The Palisades are markedly different in appearance from all other sections of the Hudson River. Rising to a height of over five hundred feet above the river, and nearly vertical in places, the Palisades extend along the west bank of the lower Hudson River for forty miles. They have been described as "massive stone logs," "a great wall of posts," "Titanic pickets," and "a sandwich of sandstone and molten rock."[3] The word "palisade" itself refers to a fence of stakes set into the ground for defensive purposes.[4]

The Palisades were formed during the Triassic Period (160–190 million years ago) when massive beds of lava were forced up from the interior of the Earth and intruded between layers of shale. The lava quickly hardened, forming an igneous rock called diabase, which is made up of feldspar and pyroxene.[1,2] The sheer cliff face of the Palisades is the result of the rock tending to divide by natural fractures, forming towering columns. Although the Palisades are old by human standards, they are still in their infancy when compared to the ancient rocks that have formed the Hudson Highlands.

What makes the Palisades so unusual is that its type of rock formation is rare. Famous examples elsewhere of palisaded rocks are the Giant Causeway in Ireland, and Fingal's Cave at the Isle of Staffa on the west coast of Scotland.[5]

Thanks to the creation of the Palisades Interstate Park Commission in 1900, the wanton destruction of the Palisades for its raw materials that had been going on since 1736 was brought to a halt.

95

CASCADE IN KENNEDY–DELLS COUNTY PARK

Location: Haverstraw (Rockland County)
Delorme *New York State Atlas & Gazetteer:* p. 32, C3-4
Accessibility: 0.2-mile walk along old road
Degree of Difficulty: Easy

Description: These little cascades are formed on a small tributary to Lake Lucille, which rises northwest of New City. The fall consists of an eight-foot-high cascade that slides into a tiny pool of water at the base of a dam. The dam, in turn, supports a magnificent stone bridge that once spanned the ravine. With its towering arches and fairly complete stonework, the bridge ruins add just the right touch to make the view scenic and picturesque.

The reasonably intact foundation of an old mill, complete with remnants of machinery, stands along the east bank of the stream next to the base of the cascade.

The cascade is located in the Kennedy–Dells County Park (which is listed as the Robert F. Kennedy County Park in the *New York State Atlas & Gazetteer*).

Directions: From the junction of Rtes. 9W & 59 in Nyack, go north on Rt. 9W for over 7.0 miles until you come to a traffic light, 1.0 mile after you pass by Rt. 304 (on your left). If you are approaching from the north, drive south on Rt. 9W from the junction of Rtes. 9W & 202 for 1.9 miles. From the traffic light on Rt. 9W, turn west onto Rt. 90 (which becomes South Mountain Road). At 2.2 miles you will pass by the entrance to High Tor State Park. In another 0.3 mile (at 2.5 miles), turn left onto Zukor Road and drive south for 0.2 mile. Turn right onto Woodhaven Drive, which enters a residential section. Continue west on Woodhaven—past a little traffic circle at 0.1 mile—for 0.7 mile until you reach the end of the road where a barricade prevents further entry. Park in the limited area provided, being sure to stay clear of any private homes and driveways.

From the barricade at the end of the street, follow the old blacktopped road to your right for 0.2 mile. It will lead to the stream and a bridge, whose fairly intact ruins still remain. The cascade is directly below, under the bridge.

The Palisades. The trail to Greenbrook Falls begins here.

BUTTERMILK FALLS
(Rockland County Park)

Location: Central Nyack (Rockland County)
Delorme *New York State Atlas & Gazetteer:* p. 32, D4
Accessibility: 0.2-mile hike along well-maintained trail
Degree of Difficulty: Easy

Description: Buttermilk Falls is formed on a tiny stream that rises in Central Nyack and flows into Hackensack Creek south of West Nyack. The waterfall is located in Buttermilk Falls County Park.[1] The main waterfall is a fifteen-foot-high cascade flowing over black rock into a tiny pool at its base. Below the pool, the water continues cascading for another eight feet.

Directly above the main fall can be seen several small cascades where the stream is more serpentine.

History: The ravine was a favorite spot of former president Theodore Roosevelt.[2]

Buttermilk Falls County Park was acquired in 1976–1977. Rockland County maintains it as a nature park.

Directions: From Central Nyack (junction of Rtes. 9W & 59) drive south on Rt. 9W for 0.2 mile. At a traffic light turn right onto South Highland Avenue, which takes you towards Nyack College. Go uphill for 0.2 mile, then follow South Highland Ave as it turns right. Continue for another 0.2 mile. At this point turn right onto Bradley Hill Parkway and follow it west for 1.3 miles. Turn right onto Greenbush Road and drive north for 0.8 mile until you reach the large, paved parking area for Buttermilk Falls County Park, which will be on your right.

Start at the trailhead at the north end of the parking lot and follow the blue-blazed trail east for 0.2 mile. The trail leads right to the side of a gorge overlooking Buttermilk Falls.

PEANUT LEAP FALLS

Location: Palisades, (Rockland County)
Delorme *New York State Atlas & Gazetteer:* p. 32, D4-5
Accessibility: 0.8-mile walk, very rocky and steep for the last 0.2 mile
Degree of Difficulty: Moderate to difficult

Description: Peanut Leap Falls is a towering, eighty-foot-high cascade formed on a small stream that rises in the hills west of the Hudson River and plunges over the Palisade escarpment near the border of New York and New Jersey. The fall is located on land owned by the Palisades Interstate Park Commission.

When visiting the fall be sure to arrive shortly after a period of heavy rainfall. The soil is so thin on top of the Palisades that the stream discharges quickly and doesn't get replenished until the next rainfall.

History: The waterfall has been known by many names in the past. It was called: Half-Moon Falls by the Lamont Family (the same family whose name is attached to the Lamont–Doherty Earth Observatory) in honor of Henry Hudson's vessel; Eagle's Ledge by residents of Sneden's Landing[1]; and even simply the Cascade.[2] Peanut Leap happens to be the oldest name by which the fall has been known, dating back to an 1874 map.[1] No one is quite sure how this name originated, however.

An historic marker just north of the entrance to the Lamont–Dougherty Earth Observatory states that Skunk Hollow, through which the stream forming Peanut Leap Falls passes, was the site of a free Black community from 1806–1905. At one time over one hundred families lived in the settlement.[3]

The ruins at the base of the fall are from an Italian Garden created by Mary Lawrence-Tonetti, a local sculptress. The land was bought in the mid 1880s by Mary's mother, Mrs. H. E. Lawrence, in order to block the proposed development of a picnic site and pier that would have allowed unlimited access to the area by boaters. Years later, when Mary Lawrence acquired the land, she decided that she would create a wonderful garden with the waterfall as a backdrop to impress her New York City friends. Enlisting the help of several artistic peers, including Stanford White, Charles McKim, and Augustus Saint-Gaudens, Mary designed a pergola that was based upon a structure she had seen at Amalfi in 1887. Next, Mary had her husband, the Italian-French sculptor Francois Tonetti, construct a series of pools at descending levels accentuated by rows of flowerbeds and scrubs. For a time the gardens were beautifully maintained. After Mary's death in 1945, however, the pergola was seriously vandalized and the magnificence of the gardens blighted. Finally, in 1979–1980, the land was taken over by the Palisades Interstate Park Commission after it was offered to them by the heirs of the Lawrence-Tonetti family.[4-6]

Directions: From Sparkill (junction of Rtes. 9W & 340) drive south on Rt. 9W for 2.7 miles until you reach the left-hand turn for the Lamont–Dougherty Earth Observatory. Along the way, at 0.6 mile, you will pass by the entrance to Tallman Mountain State Park at Piermont. (From the Palisades Interstate Parkway, get off at either Exit 3 or Exit 4 to get onto Rt. 9W. It is just a short drive to the Lamont–Dougherty Earth Observatory entrance road, on your right.) Parking for a limited number of cars is available along the east side of Rt. 9W near the entrance road to the observatory.

You will see boulders blocking an old, abandoned, two-lane cement road that once led 1.0 mile to the State Line Lookout. Walk along this road south for 0.1 mile, and then turn left onto the turquoise-blazed trail and head east into the woods. After less than 0.3 mile you will come to a main intersection. Here, you will notice that the turquoise-colored Long Trail goes off to the right, crossing over the tiny creek via a footbridge, while a white-marked trail goes straight ahead. You will also notice a trail going off to the left that leads up to the Lamont–Dougherty Earth Observatory in less than 0.3 mile. Follow the white-colored Shore Trail straight ahead as it proceeds along the north bank of the creek. Be prepared for some rocky footing as you descend on this trail. After 0.2 mile you will reach the top of Peanut Leap Falls, which overlooks the Hudson River nearly directly below. Don't get too close to the top, for it is a huge drop. Follow the trail downward for 0.1 mile to the bottom of the falls. This portion of the trail has been fashioned into giant steps in the steep places. You will see the old ruins of Lawrence's Italian Gardens, as well as having excellent views of the Hudson River and New York City in the distance.

An alternate, longer approach to the fall is from the State Line Lookout, which is accessed off the Palisades Interstate Parkway 1.8 miles north of Exit 2. From the parking area at State Line Lookout, follow the turquoise-marked trail north until you reach the white-marked Shore Trail, which you will come to right after crossing over the small stream that leads to Peanut Leap Falls. Follow the white-marked Shore Trail down to the fall.

A third approach is to reach the base of the fall directly by following the white-marked Shore Trail as it snakes along the base of the Palisades. This can be done by following the blue-colored markers south from the parking area of the State Line Lookout, and then descending via the blue/white-marked trail on your left to the base of the Palisades. Should you continue too far on the blue-colored trail and miss the turnoff, you will reach the Women's Federation Monument.

Once you have descended to the white-marked Shore Trail, proceed north along the shore of the Hudson River and you will eventually come to the base of Peanut Leap Falls.

There is one final approach, and it is perhaps the most obvious—you can access the base of the waterfall directly from the Hudson River by boat.

GREENBROOK FALLS

Location: North of Englewood (Bergen County, New Jersey)

Delorme *New York State Atlas & Gazetteer:* p. 24, A/B4

Accessibility: From Englewood Basin, 3.0-mile hike along the rock-strewn Shore Trail, or 3.0-mile drive/bicycle/walk via the Henry Hudson Drive; from Alpine Basin, 2.0-mile hike along very rock-strewn Shore Trail, or 1.5-mile drive/bicycle/walk via the circle at the start of the Henry Hudson Drive

Degree of Difficulty: Difficult hike along the Shore Trail because of distance and uneven footing; Moderate along the paved, fairly level Henry Hudson Drive

Description: Greenbrook Falls is formed on Green Brook, a small stream that rises from Sanctuary Pond (Kelder's Pond) near the top of the Palisades and flows into the Hudson River near the base of the falls.[1-4] The waterfall is reputed to be the highest in New Jersey,[3] dropping nearly 250 feet as it make its way down the cliff face formed by the Palisades. The largest drop is over eighty feet high and occurs right under Henry Hudson Drive.

The view from the white Shore Trail is absolutely stunning. You can walk directly over to the base of the fall and look straight up, taking in the enormity of the lower section of Greenbrook Falls as it cascades down from below the Henry Hudson Drive bridge. Unfortunately, it is not possible to see the other, higher parts of the fall; nor is it possible to see the entirety of Greenbrook Falls from any spot. A forty-foot section of Greenbrook Falls rising above the road can be observed from Henry Hudson Drive, but it is not possible to see the section of the falls directly below the bridge (other than to appreciate the enormity of the gulf below), nor the uppermost section of the falls.

Directions: Englewood Boat Basin Approach: Get off at Exit 1 from the Palisades Interstate Parkway and proceed east on Palisades Avenue, which leads immediately down a steep hill to the (Englewood) Boat Basin. On the drive down this road you will be treated to views of three segments of the same descending stream (Englewood Creek), where a pretty cascade can be seen each time (see next chapter on Falls on Englewood Creek). Take note that when you have driven roughly 0.4 mile downhill, you will come to a U-turn. This is where the Henry Hudson Drive begins, going north. Ignore the turn-off for the moment and complete the U-turn, proceeding down the rest of the way to the Boat Basin. When you reach the Boat Basin, drive to the parking area farthest north, which is 1.2 miles from where you started your descent down from the sign stating: "Entering Palisades Interstate Park. New Jersey Section. Englewood Picnic Area & Boat Basin. Ross Dock Area."

Be prepared to pay a seasonal parking fee, particularly on weekends.

From the northernmost parking lot, follow the white-colored Shore Trail for over 3.0 miles. Along the way you will have excellent views of the Hudson River and the skyline of New York City. The falls will be directly to your left when you reach Green Brook.

Alpine Boat Basin Approach: Get off the Palisades Interstate Parkway at Exit 2 and drive past the park headquarters, following a rapidly descending road to the base of the Palisades, a distance of roughly 1.0 mile. Near the bottom, turn left to get to the parking area for the Boat Basin. Be prepared to pay a seasonal parking fee, particularly on weekends.

From the parking area follow the white-colored Shore Trail south for slightly under 2.0 miles until you come to near the base of the fall, which will be on your right. Although this hike is shorter than the one approaching from the Englewood Boat Basin, the trail is rockier and physically more demanding.

Henry Hudson Drive Approach: The midsection of Greenbrook Falls can be seen by either driving, biking, or walking along the Henry Hudson Drive—a pretty, twenty-five-mile-per-hour highway that was opened in 1921.5 If you are traveling by car, take note that parking along the highway is not permitted; this means that the falls can only be quickly glimpsed from your car window as you drive by. It is better either to bring a bike along or to walk the distance to the bridge so that you can view the falls in a more leisurely fashion. The Henry Hudson Drive spans the distance between the Englewood Boat Basin (near Exit 1 of the Palisades Interstate Parkway) and the Alpine Boat Basin (near Exit 2 of the Palisades Interstate Parkway)—a distance of over 4.5 miles.

From the start of the Henry Hudson Drive at the U-turn above the Englewood Boat Basin, proceed north for over 3.0 miles and you will arrive at a bridge spanning Green Brook. The middle section of Greenbrook Falls can be seen to your left from the bridge.

From the start of Henry Hudson Drive next to the Alpine Boat Basin, go south on the Henry Hudson Drive for 1.5 miles and the falls will be directly to your right.

FALLS ON ENGLEWOOD CREEK

Location: Englewood (Bergen County, New Jersey)
Delorme *New York State Atlas & Gazetteer:* p. 24, A/B4
Accessibility: Roadside

Description: There is a series of cascades formed on Englewood Creek as the stream swiftly descends over a number of drops down the Palisades.

Directions: Take Exit 1 off the Palisades Interstate Parkway and drive east on Palisades Avenue. Immediately you will come to a sign stating: "Entering Palisades Interstate Park. New Jersey Section. Englewood Picnic Area & Boat Basin. Ross Dock Area." Set the odometer to 0.0 when you reach the sign, and then proceed down the hill. Along the way you will encounter segments of Englewood Creek as you zigzag your way down the escarpment. At 0.1 mile you will see a cascade on your right; at 0.2 mile there will be another one on your left; and a third fall at 0.7 mile, on your right again. But there is still more to come. Continue downhill into the parking areas for the Englewood Boat Basin. At 0.9 mile from the top of the escarpment you will pass over Englewood Creek as it readies itself to flow into the Hudson River. Park in the lot south of the stream.

Walk over to the south bank of the stream and follow it across the lawn to where the stream comes down the wooded escarpment and then across the lawn through an artificial channel. From here several more, smaller cascades are visible.

FALL ON FLAT ROCK BROOK

Location: Englewood Cliffs (Bergen County, New Jersey)
Delorme *New York State Atlas & Gazetteer:* p. 24, A/B4
Accessibility: 0.3-mile walk
Degree of Difficulty: Easy

Description: This tiny fall is formed on Flat Rock Brook, a small stream that rises near the Palisades Ridge and flows into Overpeck Creek.[1] Along the way, the stream passes through the 150-acre Flat Rock Brook Nature Center, a preserve founded in 1973 and containing 3.2 miles of trails. The preserve is managed by the Flat Rock Brook Nature Association, a nonprofit organization, and contains a nature center that is located at the end of Van Nostrand Avenue (a street that runs perpendicular to Jones Road).

The fall is half cascade and half dam, and roughly five feet in height. The beauty of the waterfall is accentuated by a footbridge that spans the top of the fall at the outlet to MacFadden's Pond. Look closely and you will notice cement walls on both sides of the stream below the fall.

Directions: From Rt. 9W in Coytesville (southwest of Englewood Cliffs), take Rt. 4 west for nearly 1.0 mile and get off at the Jones Road exit. Turn right onto Jones Road and proceed north for roughly 0.3 mile until you reach the preserve, which will be on your right opposite Fountain Road. Park on Jones Road or on one of the side streets.

Follow the main path into the preserve and cross over Flat Rock Brook via a charming footbridge. The kiosk next to the playground provides pertinent information about the park, as well as a colored map for reference. Follow the red-marked trail that parallels the east bank of the creek upstream for 0.3 mile. You will come to the dammed fall, which is at the outlet to MacFadden's Pond. A lovely footbridge spans the creek at this point.

Waterfalls were an industrial magnet during the 1800s.

Falls at Irwins Mill
Rensselaer, near Albany, N. Y.

About the Author

Russell Dunn is the author of *Adirondack Waterfall Guide: New York's Cool Cascades* (Black Dome Press, 2003), *Catskill Region Waterfall Guide: Cool Cascades of the Catskills & Shawangunks* (Black Dome Press, 2004), and *Adventures around the Great Sacandaga Lake* (Nick Burns Publishing, 2002). He is currently working on two more guidebooks, one of which will be coauthored with his wife, Barbara Delaney. Dunn has also published articles in *Adirondack Life, Kaatskill Life, Adirondac, Hudson Valley, Adirondack Explorer, Glens Falls Magazine, Sacandaga Times, National Speleological Association,* and other magazines.

Dunn works full-time as a medical social worker at the Visiting Nurse Service of Schenectady and Saratoga Counties. When not working or writing, he plays classical guitar, practices legerdemain, writes songs, and takes stereographic pictures. He and his wife divide their time between their home in Albany and their camp on the Great Sacandaga Lake.

List of Waterfalls

Notes

Preface
Types of Waterfalls

1. Rich and Sue Freeman, *200 Waterfalls in Central & Western New York: A Finders' Guide* (Fishers, N.Y.: Footprint Press, 2002), 26.

2. Gary Letcher, *Waterfalls of the Mid-Atlantic States: 200 Falls in Maryland, New Jersey, and Pennsylvania* (Woodstock, Vt.: The Countryman Press, 2004), xxii–xxiii.

3. Greg and Kate B. Watson, *New England Waterfalls: A Guide to More Than 200 Cascades and Waterfalls* (Woodstock, Vt.: The Countryman Press, 2003), xix–xx.

4. Russell Dunn, *Catskill Region Waterfall Guide: Cool Cascades of the Catskills & Shawangunks* (Hensonville, N.Y.: Black Dome Press Corp., 2004), 14.

5. Scott A. Ensminger and Douglas K. Bassett, *A Waterfall Guide to Letchworth State Park* (Castile, N.Y.: The Glen Iris Inn, 1991), 62–64.

6. T. Morris Longstreth, *The Catskills* (New York: The Century Co., 1921; reprint, Hensonville, N.Y.: Black Dome Press Corp., 2003), 85–94.

Waterfall Records

1. Peter Chapin, "New England & N.Y. Waterfalls," website: www.ecet.vtc.edu/~pchapin/water.

2. Peter Matthews, ed., *The Guinness Book of Records* (New York: Guinness Publishing, Ltd., 1994), 17.

3. Rich and Sue Freeman, op. cit., 26.

4. Edmund H. Harvey, Jr., ed., *Reader's Digest Book of Facts* (Pleasantville, N.Y.: The Reader's Digest Association, Inc., 1987), 175, 240.

Introduction: Waterfalls of the Hudson River Valley

1. Tim Mulligan, *The Hudson River Valley: A History & Guide* (New York: Random House, 1981), xvi.

2. Robert H. Boyle, *The Hudson River: A Natural and Unnatural History*, expanded edition (New York/London: W. W. Norton & Company, 1979), 16.

3. Chris W. Brown III, *Cruising Guide to New York Waterways and Lake Champlain* (Gretna, La.: Pelican Publishing Company, Inc., 1998), 20, 35.

4. Wallace Nutting, in *New York Beautiful* (Garden City, N.Y.: Garden City Publishing Co., Inc., in cooperation with the Old America Company, 1936), mentions on page 20 that the Hudson has been called "the Rhine of America."

5. Russell Dunn, *Adventures around the Great Sacandaga Lake* (Utica, N.Y.: Nicholas K. Burns Publishing, 2002).

6. Howell and Tenney, in *History of the County of Albany, New York: From 1609 to 1886 with Portraits, Biographies and Illustrations* (1886; reprint, Salem, Mass.: Higginson Book Company, undated), state in a footnote, page 15, "The fall of the river from Albany to New York is a little over three feet."

7. According to Betty Ahearn Buckell, on page 23 in *Boldly into the Wilderness: Travelers in Upstate New York, 1010–1646* (Queensbury, N.Y.: Buckle Press, 1999), riffs of rocks and stones above Waterford formed a natural barrier in the Hudson River, preventing large ships from proceeding any further.

8. Nathaniel Sylvester, in *Historical Sketches of New York and the Adirondack Wilderness* (1877; reprint, Harrison, N.Y.: Harbor Hill Books, 1973), 95, describes earlier names by which the Hudson River was known.

9. John Mylod, *Biography of a River: The People and Legends of the Hudson Valley* (New York: Bonanza Books, 1969), 4.

Rockwell Falls

1. In Roland Van Zandt's *Chronicles of the Hudson: Three Centuries of Travel and Adventure* (1971; reprint, Hensonville, N.Y.: Black Dome Press Corp., 1992), Charles Farnham is excerpted in "Running the Rapids of the Upper Hudson" in *Scribner's Monthly*, Vol. XXI (April, 1881), stating on page 260 that: "The roar of Hadley's Falls broke the spell. ... The gorge of the river here is very narrow, crooked, and walled in with precipitous rocks." An engraving of Rockwell Falls, drawn by J. R. Smith, is presented on page 254.

2. Jacques Gerard Milbert, in *Picturesque Itinerary of the Hudson River and the peripheral parts of North America*

(Ridgewood, N.J.: Gregg Press, 1968), writes on page 81: "After walking around the modest dwellings of Hadley Falls, I came to the foot of the cascade which crosses a broad open trench that was apparently abraded by the water through very hard limestone. On both sides of this opening rise rocks that are cut into pillars and arranged in a colonnade."

3. A somewhat exaggerated line drawing of Rockwell Falls can be seen in *Reminiscences of Saratoga and Ballston* (n.p.: Virtue & Yorston, 1875) by William L. Stone, 394.

Curtis Falls

1. Per Walter F. Burmeister, on page 47 in *Appalachian Waters 2: The Hudson River and its Tributaries* (Oakton, Va.: Appalachian Books, 1974), the "Corinth Dam sits at the head of an impressive ravine." Burmeister goes on to describe, on page 47, the dam as a "28-foot high barrage."

2. Nathaniel Bartlett Sylvester, in *History of Saratoga County, New York: with Illustrations and Biographic sketches of some of its Prominent Men and Pioneers* (Philadelphia, Pa.: Everts & Ensign, 1878), on page 395 describes a waterfall one-half mile upstream from Palmer Falls, which one must assume is Curtis Falls: "Its sides are steep and thickly wooded with pines. It is called 'Indian Hollow.'"

3. Mabel Pitkin Shorey, *The Early History of Corinth: Once Known as Jessup's Landing* (Corinth, N.Y.: Mabel Pitkin Shorey, 1959), 63.

4. Violet B. Dunn, ed., *Saratoga County Heritage* (Saratoga County, N.Y.: n.p., 1974), 302.

Palmer Falls

1. Roland Van Zandt, op. cit., 263. Charles Farnham states: "The Hudson returns, at Jessup's Landing, to the ways of its youth, by plunging down a great fall and then running seven miles as a wild rapid."

2. Nathaniel Bartlett Sylvester, op. cit., 391. "For beauty, and picturesque and grand effects, the scenery of Palmer's Falls may well rank with any in the State. At one point, a few rods above the falls, the river passes through a narrow channel worn in the rocks, and a

fourteen-foot plank will span from one side of it to the other. Here tradition says that several years previous to the Revolution a white trapper was pursued along the eastern bluff, and, dashing down the steep banks close to the falls, he made for this spot, and reaching it, in order to escape what was certain capture and certain death, nerved himself for the effort and vaulted over the foaming flood, alighting safely on the other side. None of his savage pursuers dared to venture the leap, and he plunged into the forest and escaped."

3. Mabel Pitkin Shorey, op. cit., 25–26.

Glens Falls

1. In Jeffrey Simpson's *The Hudson River 1850–1918: A Photographic Portrait* (Tarrytown, N.Y.: Sleepy Hollow Press, 1981), on page 36 a photo taken in April 1869 shows the Hudson River rising right out of the Glens Falls Gorge and overpowering the wooden bridge spanning the river.

2. Roland Van Zandt, op. cit., 266. An engraving of Glens Falls, drawn at the level of the river, shows the old bridge crossing the island of rock directly at the base of the falls.

3. Jacques Gerard Milbert, op cit., 71. "I visited the famous fall, which is over 50 feet in height, and its 300-foot bridge resting on pillars lodged in a cubic mass of rocks that form a kind of island."

4. Donald W. Fisher, on page 9 in *Bedrock Geology of the Glens Falls–Whitehall Region, New York*. Map and Chart Series Number 35 (Albany, N.Y.: University of the State of New York. The State Education Department/Albany, 1984), describes Glens Falls as "a drop of about 50' over the Black River and Trenton limestones."

5. In the *Encyclopedia of New York, Vol. 2* (New York: Somerset Publishing, Inc., 1996), the authors mention on page 108 that "The water power provided by the 60-foot falls in the Hudson ... determined the location of the settlement Glens Falls."

6. David Cederstrom, "Bridge & Overlook," *The Chronicle*, Vol. 25, No. 1,058 (Nov. 4–10, 2004), 1, 8.

7. Walter F. Burmeister, op. cit., 49, explains the translation of the Native American word *chepontuo*.

Bakers Falls

1. Donald W. Fisher, op. cit., 8, states that Bakers Falls is a "drop of 65' " over a "lowermost calcareous mudstone of Snake Hill formation." A picture of the falls can also be seen on the same page.

2. Jacques Gerard Milbert, op. cit., 52. "The river, very broad at this point, rushes over enormous rocks, that are visible through the clear water. A little farther along, the second cataract, of equal width, is broken into billows of foam, which, like banks of snow, vanish in the depths of the ravine. The waters pour tumultuously into the canal but become quieter as they advance."

3. A line drawing of Bakers Falls can be found in Benson J. Lossing's *The Hudson: From the Wilderness to the Sea* (1866; reprint, Hensonville, N.Y.: Black Dome Press Corp., 2000), 73. Lossing writes on page 72: "The best view is from the foot of the falls, but as these could not be reached from the eastern side, on which the paper-mills stand, without much difficulty and with some danger, I sketched a less imposing view from the high rocky bank on their eastern margin."

4. Walter F. Burmeister, op. cit., 50. "Prior to the dam construction craze and the hunger for cheap water power, this was a magnificent cataract at the head of an equally dramatic box canyon. A sheet of water dropped over 60 feet in a wild and truly impressive setting."

5. An 1820 hand-colored aquatint engraving of Bakers Falls by John Hill can be seen in Darrell Welch's article, "The Hudson River Portfolio," in *The Conservationist*, Vol. 26, No. 5 (April/May 1972).

6. Roland Van Zandt, op. cit., 317. Bakers Falls was named after Albert Baker, one of the original settlers of the Kingsbury Patent, granted in 1762, which embodied 26,000 acres.

7. *Encyclopedia of New York*, op. cit., 122. "The first white settlers came in 1760 and built gristmills and sawmills on the 70-foot falls."

8. As an interesting side point, in *An Introduction to Historic Resources in Washington County, New York* (Washington County, N.Y.: Washington County Planning Department for the Washington County Planning Board, 1984), the writers state on page 92 that "Baker's Falls, a natural falls on the Hudson River at Hudson Falls, has a fall of eighty-five feet, and is second in height only to

Niagara." There are several objections that could be made regarding this statement: 1) Bakers Falls is no longer a natural waterfall; 2) its height is probably significantly less than 85 feet; and 3) Niagara Falls is not the highest waterfall in New York State. None of this, of course, takes away from Bakers Falls being an impressive waterfall in its own right.

Fall in Pilot Knob Ridge Preserve

1. Thomas Reeves Lord, *Stories of Lake George: Fact & Fancy* (Pemberton, N.J.: Pineland Press, 1987), 58.

2. A map and brief history of the preserve is contained in a brochure entitled "Pilot Knob Ridge Preserve," distributed by the Lake George Land Conservancy (Bolton Landing, N.Y.).

3. Galen Crane, "Pilot Knob," *Adirondack Life*, Vol. XXXV, No. 8 (November/December, 2004), 96.

Kane Falls

1. Donald W. Fisher, op. cit, 9, writes that the "face of falls is a faultline scarp." A picture of the waterfall is also presented on the same page.

2. Albert Sleicher, *The Adirondacks: An American Playground* (New York: Exposition Press, 1960), 165.

3. Washington County Planning Department, op. cit., 43–45.

Dionondahowa Falls

1. Walter F. Burmeister, op. cit., 80. The gorge is described as a "set of 2 barrages above cataracts that have a 95-foot drop."

2. *A History of Greenwich, Washington Co., N.Y.*, from a paper contributed by Edwin Neilson, a 7th grade student in the Greenwich High School, who was given the manuscript in 1966. The author (unidentified) refers to the Batten Kill, and states that "At Middle Falls it drops 40 feet and at Big Falls drops 70 feet."

3. The *History and Biography of Washington County and the Town of Queensbury, New York, with Historical Notes on the Various Towns* (Richmond, Ind.: Gresham Publishing Company, 1894) states on page 19 that the Indian name for the Batten Kill was Ondawa, and that "the Batten Kill becomes a swift-flowing and strangely pictur-

esque stream whose wonderful Dionondahowa, or Middle Falls, have a descent of seventy-five feet, in the distance of three hundred."

4. Jacques Gerard Milbert, op. cit., 48. "Here the Hudson forms rapids below the mouth of the charming Battenkill River that rises in the Vermont mountains and drops about 60 feet in its course."

5. In the *History of the Town of Greenwich* (Salem, N.Y.: H. D. Morris, Book and Job Printer, 1876), compiled by Elisha P. Thurston, the falls and river are described on page 6: "at 'Big Falls' it has an abrupt descent of 70 feet. The last are called 'The Falls of the Dionondehawa' from the Iroquois name for the Battenkill. These falls attract much attention from visitors from abroad; the over-hanging trees, jagged rocks, and bounding waters uniting to make the scenery wild and thrilling."

6. In the *History of Washington County, New York: Some Chapters in the History of the Town of Easton, N.Y.* (Washington County, N.Y.: Washington County Historical Society, 1959), the writ-ers state on page 99 that "The power site at Ondawa Falls, some-times called Big Falls, is the most valuable power on the river. There the Battenkill tumbles spectacularly ninety feet into a rocky gorge." The book also provides background information on pages 99 and 100 on some of the past factories that proliferated near the fall.

7. Benson J. Lossing, op. cit., 84. "Within two miles of its mouth are remarkable rapids and falls, which the tourist should never pass by unseen; the best point of view is from the bottom of a steep precipice on the southern side of the stream. The descent is fifty or sixty feet, very difficult, and somewhat dangerous. It was raining copiously when we visited it, which made the descent still more difficult, for the loose slate and the small sparse shrubbery were very insecure. Under a shelving black rock on the margin of the abyss into which the waters pour, we found a great place for observation. The spectacle was grand. For about three hundred feet above the great fall, the stream rushes through a narrow rocky chasm, roaring and foaming; and then, in a still narrower space, it leaps into the dark gulf which has been named the Devil's Caldron, in a perpendicular fall of almost fifty feet." A line drawing of the fall made from this observation point is also presented on page 86.

8. Arthur G. Adams, *The Hudson River Guidebook,* 2nd Edition

(New York: Fordham University Press, 1996). On page 287 the author refers to the falls as the "Great Falls" of the Batten Kill.

9. In "Dionondehowa: Wildlife Sanctuary and School," *The Healing Springs*, Issue # 12 (February–March 2004), Bonnie Hoag writes on page 12 that "Dionondehowa (Die-on-on-duh-how-uh) was first recorded by the European immigrants in 1709. It is listed in *Beauchamp's Aboriginal Place Names of New York State* and translates to 'She opens the Door for Them,' which may have referred to the river itself, to some ancient sachem, or perhaps to the keeper of the Eastern Door of the Iroquois Confederacy."

10. Lawrence I. Grinnel, in *Canoeable Waterways of New York State and Vicinity* (New York: Pageant Press, Inc., 1956), states on page 53 how the Batten Kill was named, and gives brief information about canoeing the stream, albeit not by the falls.

11. Washington County Planning Department, op. cit., 65. "The greatest fall on the Battenkill and the most beautiful, is about a mile from Middle Falls––Dionondehowa Falls, the site now of Stevens and Thompson Paper Company Mills. At the turn of the last century, Dionondehowa Park, across the kill from the Stevens and Thompson Mill, was a recreation area where band concerts, picnics, and sports programs were held with people arriving by trolley from all of the communities along the Hudson Valley from Troy to Glens Falls."

Middle Falls

1. Walter F. Burmeister, op. cit., 80. The fall is described as a "seven foot barrage above a 30-foot falls."

2. *History of Washington County*, op. cit., 100. "At the Middle Falls power site the river drops fifty feet."

3. *History and Biography of Washington County and the Town of Queensbury*, op. cit., 103. "The falls here are forty-five feet high, and afford a great water power."

4. In *History of Greenwich*, op. cit., 6. "At Center Falls it has a natural fall of 17 feet, at Middle Falls one of about 40 feet."

5. Washington County Planning Department, op. cit., 65. "Formerly known as Galesville, and before that as Arkansaw, it became Middle Falls in 1875."

Center Falls

1. Walter F. Burmeister, op. cit., 80. The waterfall consists of a "six-foot barrage above 20-foot falls."

2. Elisha P. Thurston, op. cit., 6, writes: "At Center Falls it has a natural fall of 17 feet." On p. 69, Thurston states: "Center Falls was formerly a lumbering district, the fine fall in the Battenkill offering excellent facilities for sawing. It was originally settled by Smith Barber and Nathan Rogers. ... In later years a paper mill was carried on by Isaac G. Parker and others."

3. *History of Washington County, New York: Some Chapters in the History of the Town of Easton*, op. cit., 105. "At Center Falls, formerly known as Hardscrabble, the river drops twenty-five feet. In the early years of the nineteenth century Smith Barber built a cotton mill on the Easton side of the river."

4. *An introduction to Historic Resources in Washington County*, op. cit., 64. "At one time it was known as Franklin, then later Hardscrabble because of the difficulty presented to horses getting up the nearby hill." Mention is also made of various cotton mills that operated in the early days and later evolved into other kinds of mills.

Buttermilk Falls (Schaghticoke)

1. Walter F. Burmeister, op. cit., 126. Between the Rt. 40 bridge and 1.5 miles south of the Hoosic River, the Tomhannock Creek "drops 207 feet (stream distance is two and one-half miles)." Burmeister describes the falls as a "series of abrupt cataracts."

2. Jim Capossela, on page 203 in *Good Fishing in the Catskills*, 2nd Edition (Woodstock, Vt.: Backcountry Publications, 1992), gives the dimensions of the Tomhannock Reservoir.

3. Warren Broderick, author and historian, Rensselaer County.

Great Falls of the Hoosic

1. Walter F. Burmeister, op. cit., 120, 121. Referring to the dam east of the bridge and the falls downstream from the base of the dam, Burmeister states that: "This 16-foot barrage sits above cataracts that drop 85 feet within two-fifths mile."

2. Warren Broderick, author and historian, Rensselaer County.

3. A picture of the falls can be found on page 59 in *A*

Resourceful People: A Pictorial History of Rensselaer County, New York (Norfolk, Va.: The Donning Company, 1987), by Rachel D. Bliven, et al. The picture shows the Schaghticoke Woolen Mill, along the north bank, across from the waterfall. Information is also provided about the Woolen Mill itself.

Hoosic Falls

1. Rachel D. Blivens, et al., op. cit., 59. A picture of the falls is presented. On page 72, the enormity of the Walter A. Wood Mowing and Reaping Machine Company is dramatically shown in a picture.

2. A. J. Weise, on page 86 in *History of the Seventeen Towns of Rensselaer County: from the Colonization of the Manor of Rensselaerwyck to the Present Time* (Troy, N.Y.: J. M. Francis & Tucker, 1889), provides significant background about the village of Hoosick Falls.

3. Arthur G. Adams, *The Hudson River Guidebook*, op. cit., 285. Background information on the various names and spelling of the Hoosic River is provided.

4. According to Shirley W. Dunn, on page 99 in *The Mohicans and Their Land. 1609–1730* (Fleischmanns, N.Y.: Purple Mountain Press, 1994), "The Hoosick River or its tributary, the Little Hoosick, was termed the 'Wappennakuis' or Fresh River."

5. Joseph A. Parker, on page 169 in *Looking Back: A History of Troy and Rensselaer County, 1925–1982* (Troy, N.Y.: n.p, 1980), writes, "Hoosick Falls became an industrial town when the falls of the Hoosic River was harnessed to turn machines."

6. General information on Hoosic Falls can be found in *Hoosic Falls Historic Guide* (Hoosic Valley, N.Y.: Hoosic Valley Publishing Co., 1990) by Charles Davidson.

Falls on Goulds Creek at North End of Oakwood Cemetery

1. Claire K. Schmitt, on pages 45–48 in *Natural Areas of Rensselaer County, New York* (New York: Rensselaer–Taconic Land Conservancy & Environmental Clearinghouse of Schenectady, Inc., 1994), gives a detailed account of the area's natural setting. A photograph of the fall in the Devil's Kitchen can also be seen on page 47.

2. In *Picturesque Oakwood: Its Past and Present Associations* (Troy, N.Y.: Frederick S. Hills, 1897), edited by DeWitt Clinton, the dimensions of Long Lake are provided on page 151, as well as mention that "At the outlet of Long Lake a waterfall has been formed which plunges down over rugged rocks to a ravine sixty or more feet in depth, and rushing over a series of rapids, again falls to the depth of 100 feet."

3. In *An Address Delivered at the Consecration of Oakwood Cemetery* (Troy, N.Y.: Troy Cemetery Association, 1850), the Hon. David Buel, Jr. stated: "Remarkably diversified in its formation, it embodies within its bounds deeply shaded glens, living fountains and gurgling brooks--gently swelling knolls, steep declivities, hills with slopes of various inclination, groves of evergreens, woods of oak and chestnut, walnut and beach, lawns of undulating surface and at intervals along its borders precipitous rocks. To these natural varieties the skill of the Engineer has added a group of charming little lakes, in the construction of which nature has been most successfully imitated and improved by art."

4. As an educated guess, it's quite possible that the name of Goulds Creek came from George Gould--a wealthy trial lawyer who served as mayor of Troy and later became a State Supreme Court justice.

5. Warren Broderick, author and historian, Rensselaer County.

Falls on Goulds Creek at South End of Oakwood Cemetery

1. Claire K. Schmitt, op. cit., 48. A picture of the upper falls is included with the text.

Factory Hollow Falls

1. Rachael Bliven, et al., op. cit, 112. A picture of the Tomhannock Reservoir taken by Gene Baxter is included. In order to create the reservoir in 1906, 1,700 acres were flooded and 80 homes displaced, creating a body of water 0.5 mile long and 2 miles wide. A pipe 8 miles long was constructed in order to transport the water to Troy.

2. Joseph A. Parker, op. cit., 185. "Another major product in the

town is its water in the Tomhannock Reservoir which holds an average of 12 billion gallons. Troy owns the reservoir and in addition to supplying its own residents, it sells its surplus to Menands, Rensselaer and sections of East Greenbush and Brunswick."

3. In *Pittstown Through The Years* (n.p.: Pittstown Historical Society, n.d.), compiled and edited by Evelyn Bornt, Beryl Harrington, and Ellen L. Wiley, interesting historical information on what types of mills once could be found along the banks of Sunkauissia Creek is provided.

Mount Ida Falls

1. Claire K. Schmitt, op. cit., 53. Information on the falls and the history of the gorge is provided. Photos of the falls in the main gorge can be seen on page 52, and of the upper fall on page 56.

2. Jacques Gerard Milbert, op. cit., 45–46. "Beyond this promenade are the foothills, from whose gorge emerges a pretty brook called the Poesten [kill]. As you follow its course through one beautiful spot after another, you may see in the midst of a green landscape dark rocks worn by the waters of numerous cataracts formed by melting snow. Again you glimpse the Poesten itself flowing from cascade to cascade beneath a thick canopy of evergreens, then farther along the brook slows its course and spreads out into reservoirs. Industry has skillfully forced the stream to provide power for factories on the mountain slopes."

3. An 1885 photo of the falls, gorge and bridge spanning the creek at the base of the falls can be seen on page 45 in *Images of America: Troy* (Charleston, S.C.: Arcadia Publishing, 1998) by Don Rittner.

4. The *Hudson Mohawk Gateway: An Illustrated History* (Northridge, Ca.: Windsor Publications, 1985), by Thomas Phelan, contains multiple pictures of the falls: an early-19th-century lithograph made from a painting by T. Milbert, showing an idealized view of the falls, as though you could look straight through the contours of the gorge, on page 132; a picture of the falls on page 114 with eight RPI students in the foreground, taken in 1888; and a picture of the gorge on page 24 showing water issuing from a tunnel in the upper, north bank of the ravine.

5. Rachel D. Bliven, et al., op. cit., 40–41. A picture of the

Griswold Wire Works, Thompkins Brother Machine Works, J. A. Manning Paper Company, and Mount Ida Cotton Factory (later known as Wultex) can be seen. The authors also mention that all of the mills and structures along the north bank of the Poesten Kill were destroyed in the great flood of 1938, caused by a hurricane.

6. Florence M. Hill, *West of Perigo: Poestenkill Memories* (Troy, N.Y.: n.p., 1979), 106.

7. Warren Broderick, author and historian, Rensselaer County.

8. Patricia Edwards Clyne, "After the Falls: A Collection of Valley Cascades," *Hudson Valley* (Sept. 1999), 20.

Eagle Mills Falls

1. A. J. Weise, op. cit., 105. Substantial history on the hamlet's industrial past is provided.

2. Rachel D. Bliven, et al., op. cit., 64. Included is a picture of Eagle Mills (then known as Millville) with a sawmill, foundry, carriage house, hotel, and general store. The authors mention a "drop of twenty-five feet" in the stream at Eagle Mills.

Falls on Little Hoosic

1. Walter F. Burmeiser, op. cit., 123.

2. In *Petersburgh, Then & Now: A Photographic Comparison* (Town of Petersburgh, N.Y.: n.p., 1991), by Peter R. W. Schaaphok, two photographs of the falls can be seen, taken from the same spot, but possibly in different centuries. One shows the falls, dammed, next to a covered bridge; the other shows the falls no longer dammed, next to the present stone bridge.

3. In *The Mohawk Trail: Historic Auto Trail Guide* (Brookline, Mass.: Muddy River Press, 2003), on page 54 a picture of the bridge spanning the Little Hoosic River can be seen.

4. Joseph A. Parker, op. cit., 183. "The Little Hoosic River in a freak July 1, 1973 flood caused considerable havoc along its banks, including damage to about 30 trailers and several cars at Vista Campgrounds."

Falls on Wynants Kill, including Burden Falls

1. Nathaniel Bartlett Sylvester, op. cit., 231. "The Wynantskill has here worn a deep and wide gorge through the slate rock, and runs down in a series of irregular rapids and cascades into the Hudson."

2. Claire K. Schmitt, *Natural Areas of Rensselaer County*, op. cit., 59. A winter photo of Burden Pond, complete with dozens of skaters on the ice, is presented.

3. Thomas Phelen, op. cit., 143. A picture of the dam taken by G. Steven Draper in the lower Wynants Kill Gorge, downstream from Burden Falls, can be seen.

4. Don Rittner, op. cit., 87. An old map is shown revealing the location of some of the factories and mills along the Wynants Kill near its confluence with the Hudson River.

5. Sand Lake Historical Society, *Historical Highlights*, Vol. 24, No. 2 (Winter 1998), 3.

Barberville Falls

1. Claire K. Schmitt, *Natural Areas of Rensselaer County*, op. cit., 123–126. A chapter is devoted to Barberville Falls. A photograph of the fall can be seen on page 125.

2. In "Taking the Plunge," *Hudson Valley*, Vol. XXXIII, No. 1 (May 2004), Polly Sparling gives a succinct history of Barberville Falls. On page 22, she states that the "Remnants of an old mill––including a foundation and part of a spill-way––are evident at the summit." Sparling goes on to state that "Local legend has it that the mill and bridge were left incomplete when one of the project's partners ran off with most of the capital." A pretty picture of the fall, thawing out from winter, also accompanies the piece.

3. Beulah Bailey Thull, *Dictionary of Place Names of Rensselaer County, 1609–1971* (pamphlet, 1971), 1.

4. Joseph A. Parker, op. cit., 191. "The same year the Nature Conservancy received the Barberville Falls on the Poestenkill (creek) as a gift." This would be the year 1967.

5. Rachael Bliven, et al., op. cit., 189. A photograph of the old Moon's Hotel, taken by Kathe Forster, is shown.

6. Patricia Edwards Clyne, "After the Falls," op. cit., 20.

Falls at Rensselaer Technology Park

1. Claire K. Schmitt, *Natural Areas of Rensselaer County*, op. cit., 66.

2. Warren Broderick, author and historian, Rensselaer County.

3. Brochures distributed on "Tech Park Trails" by the North Greenbush Trail Committee, North Greenbush Town Offices, 2 Douglas Street, Wynantskill, New York 12198, provide information about the park and its trails.

Red Mill Falls

1. Douglas L. Sinclair, *Three Villages, One City* (Rensselaer County, N.Y.: City of Rensselaer Historical Society, 1974). On page 11, Sinclair mentions that Mill Creek was earlier called Huyck Stream. Pictures/drawings of the falls and of the W. P. Irwin Flour Mill can be found on pages 11 and 74. On page 74, Sinclair quotes an unnamed writer who visited the fall in 1800: "walked to cascade at Rensselaer Mills. ... Has a very different character to Lowdore Falls near Keswick Lake England but I think it would be generally more admired. A saw mill erected on the verge of the fall greatly improves its effect. In winter and spring this cascade is visible from Albany."

2. Warren Broderick, author and historian, Rensselaer County.

3. Beulah Bailey Thull, op. cit., 10.

4. Alfred B. Street, *The Poems of Alfred B. Street*, Vol. II (New York: Hurd and Houghton, 1867).

Fall on Upper Wynants Kill

1. A. M. Weise, op. cit., 142.

Fall on Burden Lake Road

1. A picture of the fall and bridge, taken from downstream, can be seen on page 72 in *Images of America: West Sand Lake* (Charleston, S.C.: Arcadia, 2001) by Mary D. French and Robert J. Lilly.

2. Joseph A. Parker, op. cit., 195. Burden Lake was originally known as Martin's Lake, but was changed to the latter name to honor Henry Burden, who operated a renowned factory near the Wynants Kill's confluence with the Hudson River.

Falls on Black River

1. Claire K. Schmitt, op. cit., 85–92. Schmitt devotes an entire chapter to the waterfall.

Mattison Hollow Cascade

1. Claire K. Schmitt, Norton G. Miller, Warren F. Broderick, John T. Keenan, and William D. Niemi, *Natural Areas of Rensselaer County* 2d Edition (Schenectady/Troy, N.Y.: The Rensselaer–Taconic Land Conservancy & Environmental Clearinghouse of Schenectady, Inc., 2002), 113. A picture of Mattison Hollow Falls (referred to as Davis Cascade in the picture), taken by James E. West around 1890, can be seen on page 114.

2. Rachel D. Bliven et. al., op. cit., 63. The authors provide a wonderful picture of the charcoal sheds which once existed along the hike up to Mattison Hollow Falls. In the background, you can see the two-car inclined railroad track that was gravity-powered, bringing lumber down to the kilns.

Falls on Tsatsawassa Creek

1. A. J. Weise, op. cit., 126.

2. Warren Broderick, author and historian, Rensselaer County.

3. Philip L. Lord, in *Mills on the Tsatsawassa: techniques for documenting early 19th-century water-powered industry in rural New York, a case study* (Albany, N.Y.: University of the State of New York, State Education Department, Division of Historical and Anthropological Services, 1983), provides background information on the past mills.

Falls in East Nassau

1. Wallace Nutting, op. cit., 58.

2. A. J. Weise, op. cit., 126. Mention is made that the town formed near the confluence of Kinderhook Creek and Tackawasick Creek was earlier known as Schermerhorns, after John W. Schermerhorn, a tavern owner.

Fall on Moordener Kill

1. Walter F. Burmeister, op. cit., 62. "There are falls within a

constricted gorge, dropping 110 feet along a three-fifths mile stretch."

2. Joseph A. Parker, op. cit., 201–202. Parker mentions the fact that the Fort Orange Company became part of the Sutherland Paper Company in 1955; then was acquired by the Brown Company in 1966; only to become the Fort Orange Paper Company, Inc., again in 1978.

3. Specific details about the Paper Factory are described in *Castleton History* (1948; reprint, n.p: Kiwanis Project, 1976). On the inside cover of the booklet can be seen the plant in the early 1900s following a boiler explosion.

4. Rachel D. Bliven, et. al., op. cit., 65.

5. Wallace Bruce, in *The Hudson: Three Centuries of History, Romance, and Invention*, Centennial Edition (New York: Walking News Inc., 1982), makes mention on page 179 of how the stream came to be named: a "sad story of a girl tied by Indians to a horse and dragged through the valley."

Falls on Muitzes Kill

1. Shirley W. Dunn, op. cit., 175. "The stream to be sold, called Paponicuck in the Mohican tongue, emptied into the Hudson River from the east. A beautiful divided waterfall was located close to its mouth. This creek is today called the Muitzeskill." The waterfall referred to is the one just a short distance upstream from the lowermost fall. Dunn goes on to mention on page 175 that "The stream was in the area where some Mohicans of Schodack had been receiving furs from the Mohawks and transporting them to English traders."

2. A. J. Weise, op. cit., 75.

3. In *The Muitzeskill Historic District: A typical 19th-century farm hamlet* (n.p.: Historical Society of Esquatak, 1976) valuable material is contained about how the creek came to be named, and the types of mills which once inhabited the banks of the stream.

Falls in Valatie

1. Walter F. Burmeister, op. cit., 260. "A dam blocks the northern channel while the southern arms drop over a 10-foot cataract."

2. The *History of Columbia County, New York: with illustrations and biographic sketches of some of its prominent men and pioneers*

(1878; limited facsimile edition, Old Chatham, N.Y.: Sachem Press, 1974) points out on page 226 that Valatie is the Dutch term for "little falls," used to distinguish it from the "great falls" at Stuyvesant Falls.

3. Reed Sparling, in "Valatie Now & Then," *Hudson Valley*, Vol. XXXIII, No. 2 (June 2004), on pages 17–20 provides considerable background on the town of Valatie, both past and present, including Pachaquak Park.

Davenport Falls

1. Mrs. Frank Randell, Sr., *And So It Was: Yesteryear in the Punsit Valley* (Spencertown, N.Y.: Griswold Publishing, 1993), 20. "It supplies the Taylor pond and crossing the road falls a sheer 25 feet forming a picturesque falls. (An Indian killing took place in this ravine and, while owned by Beach, still retains the name Davenport's Falls)." On page 13, Randell states that "Below the falls was another mill said to have made ox-yokes."

2. In *The Capital Region of New York State: Crossroads of Empire*, Vol. II (New York: Lewis Historical Publishing Company, Inc., 1942), Francis P. Kimball mentions on page 365 that a Spencertown resident named Beal built the forerunner to today's lawn mowing machine in the 1830s.

Falls in Beebe Hill State Forest

1. In "Hidden Treasures," *Hudson Valley*, Vol. XXXIII, No. 1 (May 2004), on page 20 Reed Sparling provides interesting background on the sixty-foot-high Beebe Hill firetower located in another section of the state forest.

Stuyvesant Falls

1. Walter F. Burmeister, op. cit., 257. The upper dam fall is a "six-foot barrage above 22-foot falls," and the lower dam fall is a "Two-to-3-foot barrage above 30-foot falls."

2. In *Our Historic Hudson* (Roosevelt, N.Y.: James B. Adler, Inc., 1968), by John S. Dyson, Stuyvesant Falls is described on page 32 as "two sets of falls, one forty-five feet tall and the other twenty-six feet"—a figure which seems to tally with that given by other writers.

3. *History of Columbia County*, op. cit., 355. Jasper Dankers and

Peter Sluyter are quoted from their 1680 journal: "The water falls quite steep in one body, but it comes down in steps, with a broad rest between them. These steps are sixty feet or more high, and are formed out of a single rock." On pages 357–358, the authors of the book state that "Unusual good water-power is here afforded by Kinderhook Creek, by two natural falls of forty-five feet and twenty-six feet in height, and about forty rods apart. At the foot of the lower and greater falls the waters of the channel are divided by a point of rock nearly a hundred feet in height, which forms the headland of an island containing about twenty acres of land." This description refers to the lower and upper falls respectively. Extensive history on the various mills in operation at Stuyvesant Falls is contained on page 358.

4. Howard Stone, *25 Bicycle Tours in the Hudson Valley: Scenic Rides from Saratoga to West Point* (Woodstock, Vt.: Backcountry Publications, 1989), 74.

Rossman Falls

1. Walter F. Burmeister, op. cit., 257. The fall consists of a "5-foot barrage above 20-foot falls."

2. In *History of Columbia County,* op. cit., 347, reference is made to Rossman's Falls—called Chittendens Falls at that time: "The other streams have, in the town, falls whose aggregate height is more than one-hundred and fifty feet; and natural water-power is afforded at Stottsville, Stockport, Chittendens Falls, and Columbiaville."

Fall on Fitting Creek

1. Walter F. Burmeister, op. cit., 204.

2. William M. Gazda, *Place Names in New York* (Schenectady, N.Y.: Gazda Associates, Inc. 1997), 76.

Fall on Claverack Creek

1. Walter F. Burmeister, op. cit., 200.

2. *History of Columbia County,* op. cit., 349. "Claverack creek here makes a descent of fifty-three feet in three successive falls, affording excellent water-power, which is used in operating Stott's

woolen mills." On the same page, the authors recount how the town was originally known as Springville until it was re-named Stottville in honor of John Stott, who operated a woolen mill there. Specific information is also provided on the Van Rensselaers, who ran a sawmill and gristmill.

3. Margaret B. Schram, *Hudson's Merchants and Whalers: The Rise and Fall of a River Port, 1783–1850* (Hensonville, N.Y.: Black Dome Press Corp., 2004), 9.

Cascade on Fish Creek

1. Walter F. Burmeister, op. cit., 114. "Approximately one-fifth mile below Schuylerville Dam the creek falls over a 3-to-4-foot ledge."

2. Jacques Gerard Milbert, op. cit., 47. "I soon reached Fish Creek, which rises in Saratoga Lake and drops a remarkable distance before emptying in the Hudson." Milbert also states, on page 48, "I visited the deep gorges where water escapes from Lake Saratoga to form Fish Creek."

3. Violet B. Dunn, op. cit. On page 572 historical information related to the area next to the cascade is provided.

4. Francis R. Taormina, in *Philip Schuyler: Who He Was, What He Did* (Schenectady, N.Y.: n.p., 1992), mentions on page 9 that "Schuyler built the first water driven flax mill in New York."

Buttermilk Falls (Cohoes)

1. Claire K. Schmitt and Mary S. Brennan, in *Natural Areas of Albany County* (Niskayuna, N.Y.: The Environmental Clearinghouse of Schenectady, 1991), provide information on Peebles Island on page 25, including a map of the island on page 24 showing the rapids which constitute Buttermilk Falls.

Cohoes Falls

1. Betty Ahearn Buckell, op. cit., 173. Johannes Megapolensis Jr.'s 1644 account of visiting Cohoes Falls is quoted: "There it [the Mohawk] flows between two high rocky banks and falls from a height equal to that of a church, with such a noise that we can sometimes hear it here with us. ... When we came there we saw not only the river falling with such a noise that we could hardly hear

one another, but the water boiling and dashing with such force in still weather, that it seemed all the time as if it were raining."

2. Walter F. Burmeister, op. cit., 272. "The final and most dramatic effect of the Mohawk, the famous Cohoes Falls, have been robbed of their water and are but a shadow of their former glory."

3. Joel Munsell, *The History of Cohoes, New York: From its Earliest Settlement to the Present Time* (1877; reprint, n.p.: Cohoes Historical Society, 1969). Many early sightings of the falls, going back into the 1600s, are cited on pages 1–14. On page 1, mention is made of how Cohoes came to be named.

4. According to Jean S. Olton (town historian and compiler), on page 52 of *The Town of Colonie: A Pictorial History* (Town of Colonie, N.Y.: n.p., 1980), "Gerrit Lansing established his grist mill near the Cohoes Falls on the Mohawk River opposite the present day factories in Watervliet and Cohoes."

5. Reed Sparling, in "City of Surprises," *Hudson Valley*, Vol. XXXIII, No. 6 (October 2004), talks about the history of the city of Cohoes on pages 21–24, including a picture taken of Cohoes Falls by Richard Buttlar on page 21.

6. C. R. Roseberry, in *Albany: Three Centuries a County* (Albany, N.Y.: Tricentennial Commission, 1983), talks about the origin of the name Cohoes on page 33. A picture of the fall is also included.

Buttermilk Falls, Underground

1. John J. McEneny, on page 73 in *Albany: Capital City on the Hudson, An Illustrated History* (Sun Valley, Ca.: American Historical Press, 1998), writes that the Beaverkill "included a stream, barely visible today at the bottom of the great ravine to the south of Park Avenue, with a pond at the bottom known as Rocky Ledge. The adjoining Hinckel (later Dobler) Brewery dumped its effluent suds into the water supply, thus giving the area its more common descriptive name of Buttermilk Falls."

2. Howell and Tenny, op. cit., 15. "The Beaver or Buttermilk, Rutten, and Foxen Kills, in Albany, are used now mostly for sewer drainage." Can there be a worse and more undignified fate for a waterfall than this?

3. In *Images of America: Albany* (Charleston, S.C.: Arcadia Publishing, 2000), Don Rittner writes on page 116 that the "Beaver Kill, or Buttermilk Falls, was once a beautiful park—today, only the ravine is still there. In the 19th century, some protests arose over the destruction of the waterfall. ... Today, the area is part of Lincoln Pond."

4. Charlotte Wilcoxen, *Seventeeth Century Albany: A Dutch Profile* (Albany, N.Y.: Education Department, Albany Institute of History and Art, 1981), 51. Wilcoxen mentions on page 51 that "there were several other breweries there in the 1650's, one being that of Jacob Gerritsen, probably located on the Beaverkill." According to Wilcoxen, on page 29, there were originally five kills (or streams) in Albany.

5. *History of Columbia County, New York*, op. cit., 73. Material is provided on Beaver Park, the Beaverkill, and Buttermilk Falls.

6. Jean S. Olton, op. cit., 52. "The small creeks which abound in the vicinity of Albany and Watervliet were early utilized in producing power for grinding wheat and other grain."

7. In an article by Duncan Campbell Crary, "Rediscovering the Beaverkill," in *Capital Neighbors: Newspaper for and about Albany's Historic Neighborhoods*, Vol. 8, No. 1 (week of March 11, 2002), an interesting story is told about the Beaverkill: "According to William Kennedy's *Oh Albany!*, a group of Mohawk Indians surprised a party of Dutchmen near the Beaverkill in 1626 and cannibalized Tymen Bouwensen, one of the men in the party." Also of interest is the fact that James Hall, the eminent nineteenth-century, New York State geologist lived nearby and built his lab near the Beaverkill.

Falls on Lower Normans Kill

1. Walter F. Burmeister, op. cit., 296. The falls are "a step-like series of formidable ledges that have the appearance of a gigantic staircase dropping 30 feet within 130 yards."

2. Roland Van Zandt, op. cit., 23. Jasper Danker gives this account of the Normans Kill in 1680: "There are two high falls on this kill, where the beautiful green water comes falling over incessantly, in a manner wonderful to behold. ... The water was the greenest I had observed, not only on the South River, but in all of New

Netherlands. ... At the falls on this river stands a fine saw-mill." It's possible that Danker may be talking about falls further upstream.

3. Betty Ahearn Buckell, op. cit., 123. The Normans Kill was named after Albert Adriaensen Bradt de Norman.

4. Shirley W. Dunn, op. cit., 84. "The Normanskill dropped as it went through the countryside, providing later mill sites for the Dutch, and ended with some rapids near its mouth. ... In the nineteenth century, a milling community called Kenwood developed at this location."

5. C. G. Hine, in *Albany to Tappan: The West Bank of the Hudson River* (1906; facsimile, Astoria, N.Y.: J. C. & A. L. Fawcett, Inc., n.d.), offers history of the lower Normanskill, 3–7.

6. Benson J. Lossing, op. cit., 141. "Norman's-Kill (the Indian Tawasentha, or Place of many Dead) ... comes down from the region of the lofty Helderbergs."

7. In *Stubborn for Liberty: The Dutch in New York* (Syracuse, N.Y.: Syracuse University Press, 1975), Alice P. Kenney mentions on pages 18–19 that Fort Nassau was established on Castle Island (now part of the Port of Albany) by the New Netherland Company. The redoubt was surrounded by a moat eighteen feet wide, had a complement of cannons, and a garrison of ten to twelve men. The fort was not destroyed by attackers, however, but rather by the annual flood swells of the Hudson, in 1617. According to tradition, Jacob Eelkins then rebuilt a fort on the nearby banks of the Normanskill. Legend has it that the first treaty between the Dutch and Mohawks was conducted from here. There is no evidence that either of these two accounts is true, although most historians suspect the former to be so.

Fall on Vloman Kill

1. Walter F. Burmeister, op. cit., 61, 62. Descriptions of the stream and falls are provided.

Falls on Coeymans Creek

1. Walter F. Burmeister, op. cit., 63. "The creek has eroded a picturesque gorge directly west of the Hudson."

2. A picture of an old mill at the mouth of Coeymans Creek, followed by a mill and dam just upstream, can be seen in Edward D.

Gidding's *Coeymans and the Past* (Coeymans, N.Y.: Tricentennial Committee of the Town of Coeymans, 1973).

3. C. R. Roseberry, op. cit., 14. "The best location for this purpose was where the Onesquethaw tumbled 75 feet over cascades to meet the Hudson." Here, Roseberry is referring to mill sites established by Barent Coeymans. It should be noted that Onesquethaw Creek flows into Coeymans Creek; therefore, it is Coeymans Creek that tumbles seventy-five feet over cascades to meet the Hudson River.

Ravena Falls

1. Claire K. Schmitt, et al., op. cit., 66, 67.

2. Walter F. Burmeister, op. cit., 63. The cascade is described as a "10-foot" waterfall, although it is not actually mentioned by name. Burmeister goes on to say that several miles upstream is Deans Mill, where a "60-foot high array of cataracts" can be found.

3. Town of New Baltimore Bicentennial Committee, *The Heritage of New Baltimore* (New Baltimore, N.Y.: Town of New Baltimore, 1976). Mention is made of the Croswell Paper Mill on page 102. A photograph of the fall and mill dam can be seen on page 103.

4. The upper falls referred to on Hannacroix Creek is located at Deans Mill in Aquetuck. In *History of Greene County, 1651–1800*, Vol. I (1927; reprint, Cornwallville, N.Y.: Hope Farm Press, 1985), J. Van Vechten Vedder mentions on page 111 that the first mill on the site at Deans Mill was deeded to Solomon Skinner, around 1780.

Falls on Coxsackie Creek

1. Walter F. Burmeister, op. cit., 63.

2. Wallace Bruce, op. cit., 175, states that the name is "derived from Kaak-aki, or place of wild geese. 'Aki' in Indian signifies place and it is singular to find the Indian word 'kaak' so near to the English 'cackle.'"

3. Raymond Beecher, in *Under Three Flags* (Hensonville, N.Y.: Black Dome Press Corp., 1991) devotes two pages, 12–13, to the possible derivations and meaning of the word "Coxsackie." Beecher also notes, on page 78, that at one time Coxsackie was the center of the Hudson River's ice trade.

Falls on Tributary to Cob Creek

1. Raymond Beecher, op. cit., 53. It was postmaster George H. Scott who stated, "We've got a Surprise and a Result, how about a Climax?" And so it was. Up until then the hamlet was known as Guinea Hill.

Cantine Falls

1. Walter F. Burmeister, op. cit., 232. The Saugerties Dam is described as a "7-foot barrage located above 35-foot falls," dropping (page 241) "over a pronounced ledge formation."

2. Benson J. Lossing, op. cit, 172.

3. Arthur G. Adams, on page 354 in *The Catskills: An Illustrated Historical Guide with Gazetteer* (New York: Fordham University Press, 1990), provides a brief history of Saugerties and how it came to be named.

Glenerie Falls

1. Walter F. Burmeister, op. cit., 241. On page 240 Burmeister writes: "Glenerie Falls is formed by a huge 50-foot high solid bench of rock of relatively smooth convex conformation. From the crest to its base the formation extends about 300 yards." Later, on the same page, he describes the lower, near-roadside waterfall as a "long diagonally positioned edge with a 7-foot drop."

2. Arthur G. Adams, *The Catskills: An Illustrated Historical Guide with Gazetteer*, op. cit., 262. A lead work was formerly at the falls.

3. Marc B. Fried, *The Early History of Kingston & Ulster County* (Marbletown, N.Y.: Ulster County Historical Society, 1975), 80.

Falls at Ashokan Field Campus— Winchell Falls, Little Falls, & Cathedral Falls

1. Materials obtained from Ashokan Field Campus, and from consultation with Tim Neu, Director of the Ashokan Field Campus.

Fall along Shaupeneak Ridge

1. Jeffrey Perls, on page 296 in *Paths along the Hudson: A Guide to Walking and Biking* (New Brunswick, N.J.: Rutgers University

Press, 1999), describes it as a "small picturesque waterfall." Perls mentions on page 295 that the property once belonged to a private hunting club, and describes the rocks forming Shaupeneak Ridge as being Ordovician.

2. According to Stella Green and H. Neil Zimmerman on page 245 in *50 Hikes in the Lower Hudson Valley* (Woodstock, Vt.: Backcountry Guides, 2002), "The waterfall is on an unnamed stream in a mossy grotto and runs except in drought conditions."

3. A picture of the fall, taken by Tom Ligamari, can be seen in a brochure entitled *Scenic Hudson: Adventure Guide to Parks, Preserves and Trails* (Poughkeepsie, N.Y.: Scenic Hudson, Inc., n.d.), which is distributed at a number of sites that Scenic Hudson oversees.

4. Peggy Turco, in *Walks and Rambles in the Western Hudson Valley: Landscape, Ecology, & Folklore in Orange & Ulster Counties* (Woodstock, Vt.: Backcountry Publications, 1996), on pages 120–124 provides a whole chapter on the hike, including a map.

Fall #1 & Fall #2 at John Burroughs Sanctuary

1. Peggy Turco, *Walks and Rambles in the Western Hudson Valley*, op. cit., 115–119. Turco devotes a chapter to the sanctuary and includes a map.

2. Jeffrey Perls, op. cit., 293–294. Information on the John Burroughs Sanctuary is provided.

Fall on Black Creek

1. Walter F. Burmeister, op. cit., page 68, writes that to get to see "a series of magnificent falls" involves a 3.5-mile hike through rugged terrain.

2. Jeffrey Perls, op. cit., 294. "Nearby is Black Creek, which descends from here toward the Hudson in a beautiful series of falls."

3. In "John Burroughs and His River View," *The Conservationist* (March–April, 1982), Edward J. Renehan, Jr. presents a picture of John Burroughs sitting next to a slablike cascade that might very well may be the one at this location on Black Creek.

4. Edward J. Renehan, Jr., *John Burroughs: An American Naturalist* (Hensonville, N.Y.: Black Dome Press Corp., 1992), 183.

Fall at the Tuthilltown Gristmill & Country Store

1. In *New York: Off the Beaten Path*, 4th Edition (Old Saybrook, Conn.: The Globe Pequot Press, 1977) by William G. & Kay Scheller, there is a line drawing of the mill and fall on page 208.

2. Ralph Erenzo, current owner.

3. Beatrice M. Mattice, on pages 89–90 in *They Walked These Hills Before Me: An early history of the Town of Conesville* (Cornwallville, N.Y.: Hope Farm Press, 1980), describes the history of mills and waterwheels.

Wright Falls

1. C. G. Hine, op. cit., 117–118. "The hill which modestly poses here as the river bank (we are in Marlboro) affords the creek an opportunity for some grand and lofty tumbling before it reaches the lower level. The series of beautiful falls and rapids thus formed were early turned to account by the major, whose mill is an ancient landmark."

2. Walter F. Burmeister, op. cit., 70. "One can ascend Marlboro Creek for two-fifths mile and then walk to the foot of falls that drop 200 feet within one-half mile. The lower, most pronounced declivity drops 100 feet within 100 yards."

3. Jeffrey Perls, op. cit., 289. Marlboro is described as "Perched on a bluff overlooking the falls and valley of the Old Man's Kill where it enters the Hudson."

4. Nathaniel Bartlett Sylvester, on page 75 of *History of Ulster County, New York: With Illustrations and Biographical Sketches of its Prominent Men and Pioneers* (Philadelphia, Pa.: Everts & Peck, 1880), gives information on the village of Marlboro.

Horseshoe Falls

1. Walter F. Burmeister, op. cit., 343. "The Wallkill forms a picturesque gorge where it drops from one plateau to the next lower elevation level."

2. Marc Newman, in *Images of America: Walden and Maybrook* (Charleston, S.C.: Arcadia Publishing, 2001), on pages 14, 21, and 42 provides extensive history on the mills and factories that utilized the hydropower of the Wallkill at Walden, and presents pictures of Horseshoe Falls.

Bash Bish Falls

1. Wallace Bruce, op. cit., 171. "A mile brings one to the lower falls; the upper falls are about a quarter of a mile further up the gorge. The height of the falls, with the rapids between, is about 300 feet above the little rustic bridge at the foot of the lower falls."

2. *History of Columbia County*, op. cit., 387. "The Bash Bish gorge is a very picturesque one, and the falls at the place where the stream breaks through the last rocky barrier, on the western face of the mountain, present a very beautiful appearance."

3. According to Charles W. G. Smith, on page 37 in *Nature Walks in the Berkshire Hills* (Boston, Mass.: Appalachian Mountain Club Books, 1997), "As the brook exits the mouth of the gorge it plummets down the final escarpment in two separate whitewater plunges divided by a massive gray godstone."

4. A photo of Bash Bish Falls can be seen on the cover of the *Massachusetts and Rhode Island Trail Guide*, 7th Edition (Boston, Mass.: Appalachian Mountain Club Books, 1995).

5. A picture of Bash Bish Falls graces the cover of Rene Laubach's *A Guide to Natural Places in the Berkshire Hills* (Stockbridge, Mass.: Berkshire House Publishers, 1992). Laubach states on page 33 that "Bash Bish Falls is the most spectacular waterfall in Berkshire. The falls are composed of two portions, with the lower splitting in two around a huge boulder and plunging 80 foot into a clear green pool. ... Bash Bish Brook has cut a 1,000-foot-deep gorge through which it flows into neighboring New York."

6. A picture of Bash Bish Falls can be seen in *The Berkshires through the Camera of Arthur Palme* (n.p.: Palme–Grove Publishing Company, 1951), pages not numbered.

7. Michael Lanza, in *New England Hiking: the Complete Guide to More than 350 of the Best Hikes in New England* (San Francisco, Ca.: Foghorn Press, 1997), states on page 308 that Bash Bish Brook "tumbles down through a vertical stack of giant boulders—splitting into twin columns of water around one huge, triangular block."

8. Elizabeth L. Dugger, in *Adventure Guide to Massachusetts and Western Connecticut* (Edison, N.J.: Hunter, 1999), describes the falls on page 354 as "twin torrents cascading mostly down 80 feet of rock face."

9. According to Anna Mundow on page 186 in *Southern New*

England (Oakland, Ca.: Compass American Guides, 1999) Bash Bish Falls is "the most dramatic waterfall in Southern New England."

10. In *Play Hard, Rest Easy. New England: The Ultimate Active Getaway Guide* (Charlotte, N.C.: Walkabout Press, Inc., 2001), on page 61 Malcolm W. Campbell describes the fall as "where water from Bash Bish Brook tumbles 200 feet, ending in a Fantasy Island-like pool at the bottom."

11. A marvelous line drawing of Bash Bish Falls can be seen on page 151 and next to the title page of Clark W. Bryan's *The Book of Berkshire* (1887; reprint, North Egremont, Mass.: Past Perfect Books, 1993). Bryan writes on page 152 that "Just opposite the perpendicular north end of Alandar, after plunging 200 feet, in all, down through a narrow rocky gorge, whose sides tower 200 and 300 feet above, over several precipitous slopes that, taken together, are the noted Bash Bish Falls; and just after the last leap of sixty feet, where the water is divided by a huge boulder on the brink, the stream turns sharp to the west, and goes dancing away to join the Hudson."

12. Greg Parsons and Kate B. Watson, op. cit., page 86. "Bash Bish Falls is a segmented 80-foot drop of Bash Bish Brook. ... A large boulder splits the falls into two sections, only then to ricochet off a rock wall and rejoin at the base. With a little imagination you could even claim that the falls take on the shape of a diamond." A picture of the fall can be seen on page 87.

13. In *Autumn Rambles of New England: An Explorer's Guide to the Best Fall Colors* (Edison, N.J.: Hunter Publishing, Inc., 1998), on page 68, Michael & Mark Tougias describe the cataract as an "80-foot falls."

14. A photograph of the fall can be seen in Bradford B. Van Diver's *Roadside Geology* (Missoula, Mont.: Mountain Press Publishing Company, 1985) on page 105. On page 106 Van Diver writes that Bash Bish Brook cuts through an "impressive mountain rampart, which rises more than 1600 feet from the valley" and "is sustained by metamorphosed shales and graywackes in an erosionally separated thrust slice, or klippe, whose western base lies near the foot of the slope visible from the road."

15. In *The Audubon Society Field Guide to the Natural Places of the Northeast: Inland* (New York: The Hilltown Press, Inc., 1984), by

Stephen Kulik, et al., the authors write on page 68 that "Bash Bish Falls drops 200 feet in a series of cascades that cut through the granite and schist outcroppings forming the steep walls of the gorge."

16. In *Hikes & Walks in the Berkshire Hills* (Stockbridge, Mass.: Berkshire House Publishing, 1990), on page 50 Lauren R. Stevens writes: "Bash Bish Brook was formed by the melting of the last glacier, 10,000 to 12,000 years ago. The quartz dike, halfway up the falls, was forced out of the earth 400 million years ago. As the sediment in the brook works in the water, it gradually destroys Bash Bish Falls."

17. In *The Berkshires: The Purple Hills* (New York: The Vanguard Press, Inc., 1948), edited by Roderick Peattie, pages 264–267 are devoted to "The Spirit of Bash Bish Falls."

18. www.berkshireweb.com

19. Roeliff-Jansen Historical Society, *A History of the Roeliff Jansen Area: A historical review of five townships in Columbia County, New York* (Columbia County, N.Y.: The Roeliff-Jansen Historical Society, 1990). The authors mention on page 30 that Douglas' Inn was established at the base of Bash Bish Falls. After the business failed, the building remained vacant for several years until it was torn down and the lumber used to construct several cottages at the Copake Iron Works. A picture postcard of the Bash Bash Inn is also presented.

20. A great deal of Bash Bish Fall's history is outlined on the kiosk at the parking lot.

Fall on Roeliff Jansen Kill (Bingham Mills)

1. Walter F. Burmeister, op. cit., 304. The falls are described as a "series of ledges that tilt 35 feet within 65 yards."

Fall on Roeliff Jansen Kill (Ancram)

1. Walter F. Burmeister, op. cit., page 304, writes that you will find "cataracts totaling 30 feet." On the same page Burmeister also mentions that the stream was once known as Livingston Creek.

2. Patricia Edwards Clyne, "After the Falls," op. cit., 19. A picture of the fall, with upper dam and stone bridge further upstream, can be seen.

3. *The Mill on the Roeliff Jansen Kill: 250 Years of American*

Industrial History (Hensonville, N.Y.: Black Dome Press Corp., 1993), edited by Harold Faber, provides relevant information about the history of the mill and falls. A picture of the dam can be seen on page 49.

4. Roeliff Jansen Historical Society, op. cit., 25. A picture of the falls, dam, and stone bridge is presented.

5. Arthur G. Adams, *The Hudson River Guidebook*, op. cit., 244. Insight is provided on how the stream came to be named.

6. Francis P. Kimball, op. cit., 363. Mention is made of how Ancram was named.

7. Patricia Edwards Clyne, *Hudson Valley Tales and Trails* (Woodstock, N.Y.: The Overlook Press, 1990), 25.

White Clay Kill Falls

1. *New York Walk Book*, 6th Edition (New York: New York–New Jersey Trail Conference, 1998), makes mention on page 176 of a waterfall near Tivoli Bay.

2. Jeffrey Perls, op. cit., 356. Perls states that Stony Creek is also known as White Clay Kill, which is how the name of the falls arose.

3. Cynthia C. Lewis and Thomas Lewis, in *Best Hikes with Children in the Catskills & Hudson River Valley* (Seattle, Wash.: The Mountaineers, 1992), describe the hike past the waterfall to Tivoli Bay.

4. The Dutchess County Tourism website, www.dutchess-tourism.com/dtours, provides information about the Tivoli Bay area and Henry Hudson's 1609 visit.

5. In *New York: A Guide to the Empire State* (New York: Oxford University Press, 1940), compiled by writers of the Writers Program of the Works Project Administration in the State of New York, the authors state on page 610 how Tivoli came to be named, which is a rather interesting story. Following the French Revolution, Peter de Labigarre decided that he would construct the model community, with streets named Friendship, Plenty, Peace, Liberty, and so on. He built Chateau de Tivoli, the first unit in his community, but the project was never completed and fell to the wayside after de Labigarre's death in 1807.

Fall near South Brace Mountain

1. Cynthia C. Lewis and Thomas Lewis, op. cit., 122. The cascade is referred to as "a breathtaking waterfall."

2. New York–New Jersey Trail Conference, *New York Walk Book*, op. cit., 215. The cascade is described as a "high waterfall and ascending cliffs."

3. Warren Broderick, author and historian, Rensselaer County.

Falls on the Saw Kill: Bard College Approach

1. Walter F. Burmeister, op. cit., 66–67. "Along a tortuously eroded mile the little stream drops 140 feet. At the end of a period of heavy precipitation, one should not miss the spectacle of the lovely falls dropping within the confines of the wooded gorge … Still water reaches virtually to the foot of the lower cataracts."

2. Jeffrey Perls, op. cit., 350. The upper fall is known as Zabriskie Falls. A sawmill once operated down near the bay.

3. The Dutchess County Tourism site:

www.dutchesstourism.com/dtours, provides information about the early mills.

Falls on the Saw Kill: Montgomery Place Approach

1. Peggy Turco, on page 121 in *Walks & Rambles in Dutchess and Putnam Counties* (Woodstock, Vt.: Backcountry Publications, 1990), states that what you will see is "a series of fast cataracts and falls."

2. Howard Stone, op. cit., 114. "Montgomery Place charms rather than overwhelms. … Footpaths curve down toward the Hudson and along the Saw Kill, a small creek that descends along small cataracts."

3. Jacques Gerard Milbert, op. cit., 37. "Here a little river on Mrs. Richard Montgomery's property murmurs as it passes between fallen trees and rocks. In the spring it forms a remarkable waterfall, but hot weather dries up most of its branches."

4. Walter F. Burmeister, op. cit., 67. "At the end of a period of heavy precipitation one should not miss the spectacle of the lovely falls, chopping within the confines of the wooded gorge."

5. New York–New Jersey Trail Conference, *New York Walk Book*, op. cit., 185. The cascade is described as a "high waterfall."

6. Benson J. Lossing, op. cit., 174. "Waterfalls, picturesque bridges, romantic glens, groves, a magnificent park, one of the most beautiful of the ornamental gardens in this country, and views of the river and mountains, unsurpassed, render Montgomery Place a retreat to be coveted, even by the most favored of fortune."

7. A picture of the cascades, taken by Mick Hales, can be seen in a publicity brochure entitled "Montgomery Place: A Historic Hudson River estate."

8. Jacquetta M. Haley, in *Pleasure Grounds: Andrew Jackson Downing and Montgomery Place* (Tarrytown, N.Y.: Sleepy Hollow Press, 1988), provides a vivid description on page 49 of the cascades on the Saw Kill: "This waterfall, beautiful in all seasons, would alone be considered a sufficient attraction to give notoriety to a rural beauty in most country neighborhoods. ... In the course of this valley [she] has given two other cataracts. These are all striking enough to be worthy of the pencil of the artist, and they make this valley a feast of wonders to the lovers of the picturesque."

9. Jeffrey Perls, op. cit., 350. "A power plant was erected here in the 1920's to use the power of the stream to generate electricity to meet the estate's energy needs."

10. The Dutchess County Tourism site, www.dutchess-tourism.com/dtours, talks about the early mills.

11. Margaret E. Herrick, in *Early Settlements in Dutchess County New York* (Rhinebeck, N.Y.: Kinship, 1994), writes how Annandale was named.

Falls on Landsman Kill

1. Walter F. Burmeister, op. cit., page 68, writes that there is much to see at the "forested gorges and falls of little Landsman Kill."

2. A picture of the waterfall on Landsman Kill, complete with an old stone bridge visible upstream from the top of the fall, can be seen on page 2 in *Rhinebeck: Portrait of a Town* (Rhinebeck, N.Y.: The River Press, 1990), by Sari B. Tietjen. Tietjen goes on to provide specific information about past industries at the fall.

3. Arthur G. Adams, *The Hudson River Guidebook*, op. cit., 221. Adams mentions Vandenburgh as another name by which the stream has been known.

4. Arthur G. Adams, in *The Hudson through the Years*, 3rd

Edition (New York: Fordham University Press, 1996), indicates on page 59 how the stream came to be named, and states that the stream at one time contained "4 grist mills; 4 saw mills; 2 paper mills; 1 tannery; 1 carding mill; and 1 plaster mill."

5. The Dutchess County Tourism site: www.dutchesstourism.com/dtours, contains background information on the Van Steenburgh Bridge, and Caspar Landsman.

Falls on Crum Elbow Creek

1. Peggy Turco, *Walks & Rambles in Dutchess and Putnam Counties*, op. cit., 141. "Crum Elbow Creek splashes noisy and wide over a concrete lip onto boulders and cliff." Turco also goes into fairly extensive detail as to how the stream came to be named.

2. In *Images of America: Hyde Park on the Hudson* (Dover, N.H.: Arcadia Publishing, 1996), Margaret Logan Marquez on page 52 presents a photograph showing a robust-looking cascade under the Vanderbilt Post Road (Rt. 9) bridge.

3. Benson J. Lossing, op. cit., 186. An account of how Crum Elbow was named is provided.

4. Arthur G. Adams, *The Hudson: A Guidebook to the River*, op. cit., 227. A fairly extensive history of the Vanderbilt Mansion is provided.

5. Charles W. Snell, in *Vanderbilt Mansion* (Washington, D.C.: National Park Service Historical Handbook Series, 1960), provides information on pages 24–25 on Frederick Vanderbilt and includes a map of the estate.

6. Michael S. Durham, in *The Smithsonian Guide to Historic America: The Mid-Atlantic States* (New York: Stewart, Tabori & Chang, Inc., 1989), 187.

7. In "The Crum Elbow Creek: Its Mills and Dams," *Year Book: Dutchess County Historical Society*, Vol. 34 (1949), Harry T. Briggs recounts on pages 38–68 the numerous dams and mills which once proliferated along the stream near its confluence with the Hudson River.

Falls at Innisfree Gardens

1. Information obtained from pamphlet/guide distributed at the gardens.

Falls at Locust Grove

1. Peggy Turco, *Walks & Rambles in Dutchess and Putnam Counties*, op cit., 153. The cascade is described as "a little waterfall that curtains over an outcrop of bedrock."

2. At the kiosk next to the trail can be obtained a beautiful brochure entitled *Locust Grove, the Samuel Morse Historic Site: Trail Guide & Suggested Walking Route*.

3. New York–New Jersey Trail Conference, *New York Walk Book*, 6th Edition, op. cit., 167–168. Historical information about the grove is detailed.

Dover Stone Church Cave Falls

1. Clay Perry, on pages 130–131 in *Underground Empire* (New York: Stephen Daye Press, 1948), gives a vivid description of the cave.

2. In *Caves for Kids in Historic New York* (Monroe, N.Y.: Library Research Associates, 1980), Patricia Edwards Clyne on pages 55–61 describes a pretty hike up to the cave.

3. Virginia Palmer, in "The Stone Church," *Year Book: Dutchess County Historical Society*, Vol. 33, 1948, provides a great deal of specific information about the cave and falls. On page 45 she writes that the stream "was used at one time by the towns-people of Dover Plains as their water supply and as a storage-cooler." On page 47, Palmer states: "In early spring and during seasons of heavy rain, the stream gathers momentum from its downward course through the woods towards the Stone Church and gushes over the tall boulders at the rear of the cave, falling on the rocks below with a rush that can be heard from a half-mile away." On page 48, Palmer describes another waterfall sighting viewed from ledges 400 feet above the streambed: "In rainy seasons, a waterfall of forty feet or more can be seen to fall directly behind the Stone Church which, from this ledge, appears only as a deep and winding fissure in the rocks below." Finally, she writes: "A short walk beyond the stone church will take a traveler to the 'grotto.' A falls thunders out of sight at the rear of the grotto, whose side are worn in hollows by the swirl of the stream-waters." On page 47 the dimensions of the Stone Church are given to be 72 feet in length, with the arch entrance totaling 30 feet high and 25 feet wide.

4. In *Historical & Statistical Gazetteer of New York State* (1859; reprint, Interlaken, N.Y.: Heart of the Lake Publishing, 1986), the authors write on page 271: "The small stream flowing from the west hills has worn deep ravines, and in several places form beautiful cascades. The most noted of these is known as 'Dover Stone Church.'"

5. Wallace Bruce, op. cit., 127. "Here a small stream has worn out a remarkable cavern in the rocks forming a gothic arch for entrance." According to Bruce, on page 129, "It is said by Lossing, in his booklet on the Dover Stone Church, that Sacassas [sic], the mighty sachem of the Pequoids [sic] and emperor over many tribes between Thames and the Hudson River, was compelled after a disastrous battle which annihilated his warriors, to fly for safety, and, driven from point to point, he at last found refuge in this cave."

6. *Dutchess Land Conservancy Newsletter,* Fall 2003, 1 & 10.

7. Margaret E. Herrick, op. cit., 25. The name Dover Plains arose either due to an early settler who was from Dover, England, or from early homesteaders who looked at the marble and limestone outcroppings in the hills above and likened them to England's Dover Cliffs.

Wappinger Falls

1. Walter F. Burmeister, op. cit., 347. Wappinger Falls is a "ledge formation tilted 70 feet in 1/5 mile below a 7 foot barrage." On page 350 Burmeister states that "From the upstream launching point one looks directly into the gorge and can enjoy the magnificent spectacle of water cascading down the great staircase of the falls."

2. Howard Stone, op. cit., 146. "Next to the bridge, the creek plunges dramatically over the falls for which the community is named."

3. In *The Hudson: A Guidebook to the River* (Albany, N.Y.: State University of New York Press, 1981), Arthur G. Adams writes on page 214 that "Here it goes over a seventy-five foot fall to tidewater."

4. *Historical & Statistical Gazetteer of New York*, op. cit. 272. "Wappinger Creek here falls 75 feet, furnishing an excellent water power."

5. Ernest Ingersoll, in *Handy Guide to the Hudson River and*

Catskill Mountains (1910; reprint, Astoria, N.Y.: J. C. & A. L. Fawcett, Inc., 1989), describes the falls on page 136: "The stream falls over a series of high ledges and dams, behind which is a considerable lake. The steep walls of the ravine, the arched stone bridge, the mill races that have been carved out long ago, and the ruins of some ancient mills lend picturesqueness to a spot already highly endowed in that respect."

6. Peggy Turco, *Walks & Rambles in Dutchess and Putnam Counties*, op. cit., 50. Turco goes into much detail about the origin of the name Wappinger.

7. According to Mary Lynn Blanks, on page 27 in *Fun with the Family in New York: Hundreds of Ideas for Day Trips with the Kids*, 3rd Edition (Guilford, Conn.: The Globe Pequot Press, 2001), Wappinger Falls was the homeland of Paleo Indians, and then later, the Wappingers. All of this changed in 1683, however, when the Wappingers decided to sell land to Francis Romboat and his partners, based upon all the land that Romboat could see. Romboat cheated. He climbed up to the top of nearby South Beacon Mountain and, from there, saw over 85,000 acres of land.

8. Dutchess County Tercentenary Advisory Committee, *Municipal Historians' Book of Dutchess County: Tercentenary Edition, 1683–1983* (Dutchess County, N.Y.: Dutchess County Tercentenary Advisory Committee, 1983), 61.

Falls on Duell Brook

1. The New York–New Jersey Trail Conference, *New York Walk Book*, op. cit., 170, states that you will find a "hemlock and fern-filled gorge through which a waterfall flows."

2. Stephen Kulik, et al., op. cit., page 23, writes that the falls are contained in "a narrow but rugged hemlock gorge where the cascading waters of Duell Brook drop 50 feet in a series of waterfalls."

3. Peggy Turco, *Walks & Rambles in Dutchess and Putnam Counties*, op. cit., 25. "The ravine bedrock is a micaceous, or mica-bearing schist veined with marble."

4. Glenn Scherer and Don Hopey, *Exploring the Appalachian Trail: Hikes in the Mid-Atlantic States, Maryland, Pennsylvania, New*

Jersey, New York (Mechanicsburg, Pa.: Stackpole Books, 1998), 337.

5. Margaret E. Herrick, op. cit., 100.

Tioronda Falls

1. A brochure entitled *Scenic Hudson: Adventure Guide to Parks, Preserves and Trails* (Poughkeepsie, N.Y.: Scenic Hudson, Inc., n.d.) can be obtained at the kiosk by the trailhead. In the section on Madam Brett Park, the fall is referred to as Tioronda Falls.

2. In *Images of America: Around Fishkill* (Dover, N.H.: Arcadia Publishing, 1996), the Fishkill Historical Society states on page 106 that the Fishkill "drops nearly two hundred feet over slate and limestone between Fishkill and the Hudson River, tumbling over nine dams."

3. A picture of the falls can be seen on page 57 of *Images of America: Historic Beacon* (Charleston, S.C.: Arcadia Publishing, 1998), by Robert J. Murphy and Denise Doring Van Buren. Included in the picture is the train trestle and dam above the falls.

4. In *Retrospect: A Pictorial Review of Beacon, New York* (n.p., n.d.), the Beacon Historical Society shows a picture of the falls with a train going over the trestle. Information is provided about the railroad line. Pages, unfortunately, are unnumbered.

Fishkill Ridge Falls

1. John Jeanneney and Mary L. Jeanneney, in *Dutchess County: A Pictorial History* (Norfolk/Virginia Beach, Va.: The Donning Company, 1983), present a picture of the falls on page 61.

2. Patricia Edwards Clyne, "After the Falls," op. cit., 26.

3. Peggy Turco, *Walks & Rambles in Dutchess and Putnam Counties*, op. cit., 210.

4. Arthur G. Adams, *The Hudson River Guidebook*, op. cit., 193. Information is provided on how Beacon came to be named.

5. Margaret E. Herrick, op. cit., 47. Matteawan and Melzingah were other contenders for the name of the town that eventually became Beacon.

Falls at Tuckers Run

1. Patricia Edward Clyne, "After the Falls," op. cit.

2. Peggy Turco, *Walks & Rambles in Dutchess and Putnam Counties*, op. cit., 17. Turco talks about the hike through Walter G. Merritt Park (as it was known then), and describes the "gorge of Tucker's Run, similar to the gorge at Pawling Preserve, but larger, and full of falls and cataracts."

Melzingah Falls

1. Warren F. Broderick, Rensselaer County historian & author.

2. In "Indian Tales," *Putnam County History* (Cold Spring, N.Y.: Putnam County Historical Society, 1969), Nelson Delaney recounts on pages 23–24 a different story about how the fall came to be named.

The Hudson Highlands

1. Y. W. Isachen, E. Landing, J. M. Lauber, L. V. Rickard, and W. B. Rogers, eds., *Geology of New York: A Simplified Account* (Albany, N.Y.: The University of the State of New York, 1991), 46, 54.

2. Bradford B. Van Diver, *Roadside Geology of New York*, op. cit., 56, 89.

3. Jerome Wyckoff, *Rock Scenery of the Hudson Highlands and Palisades: A Geological Guide* (Glens Falls, N.Y.: Adirondack Mountain Club, 1971), 9, 31, 66.

Foundry Brook Falls

1. Patricia Edwards Clyne, "After the Falls," op. cit., 18. A picture of the fall can be seen on page 19.

2. Jacques Gerard Milbert, op. cit., 34. "I encountered a brook with a pretty waterfall on Captain Phillips' property."

3. Arthur G. Adams, *The Hudson River Guidebook*, op. cit., 185–186. History on Foundry Cove's background is provided.

4. The *Historical & Statistical Gazetteer of New York State*, op. cit., 304. Information is provided on past mills in the hamlet.

5. Jeffrey Perls, op. cit., 256–257.

6. Michael S. Durham, op. cit., 183.

Indian Brook Falls

1. A line drawing of the falls can be seen in *The Hudson River Highlands* (New York: Columbia University Press, 1991) by

Frances F. Dunwell.

2. Benson J. Lossing, op. cit., 241. A line drawing of Indian Brook Falls is shown.

3. A line drawing of the falls can be seen in *The Hudson River by Pen and Pencil* (1888; facsimile reprint, n.p.: J. C. & A. L. Fawcett Inc., n.d.), page 34, showing the drawings of J. D. Woodward. According to accompanying text, Indian Falls is "a wild, crystal stream that flows down a neighboring mountain-side, and forms a fine cascade."

4. Roland Van Zandt, op. cit., 204–205. A hike up Indian Falls on June 30, 1833, is described in exquisite detail by Fanny Kemble. She describes the falls as follows: "We stood on the brink of a pool, about forty feet across, and varying in depth from three to seven or eight feet; it was perfectly circular, and except on the south—where the waters take their path down the glen—closed round with a wall of rock about thirty feet high." From Kemble's description of the rock scrabble that then ensued, you would think that she was making an ascent up the Matterhorn! In Harriet Martineau's account, written in 1835, page 213, she states: "We followed the brawling brook for that distance, when we saw the glistening of the column of water through the trees. No fall can be prettier for its size, which is just small enough to tempt one to climb."

5. Arthur G. Adams, *The Hudson: A Guidebook to the River*, op. cit., 187. "The falls on this stream are very picturesque and were a popular place of resort in the nineteenth century."

6. Peggy Turco, in *Walks & Rambles in Dutchess and Putnam Counties* (Woodstock, Vt.: Backcountry Publications, 1990), on page 183 gives an account of the legend of Indian Falls.

7. "Indian Tales," *Putnam County History*, op. cit., 20–21. Nelson Delaney recounts the tale of Indian Falls.

8. Cynthia C. Lewis and Thomas Lewis, op. cit., 57. The authors recount the same story of how Indian Brook Falls came to be known.

Falls at Manitoga Preserve

1. In *Natural New York* (New York: Holt, Rinehart & Winston, 1983), Bill and Phyllis Thomas write on page 251 that "From near-

by comes the lyrical sound of a waterfall."

2. Jeffrey Perls, op. cit., 249. The cascade is described as "an artificial waterfall."

3. Peggy Turco, *Walks & Rambles in Dutchess and Putnam Counties*, op. cit., 148.

4. New York–New Jersey Trail Conference, *New York Walk Book*, op. cit., 158.

Mineral Spring Falls

1. Bill Thomas and Phyllis Thomas, op. cit., 256. Mineral Spring Falls is "A spectacular 100-foot waterfall."

2. New York–New Jersey Trail Conference, *New York Walk Book*, op. cit., 109. The falls are referred to as "a triple cascade flowing over a series of ledges through a dark hemlock grove." The authors also make mention that the waterfall goes by the name of Green Falls.

3. Lewis Beach, in *Cornwall* (Newburgh, N.Y.: E. M. Ruttenber & Son, 1873), describes a trip to Mineral Spring Falls on pages 50–53. On page 51 he writes, "The waters whose murmur we just heard—the living waters are now seen leaping from rock to rock; the rocks forming a gigantic stairway, which might have served some Titan of old to reach his castle on the hill; A few rods from the pool at the base of these stony stairs, a small rocky basin is formed by the hand of nature, and filled to the brim with the mineral water."

Buttermilk Falls (in Highland Falls)

1. Wallace Bruce, op. cit., 91. "Buttermilk Falls, so christened by Washington Irving, is a pretty little cascade on the west bank. Like sparkling wit, it is often dry, and the tourist is exceptionally fortunate who sees it in full-dress costume after a heavy shower, when it rushes over the rocks in floods of snow-white foam."

2. Benson J. Lossing, op. cit., 255. A line drawing of Buttermilk Falls is offered, which includes the mill erected along the south bank by the shore.

3. *The Hudson River by Pen and Pencil*, op. cit., 25. A line drawing of the falls done by J. D. Woodward shows the Cranston's Hotel on the cliff edge adjacent to the top of the falls along the north bank.

In the accompanying text on page 27, the author writes: "We see Buttermilk Falls (on the left), which at times is a fine cascade, tumbling over inclined ledges a distance of a hundred feet, but which is apt in the summer heat to dwindle to a comparatively narrow stream of water."

4. Roland Van Zandt, op. cit., 82. Charles Carroll states: "[There] is another beautiful cascade called 'The Buttermilk.' This is formed by a rivulet which flows from a lake on the top of a neighboring mountain."

5. Chris W. Brown, op. cit., 76. "The watercourse that runs through the town of Highland Falls, on the west shore, has a 100-foot drop. The Dutch called it Buttermilk Falls. This rush of water once powered mills for flour, grist, sawing, and cider making." Brown mentions that you can launch a boat from Highland Falls Marina to see the falls.

6. An article that appeared in *Harper's New Monthly Magazine* entitled "The Romance of the Hudson" states on page 445: "On the brow of a rocky precipice nearer is Cozzen's summer hotel, and below it you may see the white foam of a mountain stream, as it falls in a gentle cascade into the river over a smooth rocky bed, after a turbulent passage among the bowlders above. This the prosy Dutch skippers called Buttermilk Falls." The article has been reprinted in *New York: Tales of the Empire State* (Secaucus, N. J.: Castle, 1988), compiled by Frank Oppel.

7. A close-up photo of Buttermilk Falls can be seen in *The Hudson River Valley* (New York: Bonanza Books, 1960) by John Reed, 157.

8. Jacques Gerard Milbert, op. cit., 33. "Drawing closer we saw several houses and a mill fed by a little river from Buttermilk Falls; water is conveyed through a trough on trestles built level with the falls."

9. Arthur G. Adams, *The Hudson: A Guidebook to the River*, op. cit., 176. Adams gives details about the Parry mill and hotel.

10. Arthur G. Adams, *The Hudson through the Years*, op. cit., 101. Adams gives background information about Cozzen's Hotel, located above the north bank of Buttermilk Falls, and states that

"There were cottages attached and extensive pleasure grounds with walks and rustic bridges along and across the Buttermilk Falls."

Hell Hole Falls

1. Benson J. Lossing, op. cit., 261. A line drawing entitled "Falls in Fort Montgomery Creek" is presented showing the falls below a small dam.

2. According to the New York–New Jersey Trail Conference, on page 187 in *Day Walker: 32 Hikes in the New York Metropolitan Area*, Second Edition (Mahwah, N.J.: New York–New Jersey Trail Conference, 2002), "You will soon come to a spillway over an old dam with deep pools and cascades below."

3. Walter F. Burmeister, op. cit., 73. Burmeister talks about a "fall and a low dam" approximately a mile upstream in the gorge.

4. C. G. Hine, op. cit., 146. "Hellhole" and Popolopen Creek are described, "whose roar ascends to the traveler high overhead."

5. Jerome Wyckoff, op. cit., 43. A picture of the potholes in Popolopen Creek just upstream from Hells Hole can be seen.

6. Roland Van Zandt, op. cit., 81. In 1770 Charles Carroll wrote: "I landed to examine a beautiful fall of water."

7. Ernest Ingersoll, op. cit., 80.

8. Arthur G. Adams, *The Hudson: A Guidebook to the River*, op. cit., 172. The author talks about the various names the stream has been known by, and how Hell Hole came to be named.

9. An old map showing the location of Forts Montgomery and Clinton can be seen in *Putnam County Sesquicentennial: 1812–1962* (n.p., n.d.).

10. Chris W. Brown, op. cit., 75. Information is provided on Fort Montgomery Furnace and Bear Mountain Bridge.

11. Arthur G. Adams, *The Hudson Through the Years*, op. cit., 60. The author talks about how iron was mined in the area of Popolopen Creek.

Cascade of Slid

1. Patricia Edwards Clyne, "After the Falls," op. cit., 25.

2. Stella Green and H. Neil Zimmerman, op. cit., 116. Mention is made of the Cascade of Slid, where "hemlocks shroud the cliffs

and shelter small waterfalls."

3. Jerome Wyckoff, op. cit., 12. A picture of Pine Meadow Brook, entitled "Cascade at Slid" (presumably looking downstream from below the fall) can be seen, as well as a picture of Pine Meadows Brook at the cascade on page 38.

4. The New York–New Jersey Trail Conference, *Day Walker*, op. cit., 172. The authors describe the Cascade of Slid as "a beautiful waterfall and pool."

5. New York–New Jersey Trail Conference, *New York Walk Book*, op. cit., 70. The authors describe the Cascade of Slid as "a spectacular sight during the spring runoff" and a place where there are "very large boulders along the ravine."

6. *Suffern: 200 Years, 1773–1973* (Suffern, N.Y.: Suffern Bicentennial Committee, 1973) contains a picture of the cascade on page 79 looking decidedly more waterfall-like.

Fitzgerald Falls

1. Stella J. Green and Neil Zimmerman, op. cit. Page 164 contains a picture of Fitzgerald Falls.

2. Glenn Scherer and Don Hopey, op. cit., 173. The falls are "25 ft. high and marked by pink feldspar." On page 271 information on 17,500-acre Sterling Forest is provided.

3. Peggy Turco, *Walks & Rambles in the Lower Hudson Valley*, op. cit., 235. Fitzgerald Falls is where "a 25-foot sliding cascade tumbles within a hemlock forest."

4. Patricia Edwards Clyne, "After the Falls," op. cit., 26. A picture of the fall is also found on the same page.

5. In *The Best of the Appalachian Trail Day Hikes* (Birmingham, Ala.: Menasha Ridge Press, 1994) Victoria Logue and Frank Logue state on page 97 that "Fitzgerald Falls flows twenty-five feet through a rocky cleft." On the same page they also mention that you will pass by stone walls from an abandoned settlement as you proceed further along the trail.

Ramapo Falls

1. Gary Letcher, op. cit., 37. The fall is also known as Buttermilk Falls.

2. Lucy D. Rosenfeld and Maria Harrison, *A Guide to Green New Jersey: Nature Walks in the Garden State* (New Brunswick, N.J.: Rutgers University Press, 2003), 12.

3. Arthur G. Adams, *The Hudson: A Guidebook to the River*, op. cit., 153. Information is provided on a number of other names by which Ramapo has been known.

Falls on Bear Swamp Brook

1. Gary Letcher, op. cit., 36. "Bear Swamp Brook falls over a broad rounded outcropping of gneiss into a shallow pool. There is another falls (about 12 feet high) through a cleft about 200 yards upstream."

Falls at Marion Yarrow Preserve

1. In the *Eastern New York Chapter Preserve Guide: Lower Hudson Region*, 2000 Edition (Mt. Kisco, N.Y.: The Nature Conservancy, 2000), by Chris Harmon, Matt Levy, and Gabrielle Antoniadis, on pages 17–18 a description of the preserve and map is provided. On page 18, the cascade is referred to as "a 30-foot waterfall."

2. Joanne Michaels and Mary-Margaret Barile, in *The Best of the Hudson Valley & Catskill Mountains: An Explorer's Guide*, 4th Edition (Woodstock, Vt.: The Countryman Press, 2001), state on page 267 that "Lakes, waterfalls, ponds, and trails form a perfect getaway for the outdoor lover."

Falls at Croton Gorge Park

1. George Profous, on page 41 in "The Old Croton Aqueduct," *The Conservationist*, Vol. 36, No.3 (Nov./Dec., 1981), provides information on the New Croton Reservoir. A picture of the dam, from its base, can be seen on page 40.

2. Patricia Edwards Clyne, "After the Falls," op. cit., 19. A picture of the Cornell Dam spillway can also be seen.

3. Arthur G. Adams, *The Hudson River Guidebook*, op. cit, 146.

Havemeyer Falls

1. Patricia Edwards Clyne, "After the Falls," op. cit., 25.

2. New York–New Jersey Trail Conference, *Day Walker*, op. cit., 121. The fall is described as a "waterfall cascading over variegated rock formations."

3. Stephen Kulik, et al., op. cit., 6. "The deep ravine itself was carved out by the Wisconsin glacier as it moved over the area 10,000 to 15,000 years ago."

4. Chris Harmon, et al., op. cit., 29–31. Vital information on the preserve, its history, and what to see is presented.

5. Brochure distributed at the kiosk contains much information about the gorge, including a hiking map.

The Palisades

1. Richard F. Ward, in the June–July 1959 issue of *The Conservationist,* under "Geology of the Hudson River," provides substantial geological information on the Palisades.

2. Jerome Wyckoff, op. cit. 63. Extensive information about the geology of the Palisades is provided.

3. Chris W. Brown III, op. cit, 50–51.

4. Y. W. Isachen, et al., op. cit., 277. The chapter provides information on how the Palisades were named.

5. Otto L. Schreiber, *The River of Renown: The Hudson* (New York: Greenwich Book Publishers, 1959), 26.

Buttermilk Falls (Rockland County Park)

1. Bill Thomas and Phyllis Thomas, op. cit., 236–237. Basic information is provided on the park.

2. Patricia Edwards Clyne, "After the Falls," op. cit., 20, writes that the fall in its "scenic ravine" was "favored by Theodore Roosevelt."

Peanut Leap Falls

1. www.njpalisades.org provides substantial information on previous names by which the fall has been known.

2. Patricia Edwards Clyne, "After the Falls," op. cit., 25.

3. A historic marker on Rt. 9W provides information on Skunk Hollow.

4. Alice Munro Haagensen, in *Palisades: Snedens Landing,*

From the Beginning of History to the Turn of the Twentieth Century (Tarrytown, N.Y.: Pilgrimage Publishing, 1986), provides considerable history on pages 117 and 120 on Mary Lawrence's use of the cascade, including a line drawing of the fall on page 115. In a footnote on page 118, mention is made of how the gardens fell into ruins, ultimately to be saved by the Palisades Interstate Park Commission.

5. Arthur G. Adams, *The Hudson River Guidebook*, op. cit., 126. A brief history of the falls is provided.

6. Map and guide entitled "Hiking at State Line Lookout" produced by the Palisades Interstate Park–New Jersey Section (P.O. Box 155, Alpine, New Jersey 07620–0155).

Greenbrook Falls

1. Bill Thomas and Phyllis Thomas, op. cit., 78. "Greenbrook Falls, tumbling some 250 feet down ancient cliffs into the Hudson River, creates a spectacular setting above the Hudson River. A view of the waterfall, and of all the Palisades and Highlands to the north, is possible from several promontories that look down 350 feet to the river."

2. Lucy D. Rosenfeld and Marina Harrison, op. cit. 11. The authors refer to "picturesque Greenbrook Falls, in a beautifully wooded setting."

3. Gary Letcher, op. cit., 44. Letcher states that the waterfall is "arguably the highest falls in New Jersey and the Mid-Atlantic." He goes on to state: "The largest single drop is about 80 feet, a slide immediately beneath the Henry Hudson Parkway. The basalt columns of the Palisades highlight the falls." On page xxix, Letcher further states that "Greenbrook Falls is not continuous. The longest part, at the top, is a series of cascades, with no single drop greater than about 10 feet. Below the cascades is a steep 80-foot slide, followed by a final tumble of about 20 feet."

4. Arthur G. Adams, *The Hudson River Guidebook*, op. cit., 117, 120.

5. Raymond J. Obrien, in *American Sublime: Landscape and Scenery of the Lower Hudson Valley* (New York: Columbia University

Press, 1981), page 248, mentions when the Henry Hudson Drive and Palisades Interstate Parkway were created.

Fall on Flat Rock Brook

1. Lucy D. Rosenfeld and Maria Harrison, op. cit., 12. "It was once the wooded property of a private estate, lucky enough to have its own lake, waterfall, and tumbling brook."

Bibliography

Adams, Arthur. *The Hudson River Guidebook*. 2nd Edition. New York: Fordham University Press, 1996.

———. *The Catskills: An Illustrated Historical Guide with Gazetteer*. New York: Fordham University Press, 1990.

———. *The Hudson through the Years*. 3rd Edition. New York: Fordham University Press, 1996.

———. *The Hudson: A Guidebook to the River*. Albany, N.Y.: State University of New York Press, 1981.

Appalachian Mountain Club. *Massachusetts and Rhode Island Trail Guide*. 7th Edition. Boston, Mass.: Appalachian Mountain Club Books, 1995.

Bailey, Bill. *New York State Parks: A Complete Outdoor Recreational Guide for Campers, Boaters, Anglers, Hikers, Beach and Outdoor Lovers*. Saginaw, Mich.: Glovebox Guidebooks of America, 1997.

Beach, Lewis. *Cornwall*. Newburgh, N.Y.: E. M. Ruttenber & Son, 1873.

Beacon Historical Society. *Retrospect: A Pictorial Review of Beacon, New York*. n.p., n.d.

Beecher, Raymond. *Under Three Flags*. Hensonville, N.Y.: Black Dome Press Corp., 1991.

Blanks, Mary Lynn. *Fun with the Family in New York: Hundreds of Ideas for Day Trips with the Kids*. 3rd Edition. Guilford, Conn.: The Globe Pequot Press, 2001.

Bliven, Rachel D., et al. *A Resourceful People: A Pictorial History of Rensselaer County, New York*. Norfolk, Va.: The Donning Company, 1987.

Bornt, Evelyn, Beryl Harrington and Ellen L. Wiley, eds. *Pittstown through the Years*. n.p.: Pittstown Historical Society, 1989.

Boyle, Robert H. *The Hudson River: A Natural and Unnatural History*. Expanded edition. New York: W. W. Norton & Company, 1969.

Briggs, Harry T. "The Crum Elbow Creek: Its Mills and Dams." *Year Book: Dutchess County Historical Society*. Vol. 34. (1949).

Broderick, Warren. "Ben Pie: A Native American Tale of Papscanee

Island." *Hudson Valley Regional Review*. Vol. 17, No. 1 (March 2000).

Brown, Chris W. III. *Cruising Guide to New York Waterways and Lake Champlain*. Gretna, La.: Pelican Publishing Company, Inc., 1998.

Bruce, Wallace. *The Hudson: Three Centuries of History, Romance, and Invention*. Centennial Edition. New York: Walking News, Inc., 1982.

Bryan, Clark W. *The Book of Berkshire*. 1887. Reprint, North Egremont, Mass.: Past Perfect Books, 1993.

Buckell, Betty Ahearn. *Boldly into the Wilderness: Travelers in Upstate New York, 1010–1646*. Queensbury, N.Y.: Buckle Press, 1999.

Buel, David Jr. *An Address Delivered at the Consecration of Oakwood Cemetery*. Troy, N.Y.: Troy Cemetery Association, 1850.

Burmeister, Walter F. *Appalachian Waters 2: The Hudson River and its Tributaries*. Oakton, Va.: Appalachian Books, 1974.

Campbell, Malcolm W. *Play Hard, Rest Easy. New England: The Ultimate Getaway Guide*. Charlotte, N.C.: Walkabout Press, Inc., 2001.

Capossela, Jim. *Good Fishing in the Catskills*. 2nd Edition. Woodstock, Vt.: Backcountry Publications, 1992.

Carmer, Carl. *The Tavern Lamps Are Burning: Literary Journey through Six Regions and Four Centuries of New York State*. New York: David McKay Company, Inc., 1964.

Cederstrom, David. "Bridge & Overlook." *The Chronicle*. Vol. 25, No. 1,058 (Nov. 4–10, 2004).

Chapin, Peter. "New England & N.Y. Waterfalls." Website: www.ecet.vtc.edu/~pchapin/water

Chong, Herb, ed. *The Long Path Guide*. Fifth edition. Mahwah, N.J.: New York–New Jersey Trail Conference, 2002.

Clinton, DeWitt, ed. *Picturesque Oakwood: Its Past and Present Associations*. Troy, N.Y.: Frederick S. Hills, 1897.

Clyne, Patricia Edwards. "After the Falls: A Collection of Valley Cascades." *Hudson Valley*. Sept. 1999.

———. *Caves For Kids in Historic New York*. Monroe, N.Y.: Research Associates, 1980.

———. *Hudson Valley Tales and Trails*. Woodstock, N.Y.: The Overlook Press, 1990.

Crane, Galen. "Pilot Knob." *Adirondack Life*. Vol. XXXV, No. 8 (November/December, 2004).

Crary, Duncan Campbell. "Rediscovering the Beaverkill." *Capital Neighbors: Newspaper for and about Albany's Historic Neighborhoods*. Vol. 8, No. 1 (week of March 11, 2002).

Davidson, Charles. *Hoosic Falls Historic Guide*. Hoosic Valley, N.Y.: Hoosic Valley Publishing Co., 1990.

Delaney, Nelson. "Indian Tales." *Putnam County History*. Cold Spring, N.Y.: Putnam County Historical Society, 1969.

Dugger, Elizabeth L. *Adventure Guide to Massachusetts and Western Connecticut*. Edison, N.J.: Hunter, 1999.

Dunn, Russell. *Adirondack Waterfall Guide: New York's Cool Cascades*. Hensonville, N.Y.: Black Dome Press Corp., 2003.

———. *Adventures around the Great Sacandaga Lake*. Utica, N.Y.: Nicholas K. Burns Publishing, 2002.

———. *Catskill Region Waterfall Guide: Cool Cascades of the Catskills & Shawangunks*. Hensonville, N.Y.: Black Dome Press Corp., 2004.

———. "Cooper's Cave: Fact and Fiction." *Glens Falls Magazine*. Vol. 5, #5 (spring 2004).

Dunn, Shirley W. *The Mohicans and Their Land, 1609–1730*. Fleischmanns, N.Y.: Purple Mountain Press, 1994.

Dunn, Violet B., ed. *Saratoga County Heritage*. Saratoga County, N.Y.: n.p., 1974.

Dunwell, Frances F. *The Hudson River Highlands*. New York: Columbia University Press, 1991.

Durham, Michael S. *The Smithsonian Guide to Historic America: The Mid-Atlantic States*. New York: Stewart, Tabori & Chang, Inc., 1989.

Dutchess County Tercentenary Advisory Committee. *Municipal Historians' Book of Dutchess County: Tercentenary Edition, 1683–1983*. Dutchess County, N.Y.: Dutchess County Tercentenary Advisory Committee, 1983.

Dutchess Land Conservancy Newsletter. Fall 2003.

Dyson, John S. *Our Historic Hudson*. Roosevelt, N.Y.: James B. Adler, Inc., 1968.

———. *Along the Bike Hike Trail: A Guide to the Mohawk–Hudson Bikeway in Schenectady County*. Schenectady, N.Y.: The Environmental Clearinghouse of Schenectady, Incorporated & The Schenectady County Environmental Advisory Council, 1986.

Ellis, Captain Franklin. *History of Columbia County, New York: with Illustrations and Biographic Sketches of Some of Its Prominent Men and Pioneers*. 1878. Reprint, Old Chatham, N.Y.: Sachem Press, 1974.

Encyclopedia of New York, Vol. 2, 1996. New York: Somerset Publishing, Inc., 1996.

Ensminger, Scott A., and Douglas K. Bassett. *A Waterfall Guide to Letchworth State Park*. Castile, N.Y.: The Glen Iris Inn, 1991.

Faber, Harold, ed. *The Mill on the Roeliff Jansen Kill: 250 Years of American Industrial History*. Hensonville, N.Y.: Black Dome Press Corp., 1993.

Fisher, Donald W. *Bedrock Geology of the Glens Falls–Whitehall Region, New York*. Map and Chart Series Number 35. Albany, N.Y.: University of the State of New York, The State Education Department/Albany, 1984.

Fishkill Historical Society. *Images of America: Around Fishkill*. Dover, N.H.: Arcadia Publishing, 1996.

Freeman, Rich, and Sue Freeman. *200 Waterfalls in Central & Western New York: A Finders' Guide*. Fishers, N.Y.: Footprint Press, 2002.

French, Mary D., and Robert J. Lilly. *Images of America: Sand Lake*. Charleston, S.C.: Arcadia, 2001.

Fried, Marc B. *The Early History of Kingston & Ulster County*. Marbletown, N.Y.: Ulster County Historical Society, 1975.

Gazda, William M. *Place Names in New York*. Schenectady, N.Y.: Gazda Associates, Inc., 1997.

Gemmill, Eva. "The Poestenkill—Its Power and Its Glory." *The Conservationist*. March/April, 1979.

Giddings, Edward D. *Coeymans and the Past*. Coeymans, N.Y.: Tricentennial Committee of the Town of Coeymans, 1973.

Green, Stella, and H. Neil Zimmerman. *50 Hikes in the Lower Hudson Valley*. Woodstock, Vt.: Backcountry Guides, 2002.

Grinnell, Lawrence I. *Canoeable Waterways of New York State and Vicinity*. New York: Pageant Press, 1956.

Haagensen, Alice Munro. *Palisades: Snedens Landing. From the Beginning of History to the Turn of the Twentieth Century*. Tarrytown, N.Y.: Pilgrimage Publishing, 1986.

Haley, Jacquetta M. *Pleasure Grounds: Andrew Jackson Downing and Montgomery Place*. Tarrytown, N.Y.: Sleepy Hollow Press, 1988.

Harmon, Chris, Matt Levy and Gabrielle Antoniadis. *Eastern New York Chapter Preserve Guide: Lower Hudson Region*. 2000 Edition. Mt. Kisco, N.Y.: The Nature Conservancy, 2000.

Harvey, Edmund H. Jr., ed. *Reader's Digest Book of Facts*. Pleasantville, N.Y.: The Reader's Digest Association, Inc., 1987.

Herrick, Margaret E. *Early Settlements in Dutchess County, New York*. Rhinebeck, N.Y.: Kinship, 1994.

Hill, Florence M. *West of Perigo: Poestenkill Memories*. Troy, N.Y.: n.p., 1979.

Hine, C. G. *Albany to Tappan: The West Bank of the Hudson River*. 1906. Reprint, Astoria, N.Y.: J. C. & A. L. Fawcett, Inc., n.d.

Historical & Statistical Gazetteer of New York. 1859. Reprint, Interlaken, N.Y.: Heart of the Lake Publishing, 1986.

Historical Society of Esquatak *The Muitzeskill Historic District: A Typical 19th-Century Farm Hamlet*. Historical Society of Esquatak, 1976.

History and Biography of Washington County and the Town of Queensbury, New York, with Historical Notes on the Various Towns. Richmond, Ind.: Gresham Publishing Company, 1894.

Hoag, Bonnie. "Dionondehowa: Wildlife Sanctuary and School." *The Healing Springs*. Issue # 12 (February–March 2004).

Howell and Tenney. *History of the County of Albany, N.Y. from 1609 to 1886 with Portraits, Biographies and Illustrations*. New York: W. W. Munsell & Co., 1886 (reprint, Higginson Book Company of Salem, Mass., n.d.).

Ingersoll, Ernest. *Handy Guide to the Hudson River and Catskill Mountains*. Astoria, 1910. Reprint, N.Y.: J. C. & A. L. Fawcett, Inc., 1989.

Isachen, Y. W., E. Landing, J. M. Lauber, L. V. Rickard and W. B.

Rogers, eds. *Geology of New York: A Simplified Account.* Albany, N.Y.: The University of the State of New York, 1991.

Jeanneney, John, and Mary L. Jeanneney. *Dutchess County: A Pictorial History.* Norfolk/Virginia Beach, Va.: The Donning Company, 1983.

Kenney, Alice P. *Stubborn for Liberty: The Dutch in New York.* Syracuse, N.Y.: Syracuse University Press, 1975.

Kimball, Francis P. *The Capital Region of New York State: Crossroads of Empire.* Vol. II. New York: Lewis Historical Publishing Company, Inc., 1942.

Kiwanis Project. *Castleton History.* n.p., 1948. Reprint, 1976.

Kulik, Stephen, Pete Salmansohn, Matthew Schmidt and Heidi Welch. *The Audubon Society Field Guide to the Natural Places of the Northeast: Inland.* New York: The Hilltown Press, Inc., 1984.

Lanza, Michael. *New England Hiking: The Complete Guide to More Than 350 of the Best Hikes in New England.* San Francisco, Ca.: Foghorn Press, 1997.

Laubach, Rene. *A Guide to Natural Places in the Berkshire Hills.* Stockbridge, Mass.: Berkshire House Publishers, 1992.

Letcher, Gary. *Waterfalls of the Mid-Atlantic States: 200 Falls in Maryland, New Jersey, and Pennsylvania.* Woodstock, Vt.: The Countryman Press, 2004.

Lewis, Cynthia C., and Thomas Lewis. *Best Hikes with Children in the Catskills & Hudson River Valley.* Seattle, Wash.: The Mountaineers, 1992.

Logue, Victoria, and Frank Logue. *The Best of the Appalachian Trail Day Hikes.* Birmingham, Ala.: Menasha Ridge Press, 1994.

Longstreth, T. Morris. *The Catskills.* 1921. Reprint, Hensonville, N.Y.: Black Dome Press Corp., 2003.

Lord, Philip L. *Mills on the Tsatsawassa: Techniques for Documenting Early 19th-Century Water-Powered Industry in Rural New York, a Case Study.* Albany, N.Y: University of the State of New York, State Education Department, Division of Historical and Anthropological Services, 1983.

Lord, Thomas Reeves. *Stories of Lake George: Fact & Fancy.* Pemberton, N.J.: Pineland Press, 1987.

Lossing, Benson J. *The Hudson: From the Wilderness to the Sea.* 1866. Reprint, Hensonville, N.Y.: Black Dome Press Corp., 2000.

Marquez, Margaret Logan. *Images of America: Hyde Park on the Hudson.* Dover, N.H.: Arcadia Publishers, 1996.

Matthews, Peter, ed. *The Guinness Book of Records.* New York: Guinness Publishing, Ltd., 1994.

Mattice, Beatrice M. *They Walked These Hills Before Me: An Early History of the Town of Conesville.* Cornwallville, N.Y.: Hope Farm Press, 1980.

McEneny, John J. *Albany: Capital City on the Hudson. An Illustrated History.* Sun Valley, Ca.: American Historical Press, 1998.

McMartin, Barbara, and Peter Kick. *Fifty Hikes in the Hudson Valley: From the Catskills to the Taconics, and from the Ramapos to the Helderbergs.* Woodstock, Vt.: Backcountry Publications, 1985.

Michaels, Joanne, and Mary-Margaret Barile. *The Best of the Hudson Valley & Catskill Mountains: An Explorer's Guide.* 4th Edition. Woodstock, Vt.: The Countryman Press, 2001.

Milbert, Jacques Gerard. *Picturesque Itinerary of the Hudson River and the Peripheral Parts of North America.* Reprint, Ridgewood, N.J.: Gregg Press, 1968.

The Mohawk Trail: Historic Auto Trail Guide. Brookline, Mass: Muddy River Press, 2003.

Mulligan, Tim. *The Hudson River Valley: A History & Guide.* New York: Random House, 1981.

Mundow, Anna. *Southern New England.* Oakland, Ca.: Compass American Guides, 1999.

Munsell, Joel. *The History of Cohoes, New York: From Its Earliest Settlement to the Present Time.* 1877. Reprint, n.p.: Cohoes Historical Society, 1969.

Murphy, Robert J., and Denise Doring Van Buren. *Images of America: Historic Beacon.* Charleston, N.C.: Arcadia Publishing, 1998.

Mylod, John. *Biography of a River: The People and Legends of the Hudson Valley.* New York: Bonanza Books, 1969.

Newman, Marc. *Images of America: Walden and Maybrook.* Charleston, S.C.: Arcadia Publishing, 2001.

New York–New Jersey Trail Conference, *New York Walk Book*. 6th edition. New York: New York–New Jersey Trail Conference, 1998.

———. *Day Walker: 32 Hikes in the New York Metropolitan Areas*. 2nd edition. Mahwah, N.J.: New York–New Jersey Trail Conference, 2002.

Nutting, Wallace. *New York Beautiful*. Garden City, N.Y.: Garden City Publishing Co., Inc., in cooperation with Old America Company, 1936.

Obrien, Raymond J. *American Sublime: Landscape and Scenery of the Lower Hudson Valley*. New York: Columbia University Press, 1981.

Olton, Jean S., compiler. *The Town of Colonie: A Pictorial History*. Colonie, N.Y.: Town of Colonie, 1980.

Oppel, Frank, compiler. *New York State: Tales of the Empire State*. Secaucus, N.J.: Castle, 1988.

Palme, Arthur. *The Berkshires through the Camera of Arthur Palme*. n.p.: Palme-Grove Publishing Company, 1951.

Palmer, Virginia. "The Stone Church," *Year Book: Dutchess County Historical Society*. Vol. 33. (1948).

Parker, Joe. *Looking Back: A History of Troy and Rensselaer County, 1925–1980*. Troy, N.Y.: n.p., 1982.

Parsons, Greg and Kate B. Watson. *New England Waterfalls: A Guide to More Than 200 Cascades and Waterfalls*. Woodstock, Vt.: The Countryman Press, 2003.

Peattie, Roderick, ed. *The Berkshires: The Purple Hills*. New York: The Vanguard Press, 1948.

Perls, Jeffrey. *Paths Along the Hudson: A Guide to Walking and Biking*. New Brunswick, N.J.: Rutgers University Press, 1999.

Perry, Clay. *Underground Empire*. New York: Stephen Daye Press, 1948.

Phelan, Thomas. *The Hudson Mohawk Gateway: An Illustrated History*. Northridge, Ca.: Windsor Publications, Inc., 1985.

Profous, George. "The Old Croton Aqueduct." *The Conservationist*. Vol. 36, No. 3 (November/December, 1981).

Putnam County Sesquicentennial: 1812–1962. n.p., n.d.

Randell, Sr., Mrs. Frank. *And So It Was: Yesteryear in the Punsit*

Valley. Spencertown, N.Y.: Griswold Publishing, 1993.

Reed, John. *The Hudson River Valley*. New York: Bonanza Books, 1960.

Renehan, Edward Jr. *John Burroughs: An American Naturalist*. Hensonville, N.Y.: Black Dome Press Corp., 1992.

———. "John Burroughs and his River View." *The Conservationist*. March–April, 1982.

Reynolds, Helen Wilkinson. *Poughkeepsie: The Origin and Meaning of the Word. Vol. I*. Poughkeepsie, N.Y.: Dutchess County Historical Society, 1924.

Rittner, Don. *Troy: A Collar City History*. Charleston, S.C.: Arcadia Publishing, 2002.

———. *Images of America: Albany*. Charleston, S.C.: Arcadia Publishing, 2000.

———. *Images of America: Troy*. Charleston, S.C.: Arcadia Publishing, 1998.

Roeliff-Jansen Historical Society. *A History of the Roeliff Jansen Area: A Historical Review of Five Townships in Columbia County, New York*. Columbia County, N.Y.: The Roeliff-Jansen Historical Society, 1990.

Roseberry, C. R. *Albany: Three Centuries a County*. Albany, N.Y.: Tricentennial Commission, 1983.

———. *From Niagara to Montauk: The Scenic Pleasures of New York State*. Albany, N.Y.: State University of New York Press, 1982.

Rosenfeld, Lucy D., and Maria Harrison. *A Guide to Green New Jersey: Nature Walks in the Garden State*. New Brunswick, N.J.: Rutgers University Press, 2003.

Rossi, Louis. *Cycling Along the Canals of New York: 500 Miles of Bike Riding along the Erie, Champlain, Cayugaseneca, and Oswego Canals*. College Park, Md.: Vitesse Press, 1999.

Ryan, Christopher J., ed. *AMC Massachusetts & Rhode Island Trail Guide*. 6th Edition. Boston Mass.: Appalachian Mountain Club, 1989.

Sand Lake Historical Society. *Historical Highlights*. Vol. 24, no. 2 (Winter 1998).

Scenic Hudson: Adventure Guide to Parks, Preserves and Trails. Poughkeepsie, N.Y.: Scenic Hudson, Inc., n.d.

Schaaphok, Peter R. W. *Petersburgh, Then & Now: A Photographic Comparison*. Town of Petersburgh, 1991.

Scheller, William G., and Kay Scheller. *New York: Off the Beaten Path*. 4th edition. Old Saybrook, Conn.: The Globe Pequot Press, 1977.

Scherer, Glenn, and Don Hopey. *Exploring the Appalachian Trail: Hikes in the Mid-Atlantic States, Maryland, Pennsylvania, New Jersey, New York*. Mechanicsburg, Pa.: Stackpole Books, 1998.

Schmitt, Claire K. *Natural Areas of Rensselaer County*. New York: Rensselaer–Taconic Land Conservancy & Environmental Clearinghouse of Schenectady, Inc., 1994.

Schmitt, Claire K. & Norton G. Miller & Warren F. Broderick & John T. Keenan & William D. Niemi. *Natural Areas of Rensselaer County* 2nd edition. Schenectady/Troy, N.Y.: The Rennselaer–Taconic Land Conservancy & Environmental Clearinghouse of Schenectady, Inc., 2002.

Schmitt, Claire K., and Judith Wolk. *Natural Areas of Saratoga County*. Niskayuna, N.Y.: The Environmental Clearinghouse of Schenectady, 1998.

Schmitt, Claire K., and Mary S. Brennan. *Natural Areas of Albany County*. Niskayuna, N.Y.: The Environmental Clearinghouse of Schenectady, 1991.

Schram, Margaret B. *Hudson's Merchants and Whalers: The Rise and Fall of a River Port, 1783–1850*. Hensonville, N.Y.: Black Dome Press Corp., 2004.

Schreiber, Otto L. *The River of Renown: the Hudson*. New York: Greenwich Book Publishers, 1959.

Schuman, Michael A. *New York State's Special Places: Day Trips, Weekends, and Outings in the Empire State*. Woodstock, Vt.: The Countryman Press, 1988.

Scofield, Bruce, Stella J. Green and H. Neil Zimmerman. *Fifty Hikes in New Jersey: Walks, Hikes and Backpacking Trips from the Kittatinnies to Cape May*. Woodstock, Vt.: Backcountry Publications, 1988.

Scofield, Carlton B. *Echoes for the Hills*. Peekskill, N.Y.: The Gardner Press, 1961.

Shorey, Mabel Pitkin. *The Early History of Corinth: Once Known as*

Jessup's Landing. Corinth, N.Y.: Mabel Pitkin Shorey, 1959.

Simpson, Jeffrey. *The Hudson River 1850–1918: A Photographic Portrait*. Tarrytown, N.Y.: Sleepy Hollow Press, 1981.

———. *An American Treasure: The Hudson River Valley*. Tarrytown, N.Y.: Sleepy Hollow Press, 1986.

Sinclair, Douglas L. *Three Villages, One City*. Rensselaer County, N.Y.: Rensselaer County Historical Society, 1974.

Sleicher, Albert. *The Adirondacks: An American Playground*. New York: Exposition Press, 1960.

Smith, Charles W. G. *Nature Walks in the Berkshire Hills*. Boston, Mass.: Appalachian Mountain Club Books, 1997.

Snell, Charles W. *Vanderbilt Mansion*. Washington, D.C.: Historical Handbook Series, 1960.

Sparling, Polly. "Taking the Plunge." *Hudson Valley*. Vol. XXXIII, No. 1 (May 2004).

Sparling, Reed. "City of Surprises." *Hudson Valley*. Vol. XXXIII, No. 6 (October 2004).

———. "Hidden Treasures." *Hudson Valley*. Vol. XXXIII, No. 1 (May 2004).

———. "Valatie Now & Then." *Hudson Valley*. Vol. XXXIII, No. 2 (June 2004).

Stevens, Lauren R. *Hikes & Walks in the Berkshire Hills*. Stockbridge, Mass.: Berkshire House Publishers, 1990.

Stiles, Fred Tracy. *From Then till Now: History and Tales of the Adirondack Foothills*. Washington County, N.Y.: Washington County Historical Society, 1978.

Stone, Howard. *25 Bicycle Tours in the Hudson Valley: Scenic Rides from Saratoga to West Point*. Woodstock, Vt.: Backcountry Publications, 1989.

Stone, William L. *Reminiscences of Saratoga and Ballston*. n.p.: Virtue & Yorston, 1875.

Street, Alfred B. *The Poems of Alfred B. Street*. Vol. II. New York: Hurd and Houghton, 1867.

Suffern Bicentennial Committee. *Suffern: 200 Years, 1773–1973*. Suffern, N.Y.: Suffern Bicentennial Committee, 1973.

Sylvester, Nathaniel Bartlett. *Historical Sketches of Northern New York and the Adirondack Wilderness*. 1877. Reprint, Harrison,

N.Y.: Harbor Hill Books, 1973.

———. *History of Saratoga County, New York: With Illustrations and Biographic Sketches of Some of Its Prominent Men and Pioneers.* Philadelphia, Pa.: Everts & Ensign, 1878.

———. *History of Ulster County, New York: With Illustrations and Biographical Sketches of Its Prominent Men and Pioneers.* Philadelphia, Pa.: Everts & Peck, 1880.

Taormina, Francis R. *Philip Schuyler: Who He Was, What He Did.* Schenectady, N.Y.: n.p., 1992.

Thomas, Bill, and Phyllis Thomas. *Natural New York.* New York: Holt, Rinehart & Winston, 1983.

Thull, Beulah Bailey. *Dictionary of Place Names of Rensselaer County, 1609–1971.* Pamphlet. 1971.

Thurston, Elisha P., compiler. *History of the Town of Greenwich.* Salem, N.Y.: H. D. Morris, Book and Job Printer, 1876.

Tietjen, Sari B. *Rhinebeck: Portrait of a Town.* Rhinebeck, N.Y.: The River Press, 1990.

Toole, Robert M. *A Look at Metroland: A New Guide to Its History and Heritage.* Saratoga Springs, N.Y.: Office of R. M. Toole, Landscape Architects, 1976.

Tougias, Michael , and Mark Tougias. *Autumn Rambles of New England: An Explorer's Guide to the Best Fall Colors.* Edison, N.J.: Hunter Publishing, Inc., 1998.

Town of New Baltimore Bicentennial Committee. *The Heritage of New Baltimore.* New Baltimore, N.Y.: Town of New Baltimore, 1976.

Turco, Peggy. *Walks & Rambles in Dutchess and Putnam Counties.* Woodstock, Vt.: Backcountry Publications, 1990.

———. *Walks and Rambles in the Western Hudson Valley: Landscape, Ecology, & Folklore in Orange & Ulster Counties.* Woodstock, Vt.: Backcountry Publications, 1996.

United States Bicentennial Commission of Cohoes, N.Y. *Cohoes in '76: American Bicentennial, 1776–1976.* Cohoes, N.Y.: United States Bicentennial Commission of Cohoes, N.Y., 1976.

Van Diver, Bradford B. *Roadside Geology of New York.* Missoula, Mont: Mountain Press Publishing Company, 1985.

———. *Upstate New York.* Dubuque, Iowa: Kendall/Hunt Publishing

Company, 1980.

Van Zandt, Roland. *Chronicles of the Hudson: Three Centuries of Travel and Adventure.* 1971. Reprint, Hensonville, N.Y.: Black Dome Press Corp., 1992.

Vedder, J. Van Vechten. *Official History of Greene County. Vol. I, 1651–1800.* 1927. Reprint, Cornwallville, N.Y.: Hope Farm Press, 1985.

Ward, Richard F.. "Geology of the Hudson River." *The Conservationist.* June/July 1959.

Washington County Historical Society. *History of Washington County, New York: Some Chapters in the History of the Town of Easton, N.Y.* Washington County, N.Y.: Washington County Historical Society, 1959.

Washington County Planning Department. *An Introduction to Historic Resources in Washington County, New York.* 2nd edition. Washington County, N.Y.: Washington County Planning Department for the Washington County Planning Board, 1984.

Weise, A. M. *History of the Seventeen Towns of Rensselaer County: From the Colonization of the Manor of Rensselaerwyck to the Present Time.* Troy, N.Y.: J. M. Francis & Tucker, 1880.

Welch, Darrell. "The Hudson River Portfolio." *The Conservationist.* Vol. 26, # 5 (April/May 1972).

Wilcoxen, Charlotte. *Seventeenth Century Albany: A Dutch Profile.* Albany, N.Y.: Education Department, Albany Institute of History and Art, 1981.

Woodward, J. D. *The Hudson River by Pen and Pencil.* 1888. Reprint, J.C. & A.L. Fawcett Inc., n.d.

Workers of the Writers' Program of the Work Projects Administration in the State of New York, compiler. *New York: A Guide to the Empire State.* New York: Oxford University Press, 1940.

Wyckoff, Jerome. *Rock Scenery of the Hudson Highlands and Palisades: A Geological Guide.* Glens Falls, N.Y.: Adirondack Mountain Club, 1971.

Index